Caribbean Connections

THE DOMINICAN REPUBLIC

Other titles in the Caribbean Connections series:

Jamaica

Moving North

Overview of Regional History

Puerto Rico

Teaching about Haiti

Also published by Teaching for Change:

Beyond Heroes and Holidays:
A Practical Guide to K–12 Anti-Racist,
Multicultural Education and Staff Development

Putting the *Movement* Back into Civil Rights Teaching:
A Resource Guide for Classrooms and Communities

Caribbean Connections

THE DOMINICAN REPUBLIC

Edited by
Anne Gallin, Ruth Glasser, and Jocelyn Santana
with Patricia R. Pessar

Foreword by Julia Alvarez

Council on Latin American and Iberian Studies
Yale Center for International and Area Studies

WASHINGTON, DC

For permission to reprint other portions of the book, contact:

    Teaching for Change
    P.O. Box 73038
    Washington, DC 20056
    PHONE: (800) 763-9131
    E-MAIL: tfc@teachingforchange.org
    www.teachingforchange.org

Cover photo of North Rockland High School students Stephanie Ventura and Ana Medrano by Luis J. Pomales.

Book design by Gene Kim Graphics, Washington, DC

Printed in the United States of America

Library of Congress Cataloging-in-Publication Data

    Caribbean connections: The Dominican Republic / edited by Anne Gallin,
    Ruth Glasser, and Jocelyn Santana, with Patricia R. Pessar
        p.   cm.
        1. American literature—Dominican American authors. 2. Dominican
    Republic—Emigration and immigration—Literary collections. 3. Dominican
    Americans—Literary collections. 4. Dominican Americans. 5. Dominican
    Republic—history. I. Gallin, Anne. II. Glasser, Ruth. III. Santana, Jocelyn. IV.
    Pessar, Patricia R.

ISBN 978-1-878554-19-2

CONTENTS

Part One—Geography, History, Economy

Part Two—Migration and the Dominican Diaspora

Part Three—Shaping a Dominican Identity: Language, Race, and Gender

FOREWORD

Years ago, I remember reading a moving story about a ship of European immigrants leaving for America, early in the nineteenth century. Some members of the soon-to-be-divided families had brought balls of string to the docks, and as their departing loved ones went on board, they were given an end to hold. The ship sailed off, and the families on shore played out string until their spools ran out, then they let go. Out of sight already, the immigrants on deck knew—as the strings went taut—that this was their last actual connection with their past. They wound up the loose ends, creating new balls to take with them to America.

I remember being flooded with sadness at this plaintive and last-ditch effort to hold on. Those were the days before telephones or e-mail, before cheap flights and traffic back and forth allowed people to stay in touch. I also found myself wondering what the new immigrants did with that ball of string. Did they use it to tie up their first tomato plants or string beans in a garden? Did they braid pieces together to make a strong rope for a clothesline? Did they keep the ball in a drawer to be discovered some future day by their grandchildren, who would ask, "What is this for?"

It is the very question that I imagine a reader of this book, *Caribbean Connections: The Dominican Republic,* might ask. What is this book for? As the writer of its foreword, I feel compelled in some way to answer that question.

My first response is to urge you to read on. Hold tight to the string of print, and slowly spool the stories, the poems, the essays, the testimonials into yourself, and you will discover something of what it means to be an immigrant who both leaves and also, as the Brazilian musician and poet Caetano Veloso tells us, immediately begins preparing the hour of return. *(No me estoy yendo: estoy preparando la hora de volver.)*

More specifically, you will discover what it means to be a Dominican immigrant, bringing to the United States of America a rich and complicated history, a set of assumptions, expectations, dreams and fears. You will discover what it means to be a Dominican in *Nueva York* as opposed to Rhode Island or South Florida, what it means to carry another world inside you until it feels so heavy you have to go back on one of those cheap flights or call home because otherwise your heart will split from *tristeza y desesperación.*

You will discover what it means to be a child of these Dominicans, to find balls of string knotting up your spanking-new U.S.A. skein of ideas about who you are. To have new names and responses for situations the old people used to live with or emigrate from: racism, sexism, poverty. To be haunted with dark moments of your island history: dictatorships that victimized or compromised your kin; Marine occupations that taught them to buckle under; economic situations that forced them to become huddled masses yearning to breathe free, arriving, not from Europe in the holds of ships, but on *yolas* and cheap flights with and without visas to Miami, *Nueva York,* Rhode Island, Puerto Rico.

You will discover what it means to travel that trail of tears and that trail of blood, carrying in your *sub-consciencia* the ones you left behind, the ones you want to forget, your Haitian brothers and sisters, massacres and injustices that *los viejos* many times don't want to talk about.

You will discover a diverse population of hyphenated people who know that the only victims are not the ones left behind in poverty or *compromisos,* but their counterparts here, stuck in substandard housing, with low-paying or no jobs, walking *las calles,* injecting, sniffing up, peddling, *porque que se va hacer* when the dream of America ends up as ashes in the mouths of those too dark, too poor, too hopeless and desperate to be able to turn the green of their cards into the cash of survival.

You will also discover the warmth and inventiveness of a complex collection of people, *de todos colores* and backgrounds, whose energy is boundless, who have not lost faith, who can laugh at themselves and cleverly invent the stories, the jokes, the lyrics to make meaning of experience,

Stone steps in the Dominican Republic.

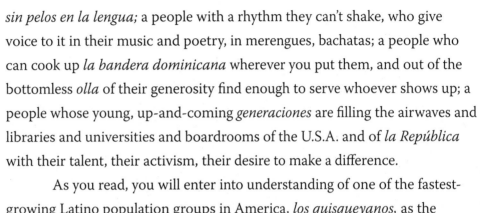

sin pelos en la lengua; a people with a rhythm they can't shake, who give voice to it in their music and poetry, in merengues, bachatas; a people who can cook up *la bandera dominicana* wherever you put them, and out of the bottomless *olla* of their generosity find enough to serve whoever shows up; a people whose young, up-and-coming *generaciones* are filling the airwaves and libraries and universities and boardrooms of the U.S.A. and of *la República* with their talent, their activism, their desire to make a difference.

As you read, you will enter into understanding of one of the fastest-growing Latino population groups in America, *los quisqueyanos,* as the Dominicans affectionately refer to themselves, from *Quisqueya,* a pre-conquest name for the island. (The native *Taínos* also called the island Haiti, "the mountainous country," both names used interchangeably, before Europeans conquered, divided, and renamed it.) You will also partake of a process, an ongoing conversation by voices gathered here, trying to make sense of what it means to be this new kind of immigrant. For the old model no longer applies, the one in which the carriers of balls of string never went back to their villages, but severed themselves completely from their pasts. These days, we stay in touch; we do not disconnect; the balls of string play out and out. This new model of immigration is ultimately about connections, and the only string long enough to stretch across those distances is the string of our words, our stories, our conversations.

And so you, reader, are now holding one end of a string of many voices. I can't help but hope in these times of division and wars and rumors of wars, that the string played out in books such as this one might indeed provide lifelines. In place of glib sound bites and the violence of chauvinistically severing connections, dividing people into *us* and *them,* we can posit connection. By reading, by listening, by speaking in turn, we can create a string of understanding that circles the world. ❀

Julia Alvarez
May 2, 2004

ACKNOWLEDGMENTS

This book would not have been possible without the generous support of the writers and photographers whose work is presented here. Thanks to all who wrote for this volume, gave oral history interviews, or gave permission for their published work to appear.

Sixteen scholars with expertise in Dominican studies provided guidance to the project. We are grateful to the following members of the Faculty Advisory Board:

Julia Alvarez, Middlebury College

Paul Austerlitz, Brown University

Ginetta E. B. Candelario, Smith College

Daisy Cocco de Filippis, Eugenio María de Hostos Community College, CUNY

Junot Díaz, Massachusetts Institute of Technology

Jorge Duany, University of Puerto Rico

Rosario Espinal, Temple University

Ramona Hernández, CUNY-Dominican Studies Institute, City College of New York

Peggy Levitt, Wellesley College

Samuel Martínez, University of Connecticut

Patricia R. Pessar, Yale University

Ydanis Rodríguez, Gregorio Luperón High School

Rob Ruck, University of Pittsburgh

Ernesto Sagás, Southern New Hampshire University

Andrew Schrank, Yale University

Silvio Torres-Saillant, Syracuse University

Teachers and students were closely involved in creating this resource and testing it in the classroom. Six teachers from Connecticut and New York drafted many of the lesson plans at a week-long curriculum writing workshop at Yale University in August 2002: Claudia Bedoya-Rose, Rebecca Ford, Lola Lopes, Josue Saint-Fleur, Pedro Tavarez, and María Tecocoatzi. Seven teachers and their students in Connecticut, New York, and Massachusetts took time out of their busy schedules to test the lesson plans and provide feedback, while we observed in the classroom. These teachers are Claudia Bedoya-Rose, Julian Cohen, Francisco García-Quezada, Amy Halloran, Grismaldy Laboy, Lola Lopes, and Sean McCarthy. Sonia Nieto of the University of Massachusetts–Amherst and Karla Spletzer, a consultant with Upstart in Education, also provided valuable feedback. We thank them all for their dedication and creativity.

With great pleasure we acknowledge the faculty, staff, and students at Yale University and the University of Connecticut who have contributed to this project since 2001. Patricia R. Pessar, principal investigator of the grant that funded this project, professor of American studies and anthropology at Yale, and one of the leading experts on Dominican migration to the United States provided guidance throughout the project. Her critical analysis of the manuscript and her sensitivity to issues that arose during the writing and editing are deeply appreciated.

Important support was provided by staff of the Council on Latin American and Iberian Studies, housed within the Yale Center for International and Area Studies. Gilbert M. Joseph, chair of the Council, recognized the book as an important contribution to the curricular resources on Latin America and lent the continuous support of the Council's Outreach Program. Beatriz Riefkohl, assistant chair of the Council and a gifted grant writer, helped us set forth our vision of the book and explain how it would serve teachers and students. She also spent long hours (often late into the night) revising the narrative with the editors. Sarah Morrill, the Council's program assistant, provided expert and good-humored office support, keeping payments, mailings, photocopying, phone and e-mail messages all in order.

Yale students Cynthia Oquendo and Patricio Zambrano-Barragán assisted with research, transcription of interviews, translation, and communication with publishers, and made countless trips to the Yale libraries. University of Connecticut student Delmaliz Medina conducted, transcribed, and translated interviews with Dominicans in Waterbury, and UConn students Kevin Fitzpatrick and Jayra Quiles also conducted interviews with Dominicans in Connecticut.

The CUNY Dominican Studies Institute at City College of New York was an invaluable resource at every step of the way. Sarah Aponte, the Institute's librarian, welcomed us and helped steer us to appropriate resources and contacts, and obtained permission for us to use photographs from the

Institute's collection. We also thank the staff at the National Archives and the Library of Congress in Washington, DC, who pointed us toward useful historical photographs and maps.

We are grateful to the professionals of our copyediting, translating, and graphic design team. Editor Catherine Sunshine transformed the manuscript from a diamond in the rough into a real gem. Translators Elisa Davila and Claudia Isaza of the State University of New York at New Paltz, and Spanish copyeditor Pablo Landa turned the Spanish companion reader, *Conexiones caribeñas: la República Dominicana, selección de lecturas en español,* into a wonderful resource for Spanish-speaking teachers and students. Graphic designer Eugenia Kim brought this book to life with her beautiful design.

Deborah Menkart, director of Teaching for Change and publisher of five earlier books in the *Caribbean Connections* series, helped us develop the concept for this volume. Her dedication to publishing multicultural, antiracist curricular resources that promote equity and social justice is unparalleled. Kate Munning, publications and communications coordinator at Teaching for Change, provided helpful guidance on permission requests, publishing costs, and distribution.

A special thanks to Luis J. Pomales, who provided photographs of Dominicans in Waterbury and of students at North Rockland High School in Thiells, New York; to Jocelyn's daughter, Darilyn Castillo, who entertained us during editing sessions with song and dance routines and tales of the seventh grade; to Mel Shaw, who supplied strong coffee and delicious lunches during those editing sessions; to Anne's mother, Joyce McKelvey, who read the entire text aloud as a final review; to Anne's newborn daughter, Ruby, who slept throughout the review process; and to Jonathan Gallin, who inspired Anne to get this project off the ground.

Finally, we gratefully acknowledge funding assistance from the Council on Latin American and Iberian Studies at the Yale Center for International and Area Studies; the U.S. Department of Education, through its International Research and Studies and National Resource Centers programs; and the Connecticut Collaborations for Teaching the Arts and Humanities grant program, a partnership of the Connecticut Department of Higher Education and the Connecticut Humanities Council. ❀

INTRODUCTION

Anne Gallin, Ruth Glasser, and Jocelyn Santana

In Francisco García-Quezada's ninth-grade Spanish class for native speakers at North Rockland High School in Thiells, New York, students read a story by author Junot Díaz. Like many of García's students, Díaz was born in the Dominican Republic and moved to the United States with his family as a child. After reading the story, the students write a letter to one of the fictional characters: Yunior, Rafa, Abuelo, Mamá, or the absent Papá. On another day, the students share photographs and describe their own families' journeys from the Dominican Republic to new lives in New York.

At Lawrence High School in Lawrence, Massachusetts, students in Sean McCarthy's eleventh-grade English class read a poem by Dominican-born poet Rhina Espaillat, describing the small bodegas or corner stores found in every Dominican town and neighborhood. Students then write their own poems describing their favorite bodegas and their tastes, aromas, sights, and sounds.

In New Haven, Connecticut, at Gateway Community College, Claudia Bedoya-Rose's English as a Second Language students watch a scene from "In the Time of the Butterflies." Based on the novel by Julia Alvarez, the film follows the lives of three of the four Mirabal sisters, who were assassinated by the Trujillo regime in 1961 because of their struggle against the dictatorship. After viewing the film, students learn about the International Day Against Violence Towards Women, established in honor of the Mirabal sisters, and write an essay on the sisters' lives.

These are just a few examples of how students in U.S. classrooms are learning about the Dominican Republic and the experiences of Dominicans in the diaspora. As the Dominican American community grows, interest in Dominican studies is growing apace. More than a million Dominicans now live in the fifty states and Puerto Rico, according to independent researchers. Dominicans rank fourth in size among Hispanic groups in the United States, following Mexicans, Puerto Ricans, and Cubans. If current growth rates continue, Dominicans will surpass Cubans by 2010 and become the third-largest Latino group in the country.

For decades, New York City has been a magnet for Dominican immigrants. The northern Manhattan neighborhood of Washington Heights is still home to the largest Dominican community in the country. But in recent years Dominicans have fanned out from this core in search of jobs and a quieter and safer place to live. They have settled in the other boroughs of New York, in the city's suburbs, and beyond, in upstate New York, New Jersey, Connecticut, and other states. Communities such as Yonkers and Haverstraw, New York, now have an unmistakable Dominican flavor. Dominicans have also flocked to other large East Coast cities such as Providence, Boston, and Miami, and to smaller cities such as Lawrence, Massachusetts. Most families who migrate reach back and help others make the same trip, welcoming them and helping them set down roots when they arrive.

How does the growing presence of Dominicans in U.S. communities and classrooms influence school curricula? As educators, how can we best teach the history of the Dominican Republic and help students understand its long and close relationship with the United States? How can we accurately present the perspectives of Dominican Americans, the challenges they face, and the contributions they have made to their adopted country?

Caribbean Connections: The Dominican Republic is intended to help meet these goals. Designed for secondary and community college students and educators, it explores the rich history and culture of the Dominican Republic, the migration experience, and the lives of Dominicans in the diaspora. The stories that unfold in these pages tell of island childhoods and of leaving loved ones, coming to a new land, learning a new language, and forging an identity that draws from the past and the future, from "there" and "here." We travel back and forth with Dominicans as they lead transnational lives and undergo, to varying degrees, the process of Americanization. This collection gives voice to

Dominicans in the homeland and to those in the United States and Puerto Rico who dream of home every day—who are, in the words of popular merengue singer José Peña Suazo, *aquí, pero allá.*

The Readings

The readings in this volume fall into three broad categories: 1) academic articles, 2) fiction and poetry, and 3) oral history narratives and interviews.

The articles were written by scholars in a variety of disciplines— sociology, literature, anthropology, history, economics, political science—who have studied the Dominican Republic and Dominican migration. Several articles were written especially for this book, while others were previously published and have been adapted for use in secondary and community college classrooms.

Fiction and poetry in the book are drawn from novels, short stories, and poetry collections by authors mainly of Dominican descent. They bring to life the history and ideas discussed in the academic articles. In "Minerva," for example, Julia Alvarez describes how a student at a private Catholic boarding school learns of the horrors of the Trujillo dictatorship through the experiences of a friend. "Aguantando," by Junot Díaz, shows the estrangement between parent and child that sometimes results when a parent migrates to the United States, leaving family members behind. And in "Perejil," novelist Edwidge Danticat, born in Haiti, explores the tense relations between the two countries that share the island of Hispaniola. We are particularly pleased to include poems written by students at Lawrence High School in Lawrence, Massachusetts, reflecting on their memories of the Dominican Republic and the experience of saying goodbye.

Oral histories and interviews in the book are first-person accounts by Dominicans and Dominican Americans from many walks of life, including teachers, community activists, scholars, a home health aide, and a musician, among others. In one interview Doña Dedé Mirabal, sister of the martyred Mirabal sisters, shares memories of their years growing up and recalls the obstacles that Dominican women faced as they struggled to transcend narrow gender roles during the last century.

Several of the poems in this book are presented here in the original Spanish as well as in English translation. In other instances, authors writing in English use selected Spanish words and phrases to convey specific concepts within Dominican culture. These words are defined in a glossary at the end of each reading. A Spanish companion reader, *Conexiones caribeñas: la República Dominicana, selección de lecturas en español,* offering a selection of articles from this volume is also available from Teaching for Change.

The Lesson Plans

The twenty-six lesson plans were created in part by six educators who attended a curriculum-writing workshop at Yale University in 2002. Each lesson plan is designed to be used with one or more of the readings, and suggests the duration of the activity, a goal, objectives, activities, assessment techniques, and materials. The lesson plans are aligned with national standards for language arts, foreign languages, and social studies[1].

The video and book resources listed under "Materials" at the end of each lesson plan are available for loan without charge through the Programs in International Educational Resources (PIER) at Yale University (www.yale. edu/ycias/pierresource.htm). Many of the books from which the readings are drawn are also available at the PIER Resource Center for teachers and students interested in conducting further research.

Organization of the Book

Part 1 provides background on the geography, history, and economy of the Dominican Republic, focusing on the political and economic conditions that gave rise to large-scale migration in the mid-twentieth century. Maps and a timeline of Dominican history are included.

Part 2 explores the migration experience and the lives of Dominicans in the diaspora. It highlights eight destinations that have attracted large numbers of Dominican immigrants: Puerto Rico, New York, New Jersey, Massachusetts,

Connecticut, Rhode Island, Washington, DC, and South Florida. Population data from the 2000 census are provided to help sketch a comparative picture of Dominican settlement in U.S. cities and states.

In Part 3, scholars and writers look at the role of language, race, and gender in shaping Dominican American identities. This section also looks at racism in the United States and its impact on Dominican Americans of different backgrounds.

Part 4 focuses on the intertwined histories of Haiti and the Dominican Republic, including the horrific massacre of Haitians by the Trujillo regime in 1937, and the present-day ties between the two neighboring peoples.

Finally, Part 5 takes a look at two beloved aspects of Dominican life: music and baseball. Musicians and baseball players have gone forth as ambassadors of Dominican culture, the merengue and bachata players making their names in the international Latin music scene and the *peloteros* (ballplayers) featuring prominently in the lineups of the U.S. major leagues.

A Dedication

Work on this book began in early November 2001, one week before American Airlines flight 587 en route to Santo Domingo crashed in Queens, New York. The 255 people who perished were mostly Dominicans returning home for a vacation. With sadness and respect, we dedicate this book to their memory and to the legacy of hope and strength they left behind. We see this hope in the Dominicans who contributed to this anthology, who opened their hearts and lives to us and shared their dreams, failures and victories. We celebrate their achievements, and hope that this book may contribute in some small way to the efforts of all Dominicans working to build strong communities—in the island homeland and in the diaspora, their home away from home.

The editors welcome feedback on the readings and lesson plans from teachers and students who have used them in the classroom. These experiences will be invaluable in shaping future editions of the book. Comments may be sent to tfc@teachingforchange.org. ❀

---

1. The following three resources were used to cite the national standards:

   Expectations of Excellence: Curriculum Standards for Social Studies (Silver Spring, MD: National Council for the Social Studies, 1994).

   Standards for the English Language Arts (Newark, DE: International Reading Association; Urbana, IL: National Council of Teachers of English, 1996).

   Standards for Foreign Language Learning in the 21st Century (Alexandria, VA: National Standards for Foreign Language Education/American Council on the Teaching of Foreign Languages, 1999).

ABOUT THE EDITORS

ABOVE: *Co-editors Anne Gallin, Ruth Glasser and Jocelyn Santana test the Dominican cake recipe.*
BELOW: *Patricia R. Pessar.*

Anne Gallin developed the Outreach Program at the Council on Latin American and Iberian Studies at Yale University. As director of the program from 1998 to 2004, she wrote curriculum materials, organized summer institutes for K–12 and community college educators, led study tours to the Dominican Republic and Puerto Rico, and taught Caribbean dance in schools. She holds an M.A. in International studies (Latin America) from the University of Connecticut.

Ruth Glasser is the author of two books: *My Music Is My Flag: Puerto Rican Musicians and Their New York Communities, 1917–1940* (University of California Press, 1995) and *Aquí Me Quedo: Puerto Ricans in Connecticut* (Connecticut Humanities Council, 1997). She has written curriculum materials and museum exhibit scripts on community and ethnic history. The holder of a Ph.D. in American studies from Yale University, she currently teaches in the Urban and Community Studies Program at the University of Connecticut–Tri-Campus.

Jocelyn Santana migrated from the Dominican Republic to New York City at the age of fourteen. She holds a Ph.D. in English education from New York University and has served as a teacher of ESL, Spanish, and English, and as a curriculum and staff developer. She is currently the English Language Learners Curriculum Instructional Specialist for District 79 in New York City. She has written extensively on language and identity issues among immigrants and is currently at work on a memoir, *Dominican Dream, American Reality.*

Patricia R. Pessar is professor of American studies and anthropology at Yale University. She is the author of *Between Two Islands: Dominican International Migration* with Sherri Grasmuck (University of California Press, 1991), *A Visa for a Dream: Dominicans in New York* (Allyn & Bacon, 1995), and *Caribbean Circuits: New Directions in the Study of Caribbean Migration* (Center for Migration Studies, 1997). Her current research focuses on Guatemalan refugees and returnees and the social production of Brazilian millenarian beliefs and movements. *From Fanatics to Folk: Brazilian Millenarianism and Popular Culture* (Duke University Press, 2004) is the title of her latest publication.

Caribbean Connections

THE DOMINICAN REPUBLIC

PART ONE

GEOGRAPHY, HISTORY, ECONOMY

Milk chocolate, Oreo® cookies and Ritz® crackers are among the many commodites sold at this bodega in Santo Domingo.

REMEMBERING DOMINICAN CHILDHOODS: THREE BODEGA POEMS

At Lawrence High School in Lawrence, Massachusetts, 87 percent of the student body is of Dominican descent, and students have many opportunities to explore their cultural heritage. The school's baseball team has had lunch with Boston Red Sox pitcher Pedro Martínez, who is Dominican. A Spanish class talked about writing with author Junot Díaz. And students in an English class worked with poet Rhina Espaillat, whose published poetry collections include Lapsing to Grace, Where Horizons Go, *and* Rehearsing Absence.

Born in Santo Domingo, Espaillat came to the United States in 1939 at the age of seven. In "Bodega," she evokes the aromas, flavors, sights, and sounds of her childhood, describing the small corner groceries found in neighborhoods throughout the Dominican Republic. Students in Sean McCarthy's tenth- and eleventh-grade English classes—most of them also Dominican-born—discussed Espaillat's poem and, following her example, wrote about bodegas they have known. The students were asked to begin their poems by describing a sound inside the bodega (or colmado, as these stores are also called). The poems by Paola Capellán and Esthefany Melo capture the sensory richness and nostalgia of these childhood memories.

ANNE GALLIN

Lawrence High School.

Bodega

Rhina P. Espaillat

Bitter coffee, musty beans,
caramel and guava jam,
rice and sausage, nippy cheese,
saffron, anise, honey, ham,

rosemary, oregano,
clove, allspice and bacalao.
Fifty years have flown away:
childhood falls around me now,

childhood and another place
where the tang of orange sweets
golden on the vendor's tray
drifts like laughter through
        the streets.

Memory is filament
weaving, weaving what I am:
bitter coffee, musty beans,
caramel and guava jam.

Bodega

Rhina P. Espaillat

Café amargo, frijol seco,
guayaba y caramelón,
salchicha, arroz, queso criollo,
anís, azafrán, miel, jamón,

clavo, orégano y romero,
malagueta y bacalao.
Cincuenta años en un soplo:
mi niñez vuelve en el vaho

de jalea de chinas—oro
en la batea del pulpero—
que se esparce como risas
por callejuela y sendero.

Los recuerdos son hilazas;
me tejen de lo que son:
café amargo, frijol seco,
guayaba y caramelón.

Rhina P. Espaillat.

English poem reprinted from Rhina P. Espaillat, *Lapsing to Grace* (East Lansing, MI: Bennett & Kitchel). © 1992 by Rhina P. Espaillat. Used by permission of the publisher. Spanish translation provided by Rhina P. Espaillat and used by permission of the author.

Mi Colmado

Paola Capellán

As I walk into the colmado,
I spy the good equimalitos
and the tasty suspiros.
I can hear the shouting,
"ey deme un peso eh plátano" and other
people playing dominoes with their
fresh Presidente.
I smell the good
queso dominicano and the great
sopita with its sazón.
As I walk into the colmado,
I remember my people with the "din din don"
of the bachata and our merengues
"tiri tiri tiri . . ." with their amazing
sabor dominicano.
As I walk into the colmado,
I see my people dancing
having the time of their lives
being "puro dominicanos."
And I walk into our great colmado.

El Colmado de Mi Abuelo

Esthefany Melo

As I walk into the colmado,
I can hear the music:
salsa, merengue, bachata
and the "buenos días" of the dueño.
The papitas hanging from the wall
catch my eye every time.
The smell of pastelitos
makes me so hungry,
and the pink gums—bolachos
stuck inside their jar,
waiting for me to grab one.
And the look on that man's face
always kind and gentle;
smiling at me,
Willing to hug me, kiss me,
take me to the stars.
A memory that will never go away
that will be eternal like the universe
because it makes me want to go back.
Back to the colmado
where the pink bolachos
wait in the jar
waiting for me to grab them
where the man stands waiting for me
to hug and kiss him.

bacalao: dried cod
bachata: Dominican popular music
bodega: small grocery store
bolachos: candy balls
buenos días: good morning
colmado: small grocery store
dueño: owner
equimalitos: ice pops
ey deme un peso eh plátano: hey, give me a dollar's worth of plantains
guava: tropical fruit
merengue: Dominican popular music
papitas: potato chips
pastelitos: meat pastries
Presidente: brand of Dominican beer
puro dominicanos: true Dominicans
queso: cheese
sabor dominicano: Dominican flavor or flair
sazón: seasoning, flavoring
sopita: chicken broth
suspiros: frosted cookies

BRYAN TIGHE

Plantains.

UNIT 2 · LESSON PLAN

LA BODEGA

USE WITH: Unit 1

DURATION: 1 class

STANDARDS:

English Language Arts: 1, 2, 3, 5, 6, 9, 10

Social Studies: 1b, 1c, 1d, 1e, 4b

Foreign Language: 1, 2, 3, 4.2

GOALS: To experience a written text using the five senses.

OBJECTIVES:

- To analyze the poet's use of the five senses.
- To identify connections between the text and Dominican culture.
- To write a poem using sensory devices that reflect the student's own culture.

ACTIVITIES:

1. On a sheet of paper, each student names a favorite neighborhood store that he or she frequents or has frequented in the past. Students list 1 smell, 1 visual image, and 1 sound that remind them of the shop. Students share their lists.

2. The teacher or a student reads Rhina Espaillat's poem "Bodega" aloud in English and/or Spanish (unit 1). Students identify all of the items named in the poem, and explain or guess how they are used. If time allows, the class can also read the other two poems in the unit and identify the items named.

3. Ask the class, "What senses are involved in the poem? What are some of the smells, tastes, sounds, and visual images from your own childhood?" Write the answers on a transparency overhead.

4. If possible, show a clip from *Washington Heights,* which was filmed, in part, inside a bodega.

5. Students write their own poems describing a store they have known. The poem should include at least three factual references and three sensory references. Factual references could be, for example, the store's location, its size, the type of building, the goods sold, or common activities inside and outside the store. Sensory references include smells, tastes, sights, sounds, and textures, such as the scent of cigars, the sounds of merengue

Lesson plan prepared by Lola Lopes.

music, or the taste of guava jam. Students can use the list from the opening activity or start fresh. To get started, students may find it helpful to complete the rubric below.

Factual references	Sensory references
Example: small building made of wood	Example: tang of orange sweets
1.	1.
2.	2.
3.	3.

ASSESSMENT: Teacher assesses students' ability to incorporate at least 3 factual references and 3 sensory references into their poems.

MATERIALS:

- Products described in the poem (optional)

- Blank transparency

- *Washington Heights* (directed by Alfredo De Villa, Lions Gate Home Entertainment, 2003)

Selling jalao (coconut candies) to a tourist in the resort town of Boca Chica.

THE DOMINICAN REPUBLIC IN MAPS

This unit contains nine maps that can be used with various other units in the book. Maps 1 through 8 are suggested for use with units 4 through 8. Map 9 is suggested for use with unit 15; it can also be used with general discussions of migration and any of the units in part 2 of the book.

Map 1. The Caribbean Region

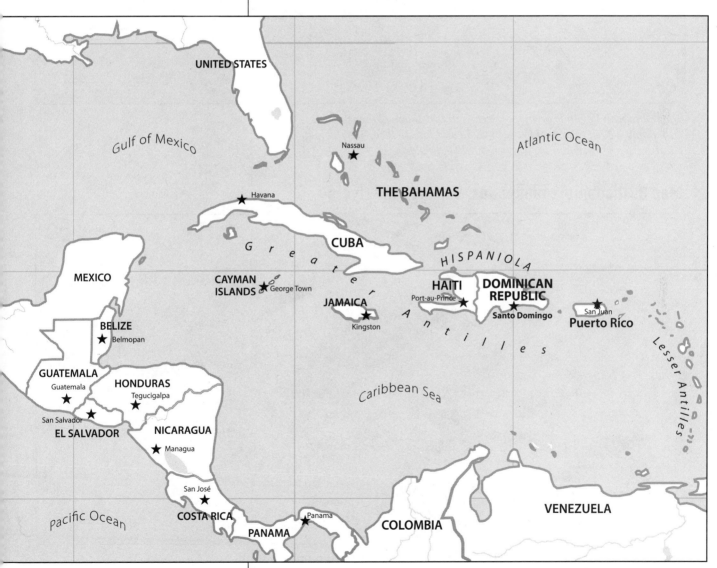

Hispaniola is the second-largest of the Greater Antilles in the Caribbean archipelago. Situated about 600 miles southeast of Florida and 310 miles north of Colombia and Venezuela, it is flanked on the north by the Atlantic Ocean and on the south by the Caribbean Sea.

Map 2. The Dominican Republic

The Dominican Republic occupies the eastern two-thirds of the island of Hispaniola, which is located between Cuba and Puerto Rico. The Republic of Haiti occupies the remaining western third of the island.

Map 3. Hispaniola mountains, valleys, and rivers

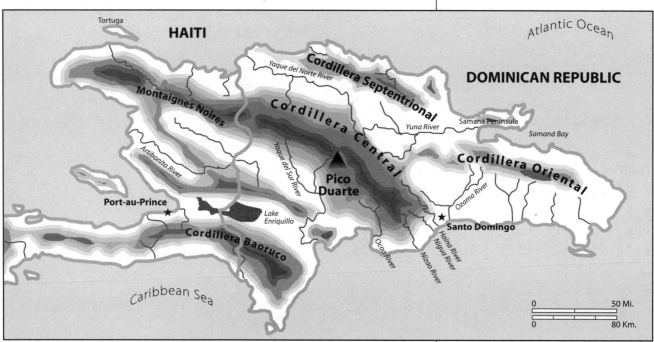

The Dominican landscape is marked topographically by its three main cordilleras, or mountain ranges: the Oriental, the Septentrional, and the Central. The Cordillera Central includes the highest mountain in the West Indian region, the 10,417-foot-tall Pico Duarte. Situated within the tropic zone, the country enjoys a mild climate, with national mean temperature of 77° F. The land offers a varied vegetation and has proven adaptable to cultivation of a wide variety of crops.

Map 4. The voyages of Columbus, 1492–1504

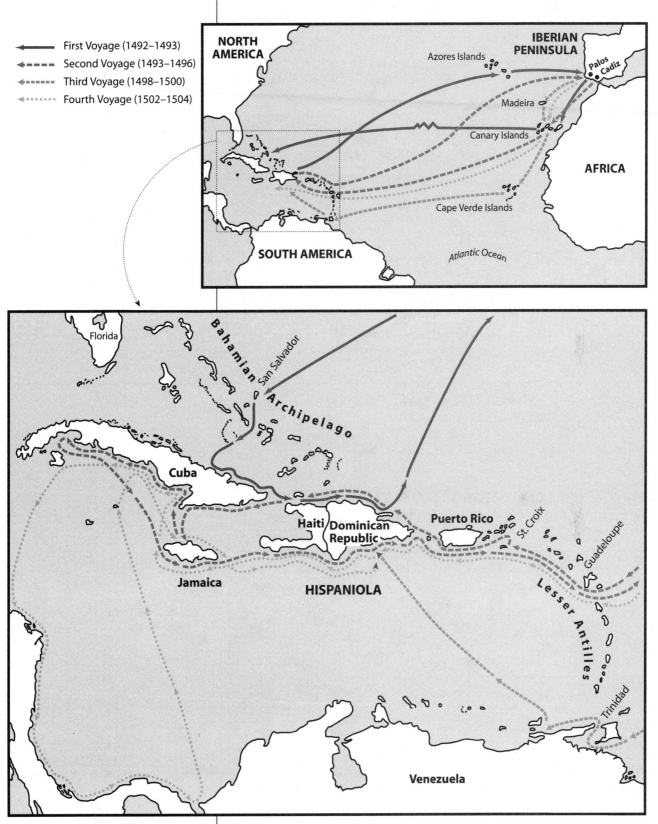

First Voyage (1492–1493)
Second Voyage (1493–1496)
Third Voyage (1498–1500)
Fourth Voyage (1502–1504)

NORTH AMERICA

IBERIAN PENINSULA

Azores Islands

Palos
Cadiz

Madeira

Canary Islands

AFRICA

Cape Verde Islands

SOUTH AMERICA

Atlantic Ocean

Florida

Bahamian Archipelago

San Salvador

Cuba

Haiti Dominican Republic

Puerto Rico

St. Croix

Guadeloupe

Jamaica

HISPANIOLA

Lesser Antilles

Trinidad

Venezuela

Christopher Columbus landed on the island of Hispaniola on his first voyage, encountered the indigenous Taínos, and built a fort. On a subsequent journey he established a colony with his brother Diego as leader.

Map 5. French expansion to the east and Spanish repopulation of the western part of Hispaniola

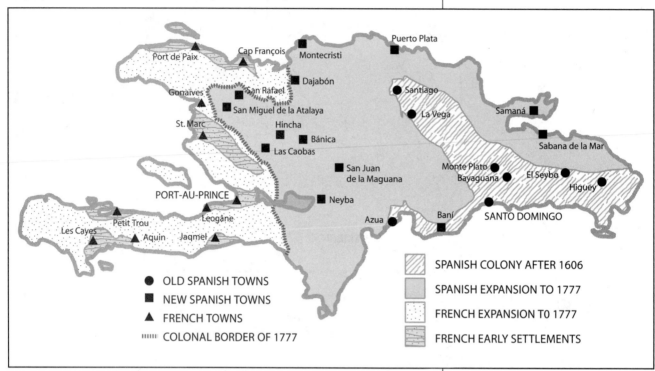

Port de Paix
Cap François
Montecristi
Puerto Plata
Dajabón
Gonaïves
San Rafael
Santiago
Samaná
San Miguel de la Atalaya
La Vega
St. Marc
Hincha
Bánica
Sabana de la Mar
Las Caobas
Monte Plato
San Juan de la Maguana
Bayaguana
El Seybo
Higuey
PORT-AU-PRINCE
Neyba
Petit Trou
Leogâne
Azua
Baní
SANTO DOMINGO
Les Cayes
Aquin
Jaqmel

● OLD SPANISH TOWNS
■ NEW SPANISH TOWNS
▲ FRENCH TOWNS
⊪⊪⊪ COLONIAL BORDER OF 1777

▨ SPANISH COLONY AFTER 1606
▨ SPANISH EXPANSION TO 1777
▨ FRENCH EXPANSION TO 1777
▨ FRENCH EARLY SETTLEMENTS

The period from the mid-1600s to the early 1800s was marked by Spanish and French struggles over political and economic dominance of Hispaniola. The division of the island into two distinct countries and cultures is in large part the result of this colonial legacy.

Map 6. Origins of the Spanish settlers of Hispaniola from the sixteenth to the nineteenth century

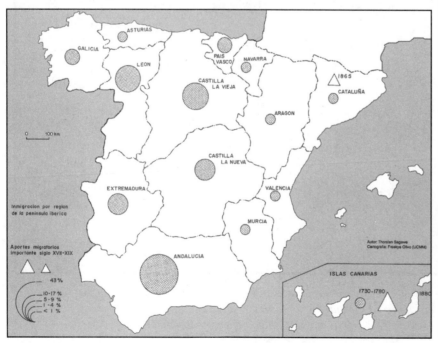

ASTURIAS
GALICIA
LEON
PAIS VASCO
NAVARRA
CASTILLA LA VIEJA
1865
CATALUÑA
ARAGON
CASTILLA LA NUEVA
EXTREMADURA
VALENCIA
MURCIA
ANDALUCIA

Inmigracion por region de la peninsula iberica

Aportes migratorios importante siglo XVII-XIX

43 %
10-17 %
5-9 %
1-4 %
< 1 %

ISLAS CANARIAS
1730-1780
1880

Autor: Thorsten Sagawa
Cartografia: Fraskya Olivo (UCMM)

Colonial Spain was a complex society composed of distinct regions, some with their own languages. This map shows the origins of Spaniards who came to the Hispaniola colony from the sixteenth to the nineteenth centuries. At times, settlers were recruited to Hispaniola from specific parts of Spain, such as the Canary Islands.

Map 7. From Africa to Hispaniola

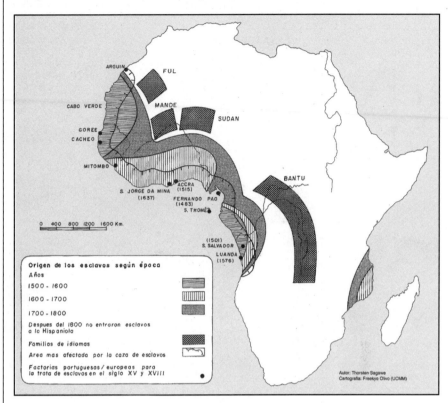

The Africans who were brought as slaves to Hispaniola from the 1500s to the beginning of the 1800s came from a number of mostly West African societies with distinct cultures and languages.

Map 8. Diverse origins of Dominican society

Through the centuries, settlers came to the Dominican Republic not only from Africa and Spain, but from other parts of the Caribbean and from France, Italy, Germany, England, and even the Middle East and Asia.

Map 9. Immigration and emigration flows, 1920–1985

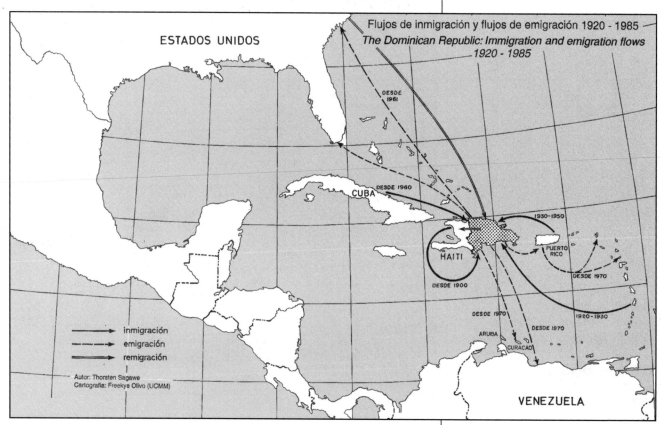

While Haitians (especially) have immigrated to the Dominican Republic in search of jobs, Dominicans have emigrated to Puerto Rico, Venezuela, Spain, and the United States, among other countries.

SOURCES:

Text for maps 1, 2, and 3 adapted from *The Dominican Americans* (Westport, CT: Greenwood Publishing Group, Inc.). © 1998 by Silvio Torres-Saillant and Ramona Hernández. Reproduced with permission of Greenwood Publishing Group, Inc. Maps 1 and 2 adapted from Peggy Levitt, *The Transnational Villagers* (Berkeley and Los Angeles: University of California Press). © 2001 by The Regents of the University of California. Used by permission of the publisher. Maps 3 and 5 adapted from *The Dominican Republic: A National History* (New Rochelle, NY: Hispaniola Books). © 1995 by Frank Moya Pons. Courtesy of the CUNY Dominican Studies Institute Library. Map 4 adapted from *The Tainos: Rise and Decline of the People Who Greeted Columbus* (New Haven: Yale University Press). © 1992 by Irving Rouse. Maps 6, 7, 8, and 9 reproduced from *Una Visión Geográfica de la Población Dominicana* (Kallmünz, Germany: Verlag Michael Lassleben). © 1992 by Thorsten Sagawe.

HAY UN PAÍS EN EL MUNDO

poema gris en varias ocasiones

Pedro Mir

Pedro Mir, poet laureate of the Dominican Republic, was born in 1913 in San Pedro de Macorís. Growing up during the Trujillo dictatorship, he criticized the regime in his writing and was forced to flee the country in 1947. He returned to live in the Dominican Republic in 1968, and in 1993 received the National Prize for Literature for his life's work. He died in 2000 at age 87.

Mir's well-known poem "Hay un país en el mundo" was written in 1949, while the poet was in exile. This excerpt from the poem speaks of the natural beauty of the Dominican Republic obscured by oppression and injustice.

Reprinted from *Countersong to Walt Whitman & Other Poems* (Washington, DC: Azul Editions). © 1993 by Pedro Mir. Translated by Jonathan Cohen and Donald D. Walsh. Used by permission of the publisher.

¡Ah, desventurados! — exclamó indignado el sirio—.
¿Cómo imaginar semejante exceso de rabia furiosa? Me
dan ganas de dar tres pasos y aplastar de tres patadas a todo
ese hormiguero de ridículos asesinos…
    No os toméis ese trabajo — le respondieron —. Ellos
mismos se encargan de su ruina.
                                    —Voltaire, *Micromegas*, cap. VII

Hay
un país en el mundo
                    colocado
en el mismo trayecto del sol.
Oriundo de la noche.
                    Colocado
en un inverosímil archipiélago
de azúcar y de alcohol.
                    Sencillamente
liviano,
        como un ala de murciélago
apoyado en la brisa.
                    Sencillamente
claro,
        como el rastro del beso en las solteras
antiguas
        o el día en los tejados.
                    Sencillamente
frutal. Fluvial. Y material. Y sin embargo
sencillamente tórrido y pateado
como una adolescente en las caderas.
Sencillamente triste y oprimido.
Sinceramente agreste y despoblado.

En verdad.
Con tres millones
                    suma de la vida
y entre tanto
                    cuatro cordilleras cardinales
y una inmensa bahía y otra inmensa bahía,

tres penínsulas con islas adyacentes
y un asombro de ríos verticales
y tierra bajo los árboles y tierra
bajo los ríos y en la falda del monte
y al pie de la colina y detrás del horizonte
y tierra desde el canto de los gallos
y tierra bajo el galope de los caballos
y tierra sobre el día, bajo el mapa, alrededor
y debajo de todas las huellas y en medio del amor.
Entonces
      es lo que he declarado.
                Hay
un país en el mundo
sencillamente agreste y despoblado.
Algún amor creerá
que en este fluvial país en que la tierra brota,
y se derrama y cruje como una vena rota,
donde el día tiene su triunfo verdadero,
irán los campesinos con asombro y apero
a cultivar
        cantando
              su franja propietaria.

Este amor
quebrará su inocencia solitaria.
          Pero no.

Y creerá
que en medio de esta tierra recrecida,
donde quiera, donde ruedan montañas por los valles
como frescas monedas azules, donde duerme
un bosque en cada flor y en cada flor la vida,
irán los campesinos por la loma dormida
a gozar
       forcejeando
          con su propia cosecha.

Este amor
doblará su luminosa flecha.
          Pero no.
Y creerá
de donde el viento asalta el íntimo terrón
y lo convierte en tropas de cumbres y praderas,
donde cada colina parece un corazón,
en cada campesino irán las primaveras
cantando
       entre los surcos
            su propiedad.
Este amor
alcanzará su floreciente edad.
         Pero no.

Hay
un país en el mundo
donde un campesino breve,
seco y agrio
       muere y muerde
descalzo
      su polvo derruido,
y la tierra no alcanza para su bronca muerte.
¡Oidlo bien! No alcanza para quedar dormido.
Es un país pequeño y agredido. Sencillamente triste,
triste y torvo, triste y acre. Ya lo dije:
sencillamente triste y oprimido.

THERE IS A COUNTRY IN THE WORLD

a poem, sad on more than one occasion

Pedro Mir

"Oh, wretched ones!" cried the Syrian
indignantly. "How can we imagine such an
excess of furious rage? I feel like taking three
steps and squashing underfoot that whole
anthill of ridiculous assassins…."
   "Don't go to all that trouble," they answered.
"They will see to their own downfall."
                    —Voltaire, *Micromegas*, VII

There is
a country in the world
                    situated
right in the sun's path.
A native of the night.
                    Situated
in an improbable archipelago
of sugar and alcohol.
                    Simply
light,
          like a bat's wing
leaning on the breeze.
                    Simply
bright,
     like the trace of a kiss on an elderly
maiden,
          or daylight on the roof tiles.
                                   Simply
fruitful. Fluvial. And material. And yet
simply torrid, abused and kicked
like a young girl's hips.
Simply sad and oppressed.
Sincerely wild and uninhabited.

In truth.
With three million
                    life's sum total
and all the while
                    four cardinal cordilleras
and an immense bay and another immense bay,
three peninsulas with adjacent isles
and the wonder of vertical rivers
and earth beneath the trees and earth
beneath the rivers and at the edge of the forest
and at the foot of the hill and behind the horizon
and earth from the cock's crow
and earth beneath the galloping horses
and earth over the day, under the map, around
and underneath all the footprints
          and in the midst of love.
Then
     it is as I have said.
                    There is
a country in the world
simply wild and uninhabited.
Some love will think
that in this fluvial country in which earth
blossoms,
and spills over and cracks like a bursting vein,
where day has its true victory,
the farmers will go amazed with their spades
to cultivate
          singing
                    their strip of ownership.

NICOLAS METIVIER

Chalk cliffs of Montecristi, Dominican Republic.

This love
will shatter its solitary innocence.

                              But no.

And it will think
that in the midst of this swollen land,
everywhere, where mountains roll through valleys
like fresh blue coins, where a forest
sleeps in each flower and in each flower life,
the farmers will walk along the sleeping ridge
to enjoy
                    struggling
                                    with their own harvest.

This love
will bend its luminous arrow.

                              But no.

And it will think
from where the wind buffets the inmost clod of
earth
and transforms it into flocks of peaks and plains,
where each hill seems a heart,
in each farmer spring upon spring will go
singing
                    among the furrows
                                    his land.

This love
will reach its flowering Age.

                              But no.

There is
a country in the world
where a farmer, cut down,
withered and bitter
                                    dies and bites
barefoot
          his defeated dust,
lacking enough earth for his harsh death.
Listen closely! Lacking earth to go to sleep in.
It is a small and beleaguered country. Simply sad,
sad and grim, sad and bitter. I've already said it,
simply sad and oppressed.

THE COUNTRY IN A POEM

USE WITH: Units 3, 4

DURATION: 2–3 classes

STANDARDS:

English Language Arts: 1, 2, 3, 4, 6, 10

Social Studies: 1c, 4h

Foreign Language: 1, 2.1, 3, 4

GOAL: To create visual representations of figures and images in the poem "Hay un país en el mundo" by Pedro Mir.

OBJECTIVES:

- To identify literal and figurative geographic images in the poem.
- To identify and locate the geographic features mentioned in the poem.
- To explain social themes suggested by the geographic images.

ACTIVITIES:

1. Using a KWL chart, ask students what they know about the geography of the Dominican Republic.

2. Read aloud the poem "Hay un país en el mundo" (unit 4), in Spanish or English or both. While listening, students draw what they see. For example, "Right in the sun's path, improbable archipelago, four cardinal cordilleras, three peninsulas with adjacent isles . . ."

3. Students share their drawings and then look at photographs and maps of the Dominican Republic to compare and contrast their drawings with these images. (See especially map 3 in unit 3.)

4. Students break into groups to discuss social themes in the poem. Each group is assigned one of the following questions:

   - Why does the poet choose to include the quote from Voltaire?

   - What is the mood and tone of the poem? What is suggested by the subtitle "a poem, sad on more than one occasion?"

   - Underline all of the adjectives used by the writer. What themes and emotions do they convey?

   - Why does the poet include the farmer? What themes are evoked by the phrase "lacking enough earth for his harsh death"?

Lesson plan prepared by Jocelyn Santana.

5. Following the discussions, students report back to the larger group. Students then return to their drawings and incorporate images that express the social themes of the poem.

ASSESSMENT: Each student writes a review of another student's picture. The review should describe how the picture conveys geographic details in the poem and the extent to which it captures an aspect of the poem's social themes.

MATERIALS:

• Large paper and markers to create drawings

• Photographs, topographical maps, and other maps of the Dominican Republic

INTRODUCTION TO DOMINICAN HISTORY

Silvio Torres-Saillant and Ramona Hernández

In this article, literary scholar and cultural critic Silvio Torres-Saillant and sociologist Ramona Hernández trace important events in Dominican history that help us understand the country's reality today. Maps 4 through 8 in unit 3 can be used with this reading.

In 1492, when the Spanish caravels commanded by Admiral Christopher Columbus successfully ventured across the Atlantic, the Caribbean was home to a thriving Taíno society with a population of approximately half a million. Scholars have traced the ethnic origins of the Taínos to a migratory wave of Arawak groups from South America that lasted several centuries. By AD 700, Taíno culture and society had evolved with well-defined characteristics. The society Columbus found in 1492 had an economic structure built around fishing, farming, and hunting. Politically, the island was divided into five confederate tribes headed by caciques. The family structure followed a mostly monogamous organization, and families usually had three to five children. Dominican historian Frank Moya Pons notes that while the father exercised central authority, consistent with a patriarchal family structure, inheritance and succession followed a matrilineal model.[1]

The Conquest

During his first encounter with Antillean indigenous people, Columbus perceived them as "well-built, with handsome bodies and fine features." Upon seeing the admiral and his men, they appeared very pleased and became so friendly that it was "a wonder to see," according to notes Columbus made in his travel journal. "Afterwards," he wrote, "they swam out to the ships' boats where we were and brought parrots and balls of cotton thread and spears and many other things."[2]

Columbus had already sailed through the Bahamas and Cuba

Taíno dwellings.

Adapted from *The Dominican Americans* (Westport, CT: Greenwood Publishing Group, Inc.). © 1998 by Silvio Torres-Saillant and Ramona Hernández. Reproduced with permission of Greenwood Publishing Group, Inc.

before arriving in Hispaniola on December 5, 1492. He decided to establish the Spanish settlements of the newly found territory on this island because of its promising gold deposits, which he and his entourage deduced from the fact that some of the aborigines wore golden ornaments. There the Spaniards built their first fort, called La Navidad. But while Columbus made his first return trip to Spain to inform the Crown about his magnificent "discoveries," the thirty-nine Spanish soldiers who staffed the fort perished at the hands of Taíno warriors, in retaliation for a rampage of rape and abuse of Taíno women perpetrated by the Spaniards during the admiral's absence.

Then followed a turbulent period of violence and depredation during which the native population was decimated as Spanish settlers spread throughout the island. A census of the colony taken in 1508 showed that a mere 60,000 Taínos remained from the nearly half a million encountered by the Spaniards in 1492. By 1519 their number was reduced to 30,000, and no available evidence exists to suggest that any Taíno communities survived by the end of the sixteenth century. They died from hunger, from alien diseases brought by the colonizers, and from the harshness of their forced labor in the gold mines set up by the Spanish. According to Moya Pons, "pregnant women systematically aborted or killed their own children to prevent them from becoming slaves." In the encomienda system, the native population was proportionally allocated as property among the white settlers.[3]

Hispaniola flourished as the first Spanish colony in a region that the Europeans viewed as the New World. In time it became the center of the entire Spanish colonization of the Western Hemisphere. Colonizing expeditions headed for Mexico, Peru, and other mainland territories had to use Hispaniola as their point of

An enslaved African and overseer in a sugar mill.

departure. As the colony developed it became known as Santo Domingo, after Saint Dominic, the Castilian who founded the Order of Friars and Preachers in the thirteenth century. The members of the order were known as Dominicans, and centuries later the inhabitants of Santo Domingo would adopt that name for their republic.

The African Population

The decimation of the indigenous population of Santo Domingo produced an acute need for labor, which the Spanish settlers sought to supply through the importation of captive workers from elsewhere. As a result, Santo Domingo became the port of entry for the first enslaved Africans who arrived in the New World. When King Ferdinand and Queen Isabella appointed Nicolás de Ovando as the new governor of Santo Domingo in 1501, they authorized him to bring "black slaves" to the colony. Ovando's fleet arrived in the island in July 1502, marking the start of the black experience in the Americas. From then on, the black population of Santo Domingo grew dramatically. The Spanish Crown overruled a decree that permitted the importation of only those enslaved blacks who had been born to Spanish masters and had thus received a Christian upbringing. This had the effect of allowing, from 1511 onward, the traffic of people directly from Africa.

As sugarcane cultivation and sugar manufacture supplanted the mineral economy of the colony after 1516, the new industry drew its labor force almost exclusively from African slaves. Soon the black population outnumbered the white by a wide margin. A 1606 census found 1,157 white settlers and 9,648 blacks, a numerical disparity that would continue to increase as the influx of Africans grew while the white Spanish settlers, disillusioned by the slim prospects for accumulating wealth, began to opt for emigration. By 1739 Archbishop Alvarez de Abreu reported that of the 12,259 people who inhabited Santo Domingo the majority were "free blacks." This was to have a decisive impact on the ethnic composition of the population.

Roots of Dominicanness

The year 1605 has been often cited as a pivotal moment for the Dominican people. In that year, having failed to contain illegal commerce between their subjects and the merchant ships of Spain's European rivals, the colonial authorities decided to burn down the areas most directly involved in the violation. Governor Antonio Osorio personally supervised the work of setting the island's whole western band on fire, having first forced the residents to vacate the region. The flames, of course, eventually cooled off, and the vacant territories became a sort of no-man's-land, until marauders of various kinds began to make use of them. The area became a favorite hideaway for pirates, filibusters, and buccaneers. Subsequently, ambitious entrepreneurs would join them, primarily from France, and by the end of the seventeenth century the western band of the island of Santo Domingo was filled with French-owned plantations that made intensive use of enslaved black labor.

Spain lost control of the western lands of the island, where a French colony developed in the course of the seventeenth century. The French colony became known as Saint Domingue. By September 1697 the Spanish acknowledged the contiguous colony and increased trade with their neighbors, encouraged by the Peace of Ryswick signed between France and Spain. By the end of the following century, Spain proved unable to sustain its colonial share on the island, causing it to relinquish jurisdiction over the entire island to France by means of the 1795 Treaty of Basel.

On the western side, enslaved people rebelled against their French colonial masters. In 1804 the black-ruled Republic of Haiti was proclaimed by a former slave, General Jean Jacques Dessalines. The fact that the newly liber-ated Haiti had to share the island with a society that remained under European colonial rule became a source of tension between the eastern and western peoples of Hispaniola. First in 1801 and later in 1822, Haitian leaders sought to safeguard their independence by unifying the entire island under their rule. The second time, the unifica-tion period lasted twenty-two years, until the tie was broken by the success of a Domini-can independence movement. On February 27, 1844, the Dominican Republic was pro-claimed as a sovereign nation.

Dominican independence, and the formal emergence of Dominicans as a people, thus occurred as a separation from the black republic of Haiti. One result of this history is that Dominican nationalist discourse has tradi-tionally emphasized perceived

The Embarcadero of Santo Domingo with "Columbus Tree" in background. Watercolor, ca. 1871.

Panoramic view (1920s) of Ozama River Bridge into Santo Domingo.

racial differences between the Dominican Republic and Haiti. At the same time, this history has complicated the racial self-identification of Dominicans: even today, the population is reluctant to affirm its blackness openly despite the overwhelming presence of people of African descent in the country.[4]

The Dominican Republic is at the core of the Caribbean historical experience despite the fact that it is seldom viewed as a member of the West Indian family. What is now the Dominican land witnessed the first settlement of Europeans, the first genocide of indigenous people, and the first cohort of enslaved Africans in the archipelago. Santo Domingo initiated racial mixture, religious syncretism, linguistic nativization, and the overall creolizing process that typifies Caribbean culture. With the splitting of Hispaniola into two distinct colonial spaces that in time became nations with their own distinguishing characteristics, a complex process of

historical evolution was set in motion. The harsh meeting of races and cultures that took place in the Dominican land during the colonial period was compounded later by the influx of a varied array of immigrants—French, German, African-American, anglophone West Indian, Arab, Jewish, Canary Islander, Chinese, Cuban, Puerto Rican, and Haitian. All of them, to varying degrees, have contributed to the ethnic and cultural formation of the Dominican people.

Precarious Autonomy

Paradoxically, the Dominican Republic, like Haiti, stands out as one of the earliest Caribbean territories to attain its national independence. Yet, like Haiti also, it has often had its sovereignty threatened by foreign forces as well as by the self-interest of its political elite. Following the proclamation of the country's independence and the founding of the republic, the conservative element invariably outsmarted the liberal patriots. Juan Pablo

Duarte, the ideological architect of the independence movement, remained in exile until his death, never having had the opportunity to participate in the new nation's governing bodies. Dominican rulers were more committed to serving themselves than to the arduous task of consolidating an independent and egalitarian society. As a result, the Dominican Republic suffered the annexation of its territory to the colonial domains of the Spanish Crown in 1861, only seventeen years after the nation came into being. The selling of the country's sovereignty by the conservative elite, represented then by President Pedro Santana, was accompanied by the formal military occupation of the land by Spanish soldiers. This gave rise to the War of Restoration, a nationalist armed struggle that lasted until July 1865. In that year the invading army completed its withdrawal, having suffered defeat at the hands of Dominican nationalists.

On December 8, 1865, Buenaventura Báez, who had been

president before and had a record of annexationist leanings, assumed the presidency. Shortly thereafter, President Báez began modifying the constitution to give himself autocratic powers and implemented economic measures that favored his allies while severely harming the tobacco industry of the Cibao region. His government met with opposition from a liberal sector represented by General Gregorio Luperón, who had excelled as a liberator during the War of Restoration. Báez had to resign the presidency the following year. The next two years were marked by political disarray in the country. Rivalries among the leaders led to a series of short-lived governments, each of which confronted the armed opposition of rebel forces. This period culminated in the installation of a triumvirate which, in addition to unleashing a reign of terror against liberal opponents, brought Báez back from exile and named him president.

President Báez took office again on May 2, 1868, beginning six years of repressive, corrupt, and autocratic rule. During that time Báez tried feverishly to annex the Dominican Republic to the United States and to sell or mortgage portions of the Dominican territory to foreign capitalists. After treating the country as a personal hacienda between 1868 and 1874, the shrewd caudillo had to resign following the armed opposition of a sector that enjoyed popular support. The old dictator, however, had not exhausted all of his tricks. He came back to power in December 1876, implementing again a corrupt, repressive, and autocratic government that lasted fourteen months. The fall of Báez was followed by a trying political period during which the leaders of the liberal sector were able to establish their control of the Dominican government until 1886.

From 1886 to 1899, Dominicans endured the cunning and tyrannical rule of Ulíses Heureaux. He ruined the country's economy and put it at the mercy of foreign governments and firms, allowing the United States to assume virtual control of the Dominican Republic. The U.S. takeover of Dominican customs in 1905 and the military occupation of the country from 1916 to 1924 clearly showed the United States as the small country's overlord.

The bloodthirsty, corrupt Rafael Leónidas Trujillo, who perpetrated thirty-one years of tyrannical rule against the Dominican people, benefited greatly from the U.S. presence in the country. Not only was he himself a graduate of the National Guard, a military police force created by the U.S. marines during the occupation, but his totalitarian government was able to achieve absolute control of the whole society thanks to the disarmament of the civilian population and the centralization of the armed forces implemented by the U.S. military government.

The period following the death of Trujillo in 1961 marked a turning point in Dominican

During Rafael Trujillo's dictatorship, every Dominican household had to prominently display the General's portrait.

A street in a poor section of Ciudad Trujillo before (top, 1936) and after (1946) public works projects under Trujillo.

history. Joaquín Balaguer was Trujillo's puppet president in 1961, when the dictator met his death. When the formal dictatorship fell, Balaguer did his best to stay in power by feigning an embrace of democracy, but he had to flee the country in 1962. Supported by the United States, the Catholic Church, the still-active military elite of Trujillo, and the Dominican oligarchy, he managed to take power as president again in 1966. He arranged for his own reelection repeatedly through 1978 and again from 1986 to 1996. In that year he decided to strike a deal with the opposition party, the Dominican Liberation Party, and helped its candidate Leonel Fernández win the election.

Balaguer proved the equal of Báez in the corruption, repres-sion, and autocracy of his governments, which largely brought back the worst vices of nineteenth-century Dominican politics. Beginning in the early 1960s, Dominican society experienced a massive and continuous exodus of people from the working-class, poor, and peasant sectors of the population. For the first time a diaspora was formed with a significant presence in Europe, the Caribbean, and the United States. As a result, future historians looking at the Dominican people from the mid-twentieth-century onward will have to widen their scope to include not only those on the eastern two-thirds of the island of Hispaniola but also those large masses of emigrants currently living in other parts of the world. ✾

Arawak: indigenous people who inhabited parts of the Caribbean in the precolonial era

cacique: chief

caudillo: leader or strongman

cordillera: mountain range

emigration: leaving one country to settle in another

encomienda: parcel of land granted to settlers that included dominion over the indigenous people living there

filibusters: military adventurers

hacienda: plantation

matrilineal: tracing descent through the maternal line

migratory: moving from one place to another

patriarchal: father-centered

syncretism: blending

Taíno: indigenous people living on Hispaniola when Columbus arrived

NOTES

1. Frank Moya Pons, *The Dominican Republic: A National History* (New Rochelle, NY: Hispaniola Books, 1995), 18–21.

2. Christopher Columbus, *Journal of the First Voyage (Diario del primer viaje),* translated and edited by B. W. Ife (Warminster, U.K.: Aris and Phillis, 1990), 29.

3. Moya Pons, *The Dominican Republic*, 34. The Spanish monarchy granted individual Spaniards parcels of land in the Caribbean colonies. These land grants, or encomiendas, included permission to enslave the native people living on them.

4. Silvio Torres-Saillant, "The Dominican Republic," in *No Longer Invisible: Afro-Latin Americans Today* (London: Minority Rights Group, 1995), 110.

A TIMELINE OF DOMINICAN HISTORY

Ruth Glasser

PERIOD	**3000 BC**	**AD 700s**	**1400s**	

POLITICAL

Several discrete Taíno tribes exist on the island, ruled by caciques, or chiefs.

Taíno tribes attempt to confederate, are interrupted by the arrival of the Spanish.

1492 Columbus arrives on Quisqueya, names it Hispaniola (Española in Spanish), and builds the fort La Navidad.

The Spanish Crown quells rebellions among the early Spanish settlers by granting them land and indigenous people as slaves.

SOCIAL/ECONOMIC

Taínos on the island have evolved into a well-defined society built around fishing, farming, and hunting.

Spanish decide to mine for gold.

DEMOGRAPHIC

Indigenous groups migrate from South America to the Caribbean, including to the island later known as Quisqueya.

As many as 500,000 Taínos live on the island.

Early Spanish settlers arrive, primarily from Andalusia.

IRVING ROUSE, *THE TAÍNOS: RISE AND DECLINE OF THE PEOPLE WHO GREETED COLUMBUS* (NEW HAVEN: YALE UNIVERSITY PRESS, 1992)

BARON CASTILLO, LIBRARY OF CONGRESS

This image of Alcázar de Colon contrasts the old and new—the 1490s fortress built by Columbus and the sculpted trees of Ciudad Trujillo, as Santo Domingo was renamed during the dictator's regime.

SOURCES: Silvio Torres-Saillant and Ramona Hernández, *The Dominican Americans* (Westport, CT: Greenwood Press, Inc., 1998); Jan Knippers Black, *The Dominican Republic: Politics and Development in an Unsovereign State* (Boston: Allen and Unwin, 1986); Frank Moya Pons, *The Dominican Republic: A National History* (New Rochelle, NY: Hispaniola Books, 1995); H. Hoetink, *The Dominican People 1850–1900: Notes for a Historical Sociology* (Baltimore: Johns Hopkins University Press, 1982); BBC News, "Timeline: Dominican Republic," http://news.bbc.co.uk/1/hi/world/americas/country_profiles/1216926.stm

PERIOD

1500s

1544 colonial map of Santo Domingo.

1600s

POLITICAL

1500

First governor of the island is appointed by the Spanish monarchs.

Spanish make Hispaniola the first Spanish colony in the New World, naming it Santo Domingo. The island becomes a base for Spanish colonizing expeditions to other parts of what is now Latin America.

Etching illustrates colonization showing Spain as angelic figure.

1519–33

Remaining Taínos attack Spanish settlements, leading to a series of wars between the settlers and the indigenous people. Peace is finally made with cacique Enriquillo in 1533.

1605

Colonial authorities burn areas where merchants are involved in smuggling. The burned-out western areas become hideouts for European pirates and other marauders.

SOCIAL/ECONOMIC

1516

Sugarcane cultivation and processing begin to supplant mining. Many Africans are brought in to provide slave labor.

Ranching and timber become important sources of income along with sugar, spawning a class of wealthy merchants.

1577

Smuggling of French and English goods becomes the basis of the economy of the northern and western parts of the island.

DEMOGRAPHIC

Taínos are decimated by European diseases, hunger, and forced labor. Some flee to the mountains.

1502

First slaves arrive in Santo Domingo, to be used mostly as domestic servants. Brought from Spain and Portugal, the first slaves are Hispanicized blacks known as ladinos. After the first slaves arrive, many more are forcibly imported directly from Africa.

1508

Only 60,000 Taínos remain.

1519

Only 30,000 Taínos remain.

1568

There are an estimated 20,000 slaves in Santo Domingo.

1606

Approximately 9,648 slaves remain in Santo Domingo. With decline of sugar production, some slaves are sold elsewhere, while others escape into the interior of the island or die of epidemic diseases.

1700s

1655
English attack on Hispaniola is defeated.

1667
French-led group attacks and pillages the city of Santiago.

1690–95
French and Spanish on the island stage attacks and counterattacks.

1697
Peace of Ryswick treaty signed, making peace between the French colony of Saint Domingue, which occupies the western third of the island, and the Spanish colony of Santo Domingo, which occupies the eastern two-thirds.

1777
Treaty of Aranjuez defines a border between the Spanish and French colonies, Santo Domingo and Saint Domingue.

1670s
Western areas of the island fill with French-owned plantations using African slave labor, and growing mainly tobacco.

1681
Spaniards on the island start selling meat and livestock to the French in exchange for European goods, and producing tobacco for French use.

Tobacco leaves.

Early 1700s
Sugar mills begin to proliferate in Saint Domingue. Cattle ranching declines and French increasingly depend on cattle from Santo Domingo.

Few new slaves are imported into the impoverished colony. Racial mixing gives rise to a demographic majority of mulattoes, which persists to this day.

1680s
Canary Islanders are brought to the island to combat the numerical superiority of the French.

1720s–60s
Santo Domingo continues to import settlers from the Canary Islands.

PERIOD

1700s *continued*

1800s

POLITICAL

1791
Slave revolts in Saint Domingue set in motion the Haitian Revolution.

1795
Spain cedes entire island to France through the Treaty of Basel.

1801–09
First Haiti, then France rules the entire island.

1801
Toussaint Louverture abolishes slavery.

1804
Republic of Haiti is declared an independent nation.

1821
In a period of "ephemeral independence," the Dominican Republic becomes an independent nation for five weeks.

1822
Haiti takes over the Spanish part of Hispaniola.

SOCIAL/ECONOMIC

1809 onward
Tobacco exports become the economic base of the central Cibao region, while mahogany is the main export in the south and cattle raising continues in the east.

Peasant farmers in all areas cultivate subsistence food and livestock.

Mahogany

AMERICAN BANK NOTE COMPANY LIBRARY OF CONGRESS

Man plowing with oxen.

DEMOGRAPHIC

1783
Spanish colony now has more than 80,000 people due to influx of Canary Islanders and immigrants from other parts of the Caribbean.

1789
Spanish colony now has about 180,000 inhabitants.

1809
War reduces population of the Spanish colony to less than 90,000.

1820s–40s
New populations come to Santo Domingo, including freed African Americans from North America and Sephardic Jews from Curaçao.

Allegorical illustration depicts the Spanish colonial relationship during the reign of Isabel II.

1838
Juan Pablo Duarte, Francisco del Rosario Sánchez, and Ramón Matías Mella form the secret society La Trinitaria in Santo Domingo to work for independence from Haiti.

1844
The Dominican Republic proclaims its independence from Haiti and becomes a sovereign nation.

1844–61
"Counterpoint" of caudillos: Pedro Santana and Buenaventura Báez alternately rule the Dominican Republic.

1861
Dominican Republic is annexed to Spain.

1863–65
War of Restoration fought to overthrow Spanish rule.

1865
Dominican Republic becomes independent once again.

1860s–1900
Dominican Republic is ruled by a number of caudillos, some of whom seek to resolve the country's chronic debt through annexation or sale of land to the U.S.

Soldiers on Parade, Santo Domingo, ca. 1904.

Juan Pablo Duarte

Buenaventura Báez

Late 1800s
Refugees come from Cuba, fleeing that island's independence struggle, and build an oligarchy based on the trading of tobacco from the central Cibao region.

Other Caribbean refugees settle in the Santo Domingo region to cultivate sugar. Santo Domingo emerges as the nation's commercial, financial, and political center.

1870s
A modern sugar industry begins, along with a rise in coffee and cacao production and decline of tobacco and mahogany. Power begins to shift toward Santo Domingo and away from Santiago, the main urban center of the Cibao.

1880s
Cibao begins to cultivate cacao and coffee.

1844
Dominican population reaches 126,000; Haitian population is 800,000.

1860s
Spanish immigrants arrive as a result of the Spanish occupation.

Tobacco plant.

1870s
Large numbers of Italians and Syrian and Lebanese Christians begin to arrive, along with some Cubans and Puerto Ricans.

1870s–1900
Haitians, Curaçaoans, and immigrants from the English-speaking Caribbean arrive to work on sugar plantations.

PERIOD # 1900–1950s

U.S. MARINE CORPS/NATIONAL ARCHIVES

POLITICAL

Early 1900s
European governments send warships to Santo Domingo to force repayment of debts.

1905
United States takes over Dominican customs collection to establish U.S. dominance and forestall European influence in the Caribbean region. U.S. is involved in managing a series of unstable governments in the Dominican Republic.

U.S. Marines patrol the Ozama River, Santo Domingo, 1919.

1916–24
U.S. military occupies the Dominican Republic.

1924
Financial crisis and popular rebellion help end the U.S. occupation, but the U.S. maintains strong financial and political control.

1929
New treaty between Haiti and the Dominican Republic resolves border questions.

SOCIAL/ECONOMIC

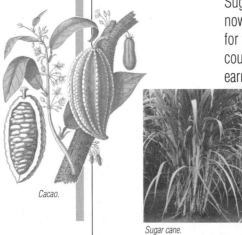

Cacao.

Sugar cane.

LINDA-ANNE REBHUN

1910
Sugar and cacao now account for four-fifths of country's foreign earnings.

1919
Most Dominican commerce, including sugar industry, now tied to U.S. interests. Post-WW I rise in sugar prices allows for importation of goods, urbanization, and health, education, and construction projects linking the country through new highways.

1920s
Flourishing agriculture, commerce, and industry permit more public works projects.

1929
Worldwide economic depression leads to collapse of export-based economy.

DEMOGRAPHIC

Thousands of Puerto Ricans and other immigrants continue to arrive in the Dominican Republic, especially the eastern region around San Pedro de Macorís and La Romana.

1920s
Increasing numbers of Haitians come to the Dominican Republic to cut sugarcane.

LIBRARY OF CONGRESS

Residents of San Pedro de Macorís, 1940.

1960s

1930
General Rafael Leónidas Trujillo Molina seizes power in a rigged election. He is a graduate of the National Guard, a police force created by the U.S. Marines during the occupation.

1937
Trujillo orchestrates massacre of approximately 15,000 Haitians in the Dominican Republic. The slaughter eliminates Haitians from border areas and allows Trujillo to establish new frontier military zones.

1952
Agreements are formalized between the Haitian and Dominican governments to bring Haitian cane cutters across the border for six-month periods.

1960
Three of the Mirabal sisters, prominent opponents of the Trujillo regime, are murdered by the dictator's henchmen.

1961
Trujillo is assassinated.

Maria Teresa, Patria, and Minerva Mirabal.

Country cemetery, Dominican Republic ca. 1904.

1930s-1960s
Three-quarters or more of the population is poor and lacks access to land, adequate food, and clean water.

1960s
U.S. companies begin to invest heavily in local agriculture, mining, and industry.

1930s–60s
Trujillo takes over industrial, agricultural, and mining operations, and fosters industrialization.

New elites form through involvement in government, military, light industry, banking, and tourism.

Tobacco plants.

1930s
Landless peasants start to move into Dominican cities.

1960s
Massive exodus begins, as people move from rural areas to cities within the Dominican Republic and from the island to cities abroad, especially New York and San Juan.

La Romana, ca. 1940.

PERIOD | **1960s** *continued* | **1970s**

POLITICAL

1963
Liberal Juan Bosch is democratically elected, governs for seven months, then is overthrown by conservatives and goes into exile.

1965
Armed insurrection erupts against the illegal regime, as liberal wing of the armed forces demands return to legality and the constitution. Civil war ensues between "constitutionalists" and conservatives. U.S. Marines invade Dominican Republic in support of conservatives and defeat the constitutionalists.

1966–78
Joaquín Balaguer, Trujillo's right-hand man, becomes president, supported by the U.S.

1978
Antonio Guzmán of the Dominican Revolutionary Party (PRD) wins the presidency in the first democratic election in modern Dominican history. The country enjoys freedom of speech and political stability.

SOCIAL/ECONOMIC

COURTESY OF THE CUNY-DOMINICAN STUDIES INSTITUTE LIBRARY, CITY COLLEGE

Juan Bosch.

1966
Dominican Republic becomes dependent on foreign—especially U.S.— aid, leading to inflation and public austerity programs.

COURTESY OF ROGER LOWENSTEIN, L.A. LEADERSHIP ACADEMY

1970s
Sugar falls from 48 percent to 35 percent of exports, while coffee, cacao, and tobacco exports increase. Mining and tourism also become important industries.

MATTHEW DULLA

DEMOGRAPHIC

DOUGLAS JONES, PHOTOGRAPHER, *LOOK* MAGAZINE, LIBRARY OF CONGRESS

U.S. troops advance on a sniper in Santo Domingo in June, 1965.

RECENT SATELLITE IMAGE OF HURRICANE OVER THE CARIBBEAN, PROVIDED BY THE SEAWIFS PROJECT, NASA/GODDARD SPACE FLIGHT CENTER, AND ORBIMAGE

1979
Two hurricanes leave more than 200,000 homeless and cause $1 billion in damage.

1980s

1990s

1980s

Urban poor riot over government-imposed price increases; industrial and agricultural unions strike to protest deteriorating work conditions and inadequate pay. Most protests are violently crushed by the government.

1986–96

Balaguer is president again.

1991

Guillermo Linares elected as first Dominican representative to the New York City Council.

1994

Dominican constitution amended to allow for dual citizenship.

1996

Adriano Espaillat wins seat in New York State Assembly.

Leonel Fernández of the Dominican Liberation Party (PLD) elected president of the Dominican Republic. Thousands of Dominican citizens living in New York and other U.S. cities fly home to Santo Domingo to vote.

1980s

Several industrial free trade zones are constructed, where foreign companies employ local workers in low-wage assembly jobs.

1985

Unemployment exceeds 30 percent.

1989

Almost six in ten Dominican households live below the poverty line.

Bavaro Beach.

Mid-1990s

Economic boom, with average growth rates of approximately 6 percent per year. Growth is concentrated in the tourism, telecommunications, and assembly sectors. However, poverty and inequality remain high.

Shanties in Santo Domingo.

Columbus statue and cathedral, 1893.

1985

800,000 Dominicans are estimated to have migrated to the United States and Puerto Rico. Remittances from overseas migrants increase purchasing power for families in the Dominican Republic.

PERIOD

1990s *cont'd* | 2000s

POLITICAL

1997
New law gives Dominican citizens—even those who also hold U.S. citizenship—the right to vote in Dominican presidential elections from polling places abroad. (However, polling places in New York and other locations are not set up until 2004.)

2000
Dominican Revolutionary Party returns to power with Hipólito Mejía as president.

COURTESY OF JOCELYN SANTANA

2004
Leonel Fernández defeats incumbent Hipólito Mejía to again win the presidency. Dominican residents of the United States, Spain and several other countries are for the first time able to vote in a Dominican election from polling places in their adopted countries.

SOCIAL/ECONOMIC

LINDA-ANNE REBHUN

Young boys work as shoe shiners in the popular Santo Domingo shopping district, El Conde.

2002–03
U.S. recession undercuts demand for the Dominican Republic's key products. Together with government borrowing, this slows growth rates and accelerates inflation.

2003
The country's second largest private bank, Baninter, collapses amid rumors of corruption and malfeasance. The resultant government bailout intensifies the economic crisis and leads to political scandal.

JENNIFER MORGAN

DEMOGRAPHIC

1998
Hurricane Georges causes widespread devastation.

BEAU McCUNE

2000
U.S. census reports more than three-quarters of a million Dominicans living in the United States and Puerto Rico; other researchers estimate the true number at over 1 million.

September 2001
The 9/11 attacks on the World Trade Center result in deaths and many job losses among Dominicans in New York City. Local Dominican organizations assist the victims.

November 2001
American Airlines flight 587 bound for Santo Domingo crashes in Queens, NY, killing all 255 people on board. Three days of national mourning are declared in the Dominican Republic.

DOMINICAN TIMELINE

USE WITH: Unit 7 (unit 6 may also be used as supplementary material)

DURATION: 2–3 classes

STANDARDS:

English Language Arts: 1, 3, 7, 8, 10

Social Studies: 1b, 1e, 1g, 2b, 2c, 2e, 4b, 4h, 5b, 6d, 7a, 7b, 7d, 9b

Foreign Language: 1, 2.1, 3, 4

GOAL: To familiarize students with important events in Dominican history.

OBJECTIVES:

- To work with and augment a timeline of Dominican history.
- To match visual and factual information.

ACTIVITIES:

1. Students read the "Timeline of Dominican History" (unit 7) and as a class answer the following questions:

   - Based on the information in the timeline, what is your understanding of the term "demography?"

   - Who are the different peoples who have settled in or emigrated to the island of Hispaniola over the centuries? How have people earned their living?

   - Which groups have governed the island of Hispaniola during its history? Which groups have challenged their rule?

   - What is the difference between political and economic domination? What are some examples of each in the Dominican context?

2. Students put their timelines away. At random, give each student a card with an important date from the timeline and an explanation of its historical significance. (The teacher should choose the dates.)

3. Students review their card and then, on a blank piece of drawing paper, draw a scene to reflect their historical information.

4. Individually and in chronological order, students hang their illustrations on the classroom wall to create a visual and written timeline. Each section of the timeline should contain a date, explanation, and picture.

Lesson plan prepared by Rebecca Ford.

ASSESSMENT: Students choose a historical event from the timeline and list the who, what, when, where, and why, and the historical significance of the event. Teacher grades students on their understanding of the event.

MATERIALS:

• Large cards with date and factual information

• Blank white paper

• Colored markers or pencils

• Tape or tacks

MINERVA

Julia Alvarez

Author Julia Alvarez was born in New York City to Dominican parents and spent her early childhood in the Dominican Republic. In 1960, when she was ten, her family had to flee their homeland. Her father, a prominent physician, was involved in a plot to overthrow Trujillo that was uncovered by the dictator's secret police. Alvarez has published highly acclaimed novels (How the García Girls Lost Their Accents, In the Time of the Butterflies), essays (Something to Declare), poetry (The Woman I Kept to Myself), and books for young readers (Before We Were Free, Finding Miracles), and is writer-in-residence at Middlebury College.

From *In the Time of the Butterflies.* Copyright © 1994 by Julia Alvarez. Published by Plume, an imprint of Penguin Group (USA), and originally in hardcover by Algonquin Books of Chapel Hill. Reprinted by permission of Susan Bergholz Literary Services, New York. All rights reserved.

Before the U.S. Marines left the Dominican Republic in 1924, they trained and equipped a National Guard and installed General Rafael Leónidas Trujillo at its head. The ruthless and murderous Trujillo made himself president in 1930. His dictatorship, supported by the United States, lasted three decades.

Growing resistance to Trujillo's brutal regime spawned secret movements dedicated to his overthrow. Three sisters from the town of Salcedo—Patria, Minerva, and María Teresa Mirabal—were among the best-known of the underground activists. Dominicans called them Las Mariposas, or "the Butterflies." The Mirabal sisters struggled to be educated and politically active women, achieving advanced degrees at a time when few Dominican women did so. As a result of their anti-Trujillo activities, the sisters and their husbands were imprisoned repeatedly. They were murdered by the regime's soldiers in 1960, becoming martyrs and symbols of resistance to the dictatorship.

In the Time of the Butterflies, a historical novel by Julia Alvarez, is a fictionalized version of the Mirabal sisters' story. In the excerpt presented here, Minerva, a student at a private Catholic boarding school, first learns of the horrors of the dictatorship from a classmate whose family members have been killed.

Complications

1938

First time I met Sinita she was sitting in the parlor where Sor Asunción was greeting all the new pupils and their mothers. She was all by herself, a skinny girl with a sour look on her face and pokey elbows to match. She was dressed in black, which was odd as most children weren't put in mourning clothes until they were at least fifteen. And this little girl didn't look any older than me, and I was only twelve. Though I would have argued with anyone who told me I was just a kid!

I watched her. She seemed as bored as I was with all the polite talk in that parlor. It was like a heavy shaking of talcum powder in the brain hearing all those mothers complimenting each other's daughters and lisping back in good Castilian to the Sisters of the Merciful Mother. Where was this girl's mother?

I wondered. She sat alone, glaring at everybody, as if she would pick a fight if you asked her where her mother was. I could see, though, that she was sitting on her hands and biting her bottom lip so as not to cry. The straps on her shoes had been cut off to look like flats, but they looked worn out, was what they looked like.

I got up and pretended to study the pictures on the walls like I was a lover of religious art. When I got to the Merciful Mother right above Sinita's head, I reached in my pocket and pulled out the button I'd found on the train. It was sparkly like a diamond and had a little hole in back so you could thread a ribbon through it and wear it like a romantic lady's choker necklace. It wasn't something I'd do, but I could see the button would make a good trade with someone inclined in that direction.

I held it out to her. I didn't know what to say, and it probably wouldn't have helped anyway. She picked it up, turned it all around, and then set it back down in my palm. "I don't want your charity."

I felt an angry tightness in my chest. "It's just a friendship button."

She looked at me a moment, a deciding look like she couldn't be sure of anybody. "Why didn't you just say so?" She grinned as if we were already friends and could tease each other.

"I did just say so," I said. I opened up my hand and offered her the button again. This time she took it.

…

After our mothers left, we stood on line while a list was made of everything in our bags. I noticed that along with not having a mother to bring her, Sinita didn't own much either. Everything she had was tied up in a bundle, and when Sor Milagros wrote it out, all it took was a couple of lines: *3 change of underwear, 4 pair of socks, brush and comb, towel and nightdress.* Sinita offered the sparkly button, but Sor Milagros said it wasn't necessary to write that down.

"Charity student," the gossip went round. "So?" I challenged the giggly girl with curls like hiccups, who whispered it to me. She shut up real quick. It made me glad all over again I'd given Sinita that button.

Afterwards, we were taken into an assembly hall and given all sorts of welcomes. Then Sor Milagros, who was in charge of the tens through twelves, took our smaller group upstairs into the dormitory hall we would share. Our side-by-side beds were already set up for the night with mosquito nets. It looked like a room of little bridal veils.

Sor Milagros said she would now assign us our beds according to our last names. Sinita raised her hand and asked if her bed couldn't be next to mine. Sor Milagros hesitated, but then a sweet look came on her face. Sure, she said. But when some other girls asked, she said no. I spoke right up, "I don't think it's fair if you just make an exception for us."

Sor Milagros looked mighty surprised. I suppose being a nun and all, not many people told her what was wrong and right. Suddenly, it struck me, too, that this plump little nun with a bit of her gray hair showing under her headdress wasn't Mamá or Papá I could argue things with. I was on the point of apologizing, but Sor Milagros just smiled her gap-toothed smile and said, "All right, I'll allow you all to choose your own beds. But at the first sign of argument"—some of the girls had already sprung towards the best beds by the window and were fighting about who got there first—"we'll go back to alphabetical. Is that clear?"

"Yes, Sor Milagros," we chorused.

She came up to me and took my face in her hands. "What's your name?" she wanted to know.

I gave her my name, and she repeated it several times like she was tasting it. Then she smiled like it tasted just fine. She looked over at Sinita, whom they all seemed partial to, and said, "Take care of our dear Sinita."

"I will," I said, standing up straight like I'd been given a mission. And that's what it turned out to be, all right.

…

A few days later, Sor Milagros gathered us all around for a little talk. Personal hygiene, she called it. I knew right away it would be about interesting things described in the most uninteresting way.

First, she said there had been some accidents. Anyone needing a canvas sheet should come see her. Of course, the best way to prevent a mishap was to be sure to visit our chamber pots every night before we got in bed. Any questions?

Not a one.

Then, a shy, embarrassed look came on her face. She explained that we might very well become young ladies while we were at school this year. She went through a most tangled-up explanation about the how and why, and finished by saying if we should start our complications, we should come see her. This time she didn't ask if there were any questions.

I felt like setting her straight, explaining things

simply the way Patria had explained them to me. But I guessed it wasn't a good idea to try my luck twice in the first week.

When she left, Sinita asked me if I understood what on earth Sor Milagros had been talking about. I looked at her surprised. Here she'd been dressed in black like a grownup young lady, and she didn't know the first thing. Right then, I told Sinita everything I knew about bleeding and having babies between your legs. She was pretty shocked, and beholden. She offered to trade me back the secret of Trujillo.

"What secret is that?" I asked her. I thought Patria had told me all the secrets.

"Not yet," Sinita said looking over her shoulder.

...

It was a couple of weeks before Sinita got to her secret. I'd forgotten about it, or maybe I'd just put it out of my mind, a little scared what I might find out. We were busy with classes and making new friends. Almost every night someone or other came visiting under our mosquito nets or we visited them. We had two regulars, Lourdes and Elsa, and soon all four of us started doing everything together. It seemed like we were all just a little different—Sinita was charity and you could tell; Lourdes was fat, though as friends we called her pleasantly plump when she asked, and she asked a lot; Elsa was pretty in an I-told-you-so way, as if she hadn't expected to turn out pretty and now she had to prove it. And me, I couldn't keep my mouth shut when I had something to say.

The night Sinita told me the secret of Trujillo I couldn't sleep. All day I hadn't felt right, but I didn't tell Sor Milagros. I was afraid she'd stick me in the sickroom and I'd have to lie in bed, listening to Sor Consuelo reading novenas for the sick and dying. Also, if Papá found out, he might change his mind and keep me home where I couldn't have any adventures.

I was lying on my back, looking up into the white tent of the mosquito net, and wondering who else was awake. In her bed next to mine, Sinita began to cry very quietly as if she didn't want anybody to know. I waited a little, but she didn't stop. Finally, I stepped over to her bed and lifted the netting. "What's wrong?" I whispered.

She took a second to calm down before she answered. "It's José Luis."

"Your brother?" We all knew he had died just this last summer. That's how come Sinita had been wearing black that first day.

Her body began to shake all over with sobs. I

crawled in and stroked her hair like Mamá did mine whenever I had a fever. "Tell me, Sinita, maybe it'll help."

"I can't," she whispered. "We can all be killed. It's the secret of Trujillo."

Well, all I had to be told was I couldn't know something for me to *have* to know it. So I reminded her, "Come on, Sinita. I told you about babies."

It took some coaxing, but finally she began.

She told me stuff I didn't even know about her. I thought she was always poor, but it turned out her family used to be rich and important. Three of her uncles were even friends of Trujillo. But they turned against him when they saw he was doing bad things.

"Bad things?" I interrupted. "Trujillo was doing bad things?" It was as if I had just heard Jesus had slapped a baby or Our Blessed Mother had not conceived Him the immaculate conception way. "That can't be true," I said, but in my heart, I felt a china-crack of doubt.

"Wait," Sinita whispered, her thin fingers finding my mouth in the dark. "Let me finish."

"My uncles, they had a plan to do something to Trujillo, but somebody told on them, and all three were shot, right on the spot." Sinita took a deep breath as if she were going to blow out all her grandmother's birthday candles.

"But what bad things was Trujillo doing that they wanted to kill him?" I asked again. I couldn't leave it alone. At home, Trujillo hung on the wall by the picture of Our Lord Jesus with a whole flock of the cutest lambs.

Sinita told me as much as she knew. I was shaking by the time she was through.

...

According to Sinita, Trujillo became president in a sneaky way. First, he was in the army, and all the people who were above him kept disappearing until he was the one right below the head of the whole armed forces.

This man who was the head general had fallen in love with another man's wife. Trujillo was his friend and so he knew all about this secret. The woman's husband was a very jealous man, and Trujillo made friends with him, too.

One day, the general told Trujillo he was going to be meeting this woman that very night under the bridge in Santiago where people meet to do bad things. So Trujillo went and told the husband, who waited under the bridge for his wife and this general and shot them both dead.

Very soon after that, Trujillo became head of the armed forces.

"Maybe Trujillo thought that general was doing a bad thing by fooling around with somebody else's wife," I defended him.

I heard Sinita sigh. "Just wait," she said, "before you decide."

After Trujillo became the head of the army, he got to talking to some people who didn't like the old president. One night, these people surrounded the palace and told the old president that he had to leave. The old president just laughed and sent for his good friend, the head of the armed forces. But General Trujillo didn't come and didn't come. Soon, the old president was the ex-president on an airplane to Puerto Rico. Then, something that surprised even the people who had surrounded the palace, Trujillo announced he was the president.

"Didn't anyone tell him that wasn't right?" I asked, knowing I would have.

"People who opened their big mouths didn't live very long," Sinita said. "Like my uncles I told you about. Then, two more uncles, and then my father." Sinita began crying again. "Then this summer, they killed my brother."

My tummy ache had started up again. Or maybe it was always there, but I'd forgotten about it while trying to make Sinita feel better. "Stop, please," I begged her. "I think I'm going to throw up."

"I can't," she said.

Sinita's story spilled out like blood from a cut.

...

One Sunday this last summer, her whole family was walking home from church. Her whole family meant all Sinita's widowed aunts and her mother and tons of girl cousins, with her brother José Luis being the only boy left in the entire family. Everywhere they went, the girls were assigned places around him. Her brother had been saying that he was going to revenge his father and uncles, and the rumor all over town was that Trujillo was after him.

As they were rounding the square, a vendor came up to sell them a lottery ticket. It was the dwarf they always bought from, so they trusted him.

"Oh I've seen him!" I said. Sometimes when we would go to San Francisco in the carriage, and pass by the square, there he was, a grown man no taller than me at twelve. Mamá never bought from him. She claimed Jesus told us not to gamble, and playing the lottery was gambling. But every time I was alone with Papá, he bought a whole bunch of tickets and called it a good investment.

José Luis asked for a lucky number. When the dwarf went to hand him the ticket, something silver flashed in his hand. That's all Sinita saw. Then José Luis was screaming horribly and her mother and all the aunts were shouting for a doctor. Sinita looked over at her brother, and the front of his white shirt was covered with blood.

I started crying, but I pinched my arms to stop. I had to be brave for Sinita.

"We buried him next to my father. My mother hasn't been the same since. Sor Asunción, who knows my family, offered to let me come to *el colegio* for free."

The aching in my belly was like wash being wrung so tightly, there wasn't a drop of water left in the clothes. "I'll pray for your brother," I promised her. "But Sinita, one thing. How is this Trujillo's secret?"

"You still don't get it? Minerva, don't you see? Trujillo is having everyone killed!"

I lay awake most of that night, thinking about Sinita's brother and her uncles and her father and this secret of Trujillo that nobody but Sinita seemed to know about. I heard the clock, down in the parlor, striking every hour. It was already getting light in the room by the time I fell asleep.

In the morning, I was shaken awake by Sinita. "Hurry," she was saying. "You're going to be late for Matins." All around the room, sleepy girls were clapping away in their slippers towards the crowded basins in the washroom. Sinita grabbed her towel and soap dish from her night table and joined the exodus.

As I came fully awake, I felt the damp sheet under me. Oh no, I thought, I've wet my bed! After I'd told Sor Milagros that I wouldn't need an extra canvas sheet on my mattress.

I lifted the covers, and for a moment, I couldn't make sense of the dark stains on the bottom sheet. Then I brought up my hand from checking myself. Sure enough, my complications had started. ⚜

---

el colegio: high school
Matins: morning religious services
novena: Catholic prayer offered for a special intention, for a special occasion, or in preparation for a feast
Sor: Sister

"BUTTERFLIES SOARING UP TO THE SKY..."

Interview with Doña Dedé Mirabal

María Teresa, Patria, and Minerva Mirabal.

Doña Dedé Mirabal was interviewed by Claudia Bedoya-Rose at the Mirabal sisters' home in Salcedo, Dominican Republic, in December 2002.

ABOVE: *Doña Dedé Mirabal.* BELOW: *Doña Dedé Mirabal is interviewed by Cladia Bedoya-Rose.*

Dominican history is full of the accomplishments of men, but women, too, have played an important role in shaping the country's political future. Minerva, María Teresa, and Patria Mirabal were patriots and feminists. They spent years fighting the dictator Trujillo until they were murdered by his henchmen only a few months before the dictator's own assassination. The three sisters, known as Las Mariposas, have been immortalized in recent years in Julia Alvarez's novel In the Time of the Butterflies. *In 2001 the novel was made into a movie starring Salma Hayek as Minerva Mirabal.*

A fourth Mirabal sister, Bélgica Adela, or Dedé, survives, and keeps a museum in memory of her martyred siblings in the house where they spent their final months of persecution. In this interview, Doña Dedé shares memories of her sisters and recalls the obstacles that Dominican women faced as they struggled to transcend narrow gender roles. The Trujillo era was an oppressive time for all Dominicans. It was doubly so for women trying to get an education and make a difference in the world around them.

In one incident recalled by Doña Dedé, Trujillo, who was known to prey on attractive women, hosted a party with the intention of seducing the beautiful Minerva. Her resistance, portrayed as a humiliating slap across the face in the novel and the movie, was really more of what Doña Dedé calls "a slap by attitude." Minerva refused to become a sexual object for Trujillo's amusement, and the incident was a turning point in the personal and political struggle that eventually cost her her life.

Interview with Doña Dedé Mirabal

I have so many memories. For example, Patria and her husband got married right here in this house. That's why I polish it like a silver cup, in order to keep it just the way they left it. This house is surrounded by memories because it's surrounded by plants grown by my sisters. I preserve the plants as best I can.

When a decision had to be made about the mausoleum, I said that my sisters needed to be surrounded by butterflies, by plants, in a place where they had dreamed their dreams and grown up. At the time of their deaths, they had been making some Dominican flags so that when the victory came they could hang them up. Two years ago, their remains were brought here for reburial on the museum grounds. It was very sad to see them wrapped in the flag. Now they are national martyrs.

Growing up with my sisters was the most beautiful part of my life.

Mirabal monument in Salcedo.

We were very close. When María Teresa was born, I was almost ten years old. Back then there was no television so we entertained ourselves by running around, dressing our dolls. In those days we were educated by our parents. Afterwards, they sent us to a small school here in the country. We went in the morning and in the afternoon until we finished third grade. Then my mother decided to send us to an academy run by Franciscan nuns in the town of La Vega, in the Cibao.

Minerva was a woman ahead of her time. She had a heron as a pet and she let it fly about freely but the heron always returned. One day the bird left and never came back. She said, "See, even animals love freedom." She wanted women to be where they are today, making decisions, getting ahead. Imagine, forty-something years ahead of her time. She

studied law when she was twenty-seven, reading law books that were heavily censored.

When the first United States invasion happened, from 1916 to 1924, my mother was a teenager. The people rebelled against the invasion. The participants in that movement—it wasn't called a revolution, but a movement—went and hid in the mountains. Among them was a distant relative of my grandmother.

At that time there was an American military barracks in Salcedo. One day one of the rebels came to ask my grandmother for help, and my grandmother said she really couldn't help since she was a widow. However, there's always a traitor, someone who plays both ends toward the middle. He informed the American government that my grandmother was helping the movement. When the soldiers came looking for my grandmother, she said she had done nothing: she had no help to give, as she was the sole support of her family. Even so, they warned her that they were going to burn down her house. That night she gathered up the whole family and went to stay with her brother nearby. The next day when she returned, the house had been burned to the ground. My mother never forgot this deliberate, vicious act.

We had an Uncle José. He was ten when the government committed this atrocity against his mother—my grandmother. He hated the American government, for as he said, "The Americans left us Trujillo. He's the product of that invasion." For that reason, from the time we were very little, there was always a feeling in our house against Trujillo. My grandmother's economic well-being declined after the loss of her house. My other uncle was shot by the American government. All those experiences contributed to Minerva's anti-Trujillo feelings.

Minerva told us that when she was at the academy there was a girl who was always very sad because her family had been murdered. That was Trujillo's style; after ordering the families killed, he'd give scholarships to the daughters. So from hearing others tell of their experiences with the regime, and because of our own grandmother's experience, Minerva began to form her own ideas about change and freedom.

Trujillo used everyone. An important person, a lawyer, a poet, a writer—if they didn't do what the dictator wanted, he killed them. He would put them in a car and have it roll over a cliff; that was his style of killing.

He liked to turn his charms on women and carry them off. The party was a pretext for the specific purpose of getting to know my sister. But since Minerva was a fervent anti-Trujillista, it turned into a duel that didn't end until Trujillo finally conquered her by taking her life. He persecuted her for eleven years. When she completed her studies at the university he refused to grant her a law degree, and this added to her martyrdom.

A young woman like Minerva was a great temptation to him. Although he never showed his feelings, his plans and desires for Minerva were well known. But she never gave in. She danced with him and spoke with him but she showed him she wasn't an ordinary woman. She was not an easy person, and for that he never forgave her. People say that Minerva gave Trujillo a hard slap, but really this slap was one of attitude.

Minerva was a brave and self-assured woman. This was an insult for Trujillo—the fact that she wouldn't give up the fight out of fear of him. My uncle said to her one day, "Minerva, you have two children. Think about what you're getting into." And she answered him, "What if my blood needs to be shed in order to save other orphans?" Each incident made her more rebellious.

My father, Enrique Mirabal, was imprisoned in order to put pressure on Minerva. He wasn't political. Minerva went with my mother to the government office to ask for clemency. He didn't want them to ask for clemency for him; he was angry because he hadn't done anything. Finally he was freed, after suffering much mistreatment, and poor Minerva and Mamá suffered a great deal, too. At the end he died of illness, but the truth is that his death was hastened by the mistreatment in the prison because they had very inhumane punishments. Little by little he had to close his business. He knew that people couldn't come to the store to buy his merchandise because they would be killed.

My mother always worried about Minerva because she was the only unmarried daughter. Eventually, though, she married Dr. Manolo Tavárez Justo and both of them devoted themselves to the struggle against the dictatorship. My mother said, "At least now she has a man by her side." A pretty, single woman was more vulnerable to all types of evils.

In 1959 a band of young revolutionaries, Dominicans who had been living in exile, mounted an expedition against Trujillo. They entered the country at Constanza, Maimón, and Estero Hondo, but the expedition was defeated and they were killed. Afterwards, Minerva and a group of young people formed the June 14 Revolutionary Movement [named for the date of the 1959 expedition], but it was discovered and most of the members were tortured and imprisoned. Minerva was one of the leaders of the June 14 Revolutionary Movement, and Trujillo persecuted her and threw her in prison along with her husband, Manolo, who was the group's principal leader.

Minerva and María Teresa were sent to Victoria Prison, and their husbands were there, too, at first. My sisters were there for three months, and for one month they were isolated in a torture chamber. Initially their sentence was for five years but later it was reduced to three. Before the three years were up, in August 1960, they were freed as a result of pressure from the Organization of American States.

On November 3, Trujillo said, "I only have two problems, the Catholic Church and the Mirabal family." Finally, the dictator gave the order to eliminate them. On November 25, 1960, they were assassinated—Minerva, Patria, and María Teresa, and their driver Rufino de la Cruz. They were murdered as they were returning to Salcedo from Puerto Plata, where their husbands were in prison.

People say that it was Minerva against Trujillo and Trujillo against Minerva. Trujillo conquered her, but he didn't conquer the people. Because now the people have complete freedom of expression and action. Women are where they are now thanks to her, even though there are still many things to be achieved.

Today when I see her children, I think of how much love Minerva had for her people—so much that she would give her life and leave her children orphans. They found a pair of "mothers" in their grandmother and me. The children remember their grandmother with great affection, as Mamá Chea, because she guided them and gave them a lot of advice.

Given their young age, we tried to raise the children normally, without rancor or hate. With the inheritance my father left we educated them. When they were young we sent them to a Christian academy. We didn't want the children to be completely isolated from society. In the academy they were treated very kindly. Today, Manolo, Minerva's son, is a businessman, a rice dealer. My son, Jaime David, was vice president and now he's a candidate for the presidency.

We have the great fortune of being a very close family and we are always sharing. Three days ago for Christmas everyone was here. There are at least fifty of us and everyone is very close, which gives me much satisfaction. Everyone in our family is healthy, they're now adults with their own families. I am seventy-seven years old and I truly feel very fortunate. This has in some way made up for the pain I have suffered. It's been very difficult but I have healed: I don't feel hatred although I always remember my sisters.

For the twenty-fifth anniversary of their death, Freddy Beras, a very well-known television personality, raised enough funds among Dominicans to donate the monument that's in front of the house. This monument has three main sections. The black part symbolizes the darkness in which our people lived. The white part represents the growth and development of my three sisters. Then there's the third part where they're oppressed, that represents Trujillo's government. On the dome there are three black branches that represent the butterflies soaring up to the sky.

In the United States they know something about Dominican history but many people don't know what happened to many families in this country. In 1981 a group of women in Colombia decided to make November 25 the "International Day Against Violence Towards Women," in homage to Minerva, Patria, and María Teresa. And in 1997 the United Nations declared that date an international day of struggle against violence against women. The movie, "In the Time of the Butterflies" has also helped people to understand this terrible era in Dominican history. ❀

anti-Trujillista: someone who strongly opposed Trujillo
Cibao: central region of the Dominican Republic
Doña: title of respect for an older woman
Las Mariposas: The Butterflies

LAS MARIPOSAS

USE WITH: Units 9, 10

DURATION: 1–2 classes

STANDARDS:

English Language Arts: 1, 2, 3, 4, 5, 9, 10

Social Studies: 2c, 4b, 4c, 5d, 6d, 6f

Foreign Language: 1, 2.1, 3, 4.2

GOAL: To research the lives of the Mirabal sisters.

OBJECTIVE:

To analyze why the Mirabal sisters are national heroines in the Dominican Republic.

ACTIVITIES:

1. Students brainstorm the characteristics of heroes and heroines from throughout the world. Who are their heroes or heroines? Why?

2. Introduce the story of the Mirabal sisters and show photographs of the Mirabal museum in the Dominican Republic (available online at several sites).

3. Students read the oral history of Doña Dedé Mirabal (unit 10).

4. The class views segments of the film, "In the Time of the Butterflies," specifically the parts to which Doña Dedé refers (see list of suggested segments below). The class can also read "Minerva," the excerpt from Julia Alvarez's novel, in connection with this activity (unit 9).

5. Afterwards, check students' comprehension by asking the following questions:

   • Who were the Mirabal sisters and why are they famous figures in Dominican history?

   • According to Doña Dedé, what did Minerva Mirabal believe about women? Why is this significant?

   • What did Trujillo think of the Mirabal family?

   • Why did the Mirabal sisters join the underground movement?

6. As a class, students make a list of the reasons why the Mirabal sisters (especially Minerva) are considered national heroines.

Lesson plan prepared by Claudia Bedoya-Rose.

ASSESSMENT: Using the list generated in class, each student writes a short essay giving three reasons why the Mirabal sisters are important figures in Dominican history. Teacher grades essay.

MATERIALS:

"In the Time of the Butterflies" (directed by Mariano Barroso, Metro-Goldwyn-Mayer, 2001)

Suggested segments:

— Minerva's friend tells her about Trujillo

— The Mirabal sisters attend Trujillo's party

— Minerva is denied her law degree

— Minerva joins the underground movement

INTRODUCTION TO THE DOMINICAN ECONOMY

Andrew Schrank

The repression of the Trujillo era and the political turmoil that followed only partly explain the difficult circumstances that have led Dominicans to migrate. As sociologist Andrew Schrank explains, the Dominican Republic's transition from an export-oriented agricultural economy, based mainly on growing sugar, to an export-oriented industrial economy, based on manufacturing and tourism, has brought few benefits to most Dominicans. Unemployment has stayed high, and the exodus of frustrated workers continues. The Dominican economy is now more dependent than ever on money sent home by Dominicans living overseas.

The Dominican Republic's economy has undergone a profound transformation in recent years. As recently as 1975, four agricultural products—sugar, coffee, cocoa, and tobacco—made up approximately 70 percent of the country's export earnings. By the late 1990s, however, their share of export earnings had fallen below 10 percent. Taking their place were new sources of hard currency: tourism, manufactured exports, and remittances from Dominicans living overseas.

What drove the change? A

Sugar cane.

LINDA-ANNE REBHUN

major factor was plummeting demand for the country's traditional exports, especially sugar. In the 1970s and 1980s, some North American consumers began to look for healthier alternatives to sweets and soft drinks. At the same time, U.S. producers of processed foods and beverages—long the biggest buyers of sugar—began to replace cane sugar with cheaper sweeteners made from corn. And, finally, the U.S. government began to subsidize domestic sugar producers against low-cost foreign imports.

With agricultural exports sagging, the Dominican government came under pressure to cultivate new sources of jobs and exports. Foreign manufacturers were invited to take advantage of the country's abundant, low-cost labor force. Foreign tourists were lured to the country's expansive beaches and to new luxury hotels and casinos. And Dominicans who emigrated to the United States or other countries were encouraged to send money back to their relatives at home. Thus, in remarkably short order the

Dominican Republic was transformed from an exporter of agricultural commodities to an exporter of manufactured goods and services—and of able-bodied immigrants who would then send those crucial dollars home.

The consequences have been profound. A country's economic structure shapes everything from where its people work to where and how they live. In the Dominican Republic, the new industries are disproportionately located on the northern and eastern fringes of the island, and this has encouraged a shift of population toward these previously less populated areas. These industries employ a disproportionately female labor force and have therefore created opportunities for women, while challenging the country's traditional patriarchal structure.

The traditional agricultural economy appears all but finished. Its investors have pulled out, while much of its workforce has emigrated. But the gains from the new industries remain more promised than tangible. Rates of poverty and inequality are still high. The raw materials needed for tourism and manufacturing come mainly from outside the country, making the Dominican economy even more dependent on foreign trade. And the economic crisis that shook the country in 2003 suggests that manufactured goods and services are no less vulnerable to economic shocks than their agricultural predecessors. ✾

WAS YOUR SCHOOL'S CAP MADE IN THIS SWEATSHOP?

UNITE! Stop Sweatshops Campaign

Wander across any college campus, and you are likely to find a bookstore or shop that sells smart-looking caps bearing the name or logo of the university. Chances are that cap was manufactured in the Dominican Republic. If so, it was very likely made at BJ&B, a seven-plant complex that employs over 2,000 workers. BJ&B is one of the world's largest producers of baseball-style caps bearing the insignia of universities, professional sports teams, and name brands. These Dominican-made caps are marketed in the United States by well-known athletic apparel companies—and command a hefty price.

In 1998 a U.S.-based trade union, the Union of Needletrades, Industrial and Textile Employees (UNITE), reported on harsh working conditions at the BJ&B factory in the Dominican Republic. That same year, on the Duke University campus, members of a student-led organization called College Students Against Sweatshops acted to ensure that goods bearing the university's name would be made under decent working conditions. In this article, student members of UNITE's Stop Sweatshops Campaign describe the working conditions at BJ&B and the code of conduct Duke University officials established to acknowledge responsibility for the human rights of the workers who make the university's signature goods.

Partly as a result of this outside pressure, workers at BJ&B eventually overcame company resistance and succeeded in forming a union. But the case may not be typical. The Dominican Republic's labor code gives workers the right to unionize, but the code is not well enforced, either inside or outside the free trade zones. Dominican workers in many workplaces are still prevented from unionizing by intimidation or the prospect of losing their jobs.

Adapted from the website of the UNITE! Stop Sweatshops Campaign, a project of the Union of Needletrades, Industrial and Textile Employees, AFL-CIO. Copyright © 2000 by UNITE. Used by permission of UNITE.

"Sixty-nine cents an hour. What I want to know is, why do we get paid so little, if these caps sell for so much?" asked a twenty-year-old woman who has been at BJ&B for one year. "I'm working fifty-six hours a week, and sometimes I can't afford clothes for my children."

In the Dominican town of Villa Altagracia outside Santo Domingo, 2,050 workers, mostly teenage girls and young women, make baseball caps bearing the names of America's great universities. Workers say that in a typical week they earn approximately $40 after fifty-six hours of work. After withholding for social security, the base pay for a full forty-four-hour workweek amounts to about $30.54, or 69 cents per hour. This is just one-third of what the Dominican government estimates to be the necessary income for a typical family to meet its basic needs.

Thousands of miles away, students, families, alumni, and sports fans buy these caps at campus stores at Harvard, Rutgers, Georgetown, Cornell, Duke, and other universities, paying about $20 a cap. The university makes about $1.50 per cap from a licensing fee, almost twenty times more than the workers, who receive only 8 cents per cap. The majority of the profits go to the factory's parent company, Yupoong, based in Seoul, Republic of Korea. (Koreans are the third-largest group of factory owners in the Dominican Republic, after Americans and Dominicans.) Based on Yupoong's sales and production information, Duke University students estimated that Yupoong sells each cap to its immediate customers—companies like Starter or Champion—for about $4.50. BJ&B is located in an industrial free trade zone, the Zona Franca Industrial de Villa Altagracia. This means the company is exempted from paying import fees and income tax to the Dominican government.

Conditions in the BJ&B factory reportedly include abusive language and physical abuse directed toward workers, unsafe drinking water, and poor health and safety conditions. Workers are also forced to work overtime, sometimes without pay. Although under Dominican law it is illegal to require overtime after forty-four hours, workers say that BJ&B began to compel overtime in early 1997. The first victims of the change were the many young workers who were also high school or college students. BJ&B used to allow students to opt out of overtime in order to attend early evening classes, but no

The Free Trade Zones

Andrew Schrank

Industrial free trade zones, or *zonas francas industriales,* were introduced in the Dominican Republic in response to the economic crisis that emerged in the aftermath of the U.S. invasion of 1965.

The strategy devised in Washington called for inviting foreign investors to the Dominican Republic to take advantage of the country's abundant, low-cost labor. Foreign investors would import capital and intermediate goods (such as sewing machines and fabric) from the United States to their factories in the Dominican Republic. There, low-paid Dominican workers would assemble the inputs into consumer goods (such as blue jeans). Finally, the manufacturers would export the finished products back to the United States to be sold to consumers there. This arrangement, U.S. aid officials believed, would create jobs for Dominicans, reduce poverty, and thereby prevent a new round of social unrest that could challenge the U.S.-backed Balaguer government.

However, Dominicans were reluctant to open their markets to foreign goods and investors. Tariffs and duties not only constituted the government's principal source of revenue, but also protected the country's manufacturing sector from foreign competition. In the absence of tariff protection, Dominican manufactur-

Trying to Make Ends Meet

A 23-year-old mother who has worked at BJ&B for two years described how she spends her daily $7.72 wage:

Rent	$1.84
Lunch from vendors	1.40
Transportation	0.70
Child care	1.08
Milk & cereal (for infant)	0.44
	$5.46

That leaves $2.26 per day for the rest of her family's food, water, electricity, clothes, school costs, personal care products, and medicine.

more. "Supervisors announced that we had to stay late or be fired," reported a twenty-six-year-old student who put in three years at BJ&B before being fired. The only alternative for some was to quit school in order to keep their jobs.

Workers also reported that on Saturdays, BJ&B had forced them to stay past the scheduled four hours until the work was done—without getting paid for the extra time. They said that two extra unpaid hours were common on Saturday, and that the company forced workers to stay by holding their paychecks. Since BJ&B workers were barely surviving week to week, this was a potent weapon.

These working conditions are not unique to BJ&B, but are common among the factories in the Dominican Republic's free trade zones. When people try to defend the impoverished conditions of workers at such plants, their arguments often sound like this: "Underdeveloped countries need low-wage jobs to grow economically. If they didn't have low wages, they wouldn't have any jobs at all!" This "sweatshops are good" argument is sometimes made by companies and sometimes by anti-labor policymakers. But such arguments ignore some of the most important issues at stake.

First, labor conditions in one country affect workers in other countries. Without real rights for workers, including the right to organize, conditions will continue to deteriorate as companies pit workers against each other in a race to the bottom. The goal of labor activists is to raise living standards for all workers by telling companies, "Wherever you produce these items, you have to treat people right."

Second, decent working conditions are affordable. Labor costs are a minor part of the costs of a cap. BJ&B could triple the amount of money it pays its production workers, and the

ers feared, they would be driven into bankruptcy by more efficient North American firms.

Ultimately, the two sides agreed to compromise. Under the agreement, the Dominican government offered special treatment to manufacturers provided they (a) located their factories in legally and geographically circumscribed "industrial free trade zones," and (b) exported all the products they made. Manufacturers that met these conditions received a wide variety of tax and tariff exemptions, including the duty-free import of capital and intermediate goods. Thus, the zones were to constitute islands of "free trade" in an otherwise protected Dominican economy. This was supposed to reconcile the needs

of exporters, who relied on low-cost imported inputs, with the needs of domestic manufacturers, who relied upon protection from North American competitors.

The first free trade zone was established in La Romana in 1969 and was followed by two more, in San Pedro and Santiago, in the early 1970s. Following this slow start, the sector expanded rapidly in the 1980s and 1990s. By 2000 the Dominican Republic's forty-six free trade zones housed almost 500 firms, employed 200,000 workers, and accounted for almost 90 percent of the country's exports.

cost per cap would go up by only about 16 cents.

Third, morality matters. Profits should flow from making a quality product efficiently, not from inflicting the most misery on the most vulnerable.

In 1998 Duke University announced a new code of conduct for companies that license the Duke name. This step was an acknowledgment of responsibility, and a step toward accountability. The Duke code includes protection of workers' right to organize, a preference for companies that show leadership in workplace practices, the right to public disclosure, and independent monitoring.

It is fitting that the university community should take leadership in this area. While universities often are at the forefront of important moral issues, the name of the university is being attached to sweatshop-made goods. Harvard provost Harvey Fineburg once said that "All members of the University and the institution as a whole benefit when its name is well used, and suffer when it is ill used." Perhaps for universities that join Duke in adopting an effective licensing code, the good use of the university name may benefit hundreds of thousands of workers.

Update

In 2003, the *New York Times* published an article about the impact of student activism against sweatshops ("Latin Sweatshops Pressed by U.S. Campus Power," March 31).

It reported that there is now a union at the BJ&B factory which "recently negotiated a labor contract that provides raises, scholarships and other benefits." Ignacio Hernández, the general secretary of the Federation of Free Trade Zone Unions, told the reporter, "I never thought a group of students, thousands of them, could put so much pressure on these brands."

The *New York Times* article also stated that members of United Students Against Sweatshops "sent thousands of letters to the factory" as well as "a student volunteer for most of last year to help the union organize. University officials, brand executives and officials from a consortium of campuses, unions and students visited with the union and factory managers."

According to Molly McGrath, development director at United Students Against Sweatshops, "We are the target market of a lot of these brands and they want a positive image on campus because they want consumers for life. We also have the moral and ethical argument being on the side of a university, so we can pressure the university to use their leverage in society to change the policies of the brands."

The workers at BJ&B also expressed their satisfaction with the progress. Patricia Graterox, a factory worker, plans to study nursing with assistance from the factory's scholarship fund. She said, "Before, you could not do that. Now you can. At least, I think I can." ❁

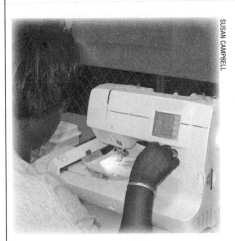

SUSAN CAMPBELL

FACTORIES AND SWEATSHOPS: MAKING THE LINKS

USE WITH: Units 12, 13, 15, 27

DURATION: 2–3 classes

STANDARDS:

English Language Arts: 1, 3, 4, 7, 9, 10

Social Studies: 1a, 2b, 4b, 4h, 7d, 7g, 7I, 9b, 9c

Foreign Language: 1, 2, 3, 4

GOAL: To explore economic aspects of globalization through the experiences of Dominicans in their home country and in the United States.

OBJECTIVES:

- To analyze the connections between deindustrialization in New York and the development of sweatshops in the Dominican Republic.

- To analyze links between deindustrialization, sweatshops, and the economic conditions of Dominicans who stay in their home country as well as those who migrate to the United States.

- To present a panel discussion to the class about the effects of deindustrialization.

ACTIVITIES:

1. Students define the term "industrialization" and give examples of industrialization in the United States.

2. Students discuss the concept of deindustrialization (the decline of manufacturing and the disappearance of factory jobs from a locality or country).

3. In three separate groups students read:

    - "Was Your School's Cap Made in This Sweatshop?" (unit 13).

    - "Roots of Dominican Migration" (unit 15).

    - "'The factories moved out . . .'" (unit 27).

    The teacher may wish to review or refer to "Introduction to the Dominican Economy" (unit 12).

4. Working together as a class, student groups answer some or all of the following questions:

    - What is the connection between industrialization in the Dominican Republic and the migration of Dominicans from rural areas to cities and from cities to the United States?

Lesson plan prepared by Ruth Glasser.

- What are industrial free trade zones (also known as export processing zones)? When did they first become important in the Dominican Republic?

- Why do Dominicans emigrate despite the creation of factory jobs in free trade zones? What other factors besides the economy might encourage Dominicans to leave?

- What kinds of jobs are available in a post-industrial economy—one no longer strongly based on industry? How has deindustrialization affected job prospects for Dominicans in cities such as New York?

- What is the connection between the "runaway factories" of cities such as New York and the establishment of factories in countries such as the Dominican Republic?

- What is the connection between cheap labor in countries such as the Dominican Republic and the price and availability of clothing in the United States?

- Why do you think factory jobs have traditionally been so important for new immigrants in the United States?

- What happened to immigrants' job prospects when "the factories moved out?" What strategies do Dominican immigrants use to earn a living in the absence of factory jobs?

5. Students examine several pieces of their own clothing, noting where it is made. Students can also go to Wal-Mart (or another store that sells clothing) and check the labels on the types of clothing they like best to see where it is made, and bring that information in to report on.

6. Using the articles and additional research as a basis, in groups of five, students develop characters and stage a panel discussion between the following:

- A Dominican worker struggling to make ends meet in an export processing zone clothing factory

- The owner of the factory, who moved it from New York to the Dominican Republic twenty years ago

- A U.S. resident of moderate income who buys inexpensive clothing with "Made in the Dominican Republic" on the label

- A U.S. high school student organizing to demand fairer wages for the Dominican workers who make his or her school's sweatshirts and caps

- A Dominican activist in New York addressing unemployment issues in his or her community

ASSESSMENT: Assess students' ability to incorporate ideas from the texts into their presentations and express their positions in an articulate manner.

ROOTS OF DOMINICAN MIGRATION

Catherine Sunshine

Both political and economic conditions in the Dominican Republic have led to mass emigration of Dominicans since the 1960s. In this article Catherine Sunshine, co-editor of an anthology on Caribbean migration to the United States, briefly traces the key factors that have spurred the exodus.

COURTESY OF ROGER LOWENSTEIN, LA LEADERSHIP ACADEMY

Adapted from *Caribbean Connections: Moving North*, eds. Catherine A. Sunshine and Keith Q. Warner (Washington, DC: Network of Educators on the Americas). © 1998 by Network of Educators on the Americas; © 2005 by Teaching for Change. Used by permission of Teaching for Change.

Across the Dominican Republic, in impoverished rural villages and sprawling urban shantytowns, people struggle day by day just to make ends meet. For many, the path to a better life leads them outside the island, to Puerto Rico, Florida, New Jersey, New York, Massachusetts, and beyond.

Why have so many Dominicans chosen to emigrate, even as they maintain strong ties to their native land and to family members left behind? To understand the Dominican exodus, one has to look at both the political and economic roots of migration.

The 1965 Invasion

During his bloody thirty-one-year rule, the dictator Rafael Trujillo allowed few people to leave the country. A few Dominicans managed to flee political persecution and settle abroad, but the vast majority remained at home. That changed following Trujillo's assassination in 1961, when a tumultuous series of events started the mass migration that continues today.

In 1962, in the country's first free elections ever, Dominicans gave a landslide victory to socialist Juan Bosch. Bosch governed only seven months before being overthrown by a right-wing military coup in 1963. Plotting continued, and in April 1965 an armed popular revolt swept the capital. Nearly the entire population of Santo Domingo poured into the streets, demanding the return of the democratically elected Bosch government and adherence to the country's constitution.

Officials in Washington, anxious to prevent another Cuban-style revolution, viewed this uprising in support of democracy as a threat. On April 28, 1965, President Lyndon Johnson sent 22,000 U.S. Marines into Santo Domingo to crush the rebellion. Afterward, new elections held under U.S. supervision brought to power the U.S.-backed candidate, Joaquín Balaguer, who had been the dictator Trujillo's right-hand man.

Before and after the election, the Dominican army continued to harass, jail, and kill Bosch supporters. Thousands fled to exile in New York. U.S. officials encouraged their departure, hoping to remove potential opponents of the new U.S.-backed Dominican government.

A Sagging Economy

The exodus had begun. Two developments caused it to continue and grow. One was a new U.S. immigration law that took effect in 1965, allowing immigrants residing legally in the United States to petition for their relatives to join them. The other was a spiraling economic crisis in the Dominican Republic that left many people more desperate than ever before.

Working hand in hand with the Balaguer government, U.S. officials set out to rebuild the Dominican economy on the basis of U.S. private investment, aid, and loans. Multinational cor-

U.S. troops advance on a sniper in Santo Domingo in June, 1965.

labor. In the fenced industrial parks known as free trade zones, workers assembled garments and other goods for wages far below what American workers earn. But export manufacturing and tourism could not provide jobs for all the farmers and workers who had been displaced from the collapsing agricultural sector. Rural Dominicans flocked to the slums of Santo Domingo and other cities, looking for some other way to make a living.

Meanwhile, loan agreements

porations took over land in the Dominican countryside. Small farmers, uprooted, drifted to the cities or emigrated.

In the 1980s the Domini- can economy went into steep decline. When world sugar prices tumbled, the United States dras- tically reduced its purchases of Dominican sugar. As an alterna- tive to sugar, the Dominican gov- ernment promoted manufactur- ing for export, agribusiness, and tourism, all dependent on cheap

with the International Monetary Fund forced the government to devalue the Dominican currency, the peso. Devaluation made the peso worth less in relation to international currencies such as the U.S. dollar. Food and other basic necessities, pur- chased abroad for dollars and imported into the Dominican Republic, now cost consumers much more in pesos than before. Life became harder than ever for most Dominicans. Remit-

tances—money sent home from relatives outside the country— became a lifeline for hundreds of thousands of Dominican families.

For three decades Balaguer held power through fraudulent elections, interrupted only by an eight-year period in which his political rivals governed. Balaguer reserved jobs and con- tracts for those loyal to him; others found their way blocked. Not only the poor but also many middle-class Dominicans saw no future for themselves if they remained in the country.

No Quick Solution

Elections in 1996 finally retired Balaguer and brought to power a younger politi- cian, Leonel Fernández Reyna. In 2000 he was replaced by Hipólito Mejía, but in 2004 voters returned Fernández to the presidency once again. Despite this new leadership, large-scale emigration from the Dominican Republic will likely continue for the foreseeable future. The country's economic crisis has no quick solution, and the earnings sent home by Dominicans living and working abroad are an increasingly vital part of the national economy.

The networks that bring Dominicans into the United States are firmly established. Many families are divided, creating an ongoing demand for U.S. visas for kin. Dominicans in the diaspora, meanwhile, are increasing their participation in U.S. civic and political life. While many maintain strong ties to their homeland, Dominican- Americans increasingly recog- nize that they are here to stay. ✸

DOUGLAS JONES, PHOTOGRAPHER, *LOOK MAGAZINE*, LIBRARY OF CONGRESS

TAKING LEAVE: POEMS OF EMIGRATION

At Lawrence High School in Lawrence, Massachusetts, many of the students left the Dominican Republic as children and moved with their families to the United States. Students in Sean McCarthy's tenth- and eleventh-grade English classes wrote poems that explore the theme of migration through the experience of saying goodbye. The students were asked to list all the places they had lived during their lives, and to provide quotes, phrases, and song lyrics remembered from these places. Each student then chose a place to say goodbye to and began to write freely and with creative license. The resulting poems bring to life their memories of the Dominican Republic and the people, places, foods, sights, and sounds they left behind.

Goodbye to Mi Abuelo

Yicaury Melo

Goodbye to the warm afternoon I had with him,
to the wind which took his laughter as far as it went,
to the lazy rainy afternoon we spent together.
Goodbye to the flowers in his yard
and the smell of the pipe he smoked.
Goodbye to Trujillo,
who ruled over my grandfather,
but could not keep his spirits low.
Goodbye to my grandfather's arms and presence:
"A moment's instant is sometimes worth a lifetime's experiences;"
"I am here to live out loud"
From now on, the distance between granddaughter
and grandfather is lifted.

© 2004 by Yicaury Melo. Used by permission of the author.

Goodbye Sancocho and Pizza

Benjamin Polanco

Goodbye to Campusanos and his obsession with coffee,
to Edgar's sporty ways and Baron's caring love.
Goodbye to the palm trees with sweet water,
the mango trees that we were obsessed with
and the *plátanos* which we put in almost anything we made.
Goodbye to the baseball made out of socks,
the bat or a piece of strong branch,
and the torn-apart gloves we used to play baseball.
"The past is a work of art, full of irrelevancies and loose ends."
Goodbye to grandma's famous, hot-right-out-of-the-oven
     sweet bread,
to roasted pork done outside with wood and fire,
and the mouth-watering tender taste of *sancocho*.
Goodbye to the cock-a-doodle-do of the rooster in the morning,
and my aunt's constant yelling at us for doing what we weren't
     supposed to do,
and the loud sound of the rain that would rock me to sleep.
Goodbye to the fresh aroma of the morning dew,
giving me energy for whatever I would do,
and the smell of my dad's cheap cologne that was not very pleasing
     to the air.
Goodbye to one of our greatest patriots Juan Pablo Duarte;
may his soul rest in peace.
Goodbye to the Dominican Republic,
my tropical island where I was born.
Let me lie down between 1986 and 2003 and see
all of the changes I have encountered.
It was all a dream, I used to read WordUp Magazine.
"It was the best of times it was the worst of times;"
From now on, the romance between *sancocho* and pizza is lifted.

❀

View from Altos de Chavón.

Mango tree.

Where I Once Lived

Esthefany Melo

Goodbye to Indhira and her pride,
to Izalia . . . she, who was always late
and goodbye to the part of me that stayed.
Goodbye to the mandarin tree
that never gave birth;
to the colmado that never let people down
to the *chichiguas* that flew around the sun.
Goodbye to the *guagüitas* bringing and taking people.
Goodbye to the best mango there is
Goodbye to the *pasteles en hoja*
sold by the poor man who always left wealthier.
Goodbye to the *kikiriki* of the morning clock
to the laughter of kids
and to the wind singing in my ears.
"Goodbye to you."
Goodbye to the smell of rain
that soaked our dreams,
to the smell of morning coffee.
Goodbye to the ghost that followed me everywhere
every moment, every second, every step.
Goodbye to Santo Domingo in '98
But don't worry, I'll go back; somehow I know it.
Let me lie down between the grass and the wind
to remember you,
To learn to love another place…
From now on, the dream between
there and here is lifted…

Goodbye

Scarlett Jimenez

Goodbye to my great-grandmother's smile, goodbye to my aunt's
    kisses, and
my uncle's arms that would lift me up to the *cereza* tree in the
    backyard.
Goodbye to that *cereza* tree where they would lift me up so I could
    pick
them down.
"I believe I can fly."
Goodbye to the rumbling sound of the *motores* passing through the
    street,
goodbye to the sounds of our next-door neighbor,
the sound of the raindrops falling on the roof top.
Goodbye to the rich creamy *maíz caquia'o* my grandmother would
    make,
to the *chivo asa'o* made in my backyard,
and let's not forget the delicious flavors of *Helados Bon.*
"Helados Bon: ¡Qué buenos son!"
Goodbye to the ever-present heat that never kept me down,
to the rainy day in which we would go out and play.
Goodbye to the smell of my grandmother's cooking which always
    filled my
stomach with joy and the smell of the cows which didn't always
    please my nose.
Goodbye to my years in the D.R.
Let me lie down between the past and the future.
"How do I say goodbye to yesterday?"
"I'll never let you go"
From now on the romance between then and now is lifted.

---

cereza: cherry
chichiguas: kites
chivo asao: roasted goat (chivo asado)
guaguitas: little buses
Helados Bon: ¡Qué buenos son!: "Helados Bon: They're delicious!" (advertising slogan for a brand of ice cream)
Juan Pablo Duarte: Dominican independence leader in the nineteenth century
kikiriki: cock-a-doodle-do
maíz caquiao: ground corn used for a dessert made with corn, milk, sugar, and cinnamon
mango: tropical fruit
motores: motorcycles
pasteles en hoja: meat pastries wrapped in green banana leaves
plátanos: plantains
sancocho: stew of meat and root vegetables
sweet water: liquid in the center of coconuts
Trujillo: Dominican dictator

PART TWO

MIGRATION AND THE DOMINICAN DIASPORA

Highways 3 and 4 in La Romana.

LA CIGUAPA

Josefina Báez

La Ciguapa is a character in Dominican folklore. The figure is drawn from the mythology of the Taíno people who lived on the island of Hispaniola before the Europeans arrived. La Ciguapa is usually pictured as a woman with long flowing hair and her feet fixed on backwards.

Poet Josefina Báez was born in La Romana, Dominican Republic, and came to New York City at the age of eleven. An actress, educator, and writer, she is the founder and director of the Latinarte/Ay Ombe theater troupe, which began in 1986. In this poem, Báez updates the traditional Dominican figure of La Ciguapa, depicting her as a Dominican immigrant in New York City.

Our deity La Ciguapa arrived in New York too.
The subway steps changed her nature.
In the ups and downs, to and from the train,
her feet became like everybody else's in the rush hour crowd.
She did not notice the drastic change.
This was the first sign of assimilation
—a concept not to be understood, but experienced.

And Ciguapa cut her hair.
Maybe to be fashionable or just to simplify her rituals.

JORGE VISMARA

Josefina Báez.

Her lover was not a hunter, as the legend goes.
He was a medical doctor by profession
turned taxi driver by necessity.
He, the gypsy taxi driver, worked for an uptown car service.
In that context, our deity was codified to a mere 10–13.
It meant companion or wife;
we never knew and she never cared.
Their love was filled with few words, passionate actions,
fast merengues, tasty sancochos,
and predictable as well as strictly scheduled trips
to la remesa "El Sol Sale Para Todos."
These trips, energized by green dollars, reforested the island.

Ciguapa works in a factory making pinkish dolls.
Dolls she never had.
Dolls dulled by the unique smell of new things.
Earning less than the minimum wage,
she managed to pay an immigration lawyer she never met.
She got her green card. It was not green.

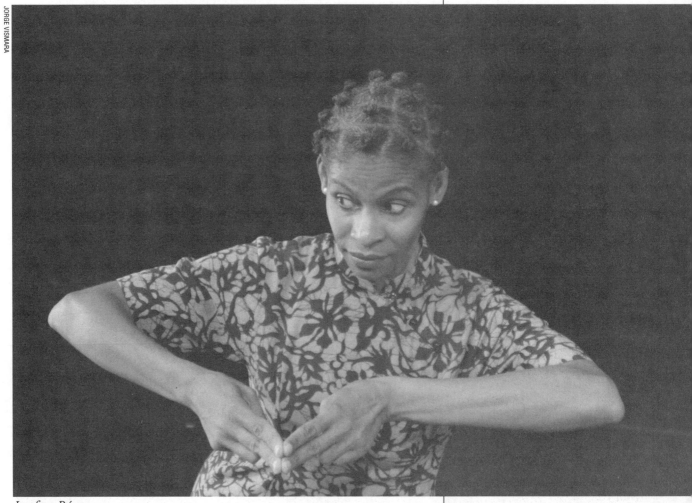

JORGE VISMARA

Josefina Báez.

By heart she knows 33 English words. Enough tools for today's communication exchange by heart.

What a triumph!
She is going to visit the Dominican Republic,
first time in seven years.
She made it!
Huge suitcases that she bought
at BBB (Bueno Bonito Barato) on 14th Street
are filled with unthinkable, unnecessary items.
To be sold at laughable prices.
Prices calculated in dollars, paid in pesos.
Laughable reality.

Her laugh is based on a constant and bitter cry.
Constant nostalgia,
bitter reality,
unheard cry.

Here in no man's land
Here in no woman's stand
You can become what you are not
by lotto, circumstance, opportunity, luck/unluck,
karma.
You might forget your divinity or from your
worldly corner
become a saint.

❀

10-13: code for wife or female companion, used in radio communications between taxi drivers and dispatchers in parts of New York City
Bueno Bonito Barrato: Good Pretty Cheap
El Sol Sale Para Todos: The Sun Shines for Everyone
green card: identifies a legal permanent resident of the United States
merengue: Dominican popular music
remesa: money transfer office, used by immigrants to send support to family members in the home country
sancocho: stew of meat and root vegetables

LA CIGUAPA

USE WITH: Unit 17

DURATION: 1 class

STANDARDS:

English Language Arts: 1, 3, 4, 6, 7, 9, 10

Social Studies: 1c, 1d, 4a, 4b, 4c, 4f, 4h

Foreign Language: 1, 2, 3, 4

GOAL: To construct cultural meaning behind poetic text.

OBJECTIVES:

• To analyze a poem and relate the imagery to real life.

• To represent imagery in a different medium from text.

ACTIVITIES:

1. Introduce the term "deity" and ask students to define it.

2. Students read "La Ciguapa" (unit 17) out loud.

3. Discuss terms and metaphors: assimilation, merengue, sancocho, la remesa, green dollars reforested the island, green card, she made it!, huge suitcases, nostalgia, no man's land, divinity, and anything else students can come up with.

4. Students draw or describe a traditional Dominican Ciguapa and a "modern" Ciguapa in New York (or another big U.S. city). The traditional Ciguapa is described in the children's story *The Secret Footprints* by Julia Alvarez.

ASSESSMENT:

Students think of a character from a folktale or legend they know, and write a poem placing that character in a modern setting.

MATERIALS:

• Julia Alvarez, *The Secret Footprints* (New York: Alfred A. Knopf, 2000)

Lesson plan prepared by Lola Lopes.

AT THE CONSULATE

Barbara Fischkin

Migration often separates families, temporarily or permanently. Each person who emigrates legally to the United States must first apply for a visa at the U.S. consulate in the home country. The rules are complicated and strict, and seldom does a whole family receive visas together.

A parent forced to migrate by economic necessity may leave children behind in the care of other family members, hoping to send for them later. In this excerpt from her book, Muddy Cup: A Dominican Family Comes of Age in a New America, *journalist Barbara Fischkin shows how the pain of separation affects one Dominican family.*

Although it reads like a story, Muddy Cup is nonfiction. The Almonte family is real. The book, based on Fischkin's interviews with members of the family over a decade, documents the lives of three generations of Almontes in the Dominican Republic and later in New York.

Reprinted from *Muddy Cup: A Dominican Family Comes of Age in a New America* (New York: Scribner). Copyright © 1997 by Barbara Fischkin. Used by permission of the author.

The U.S. consulate in Santo Domingo was a three-story, fenced, concrete building, but the immigrant visa line that wrapped around it most mornings was dressed for a party. Girls in bright ruffled dresses stood next to boys with bold, striped ties and polyester jackets "just like *Papi's.*" The adults wore sundresses and cheap suits or brand-new T-shirts blazoned with the names of towns, teams, and restaurants in New York, New Jersey, Miami. The faces were as colorful as the clothes. Complexions, even among immediate relatives, ranged from dark brown to Mediterranean white.

Mixed like that, the faces looked festive, but they reflected a small, tired land that had killed off all of its Indians, but not all of their features; a land that had imported African slaves to replace the Indians and had survived conquests by Spanish and Haitian forces, only to be occupied—twice this century—by American Marines. Everyone was afraid that they would do or say something wrong and not get a visa. The children clung to their parents as they smoothed their dresses and jackets and looked through the iron gate up at the consulate. The adults tried to hide their anxiety with chatter and laughter; a few intrepid souls read aloud from their Bibles.

Roselia Almonte and her children got on the end of the line. So many people followed them that within minutes they were in the middle of a much longer line. Roselia clutched her pocket-sized blue pamphlet of psalms. Her head hurt and she wished she had a cup of yerba buena tea. The mint flavor of the leaves in her mouth would calm her worries. Mauricio did not seem worried. Only thrilled. Her daughters thought this was a *fiesta.* They had made up their faces with blue and green eye shadow and tied bows in their hair.

As the line moved, Roselia grabbed Mauricio's hand. She nodded at her two daughters, and they followed behind her. At the gate she read a sign: TO APPLY FOR A VISA YOU NEED TO HAVE: 1. A VALID PASSPORT. 2. A VISA APPLICATION,

CAREFULLY FILLED OUT. 3. A PHOTOGRAPH: ONE AND A HALF BY ONE AND A HALF INCHES. 4. DOCU-MENTATION OF ECONOMIC SOLVENCY (LETTERS OF EMPLOYMENT, BANK LETTERS, DOCUMENTATION OF SAVINGS OR BUSINESS, CAR REGISTRATIONS, ETC.). "We have everything," she said to Elizabeth. They were led upstairs and then downstairs again, where the four of them wiggled into the last remaining spaces on a wooden bench. Behind them was a painting of Señor Ronald Reagan. He smiled at Roselia. She giggled back and felt lighthearted for a moment.

Mauricio fidgeted on the bench. Roselia put her hand on his leg and opened her Bible.

"Mami, I'm hungry," he said.

She opened her handbag and pulled out a wintergreen mint.

"This is the last one," she said.

Mauricio unwrapped it, put the hard candy in his mouth, bit it in half, and handed his sister Cristian one of the pieces.

"*Gracias,* Mauri." Cristian popped the cracked candy in her mouth.

A man came over to their bench. "Everybody raise your hands, please!"

Roselia raised hers; she looked at the girls and Mauricio so that they would do the same. They all promised to tell the truth to the government of the United States of America.

Roselia opened her Bible and began reading out loud:

He who dwells in the shelter of the Most High,
who abides in the shadow of the Almighty,
will say to the Lord, "My refuge and my fortress:
my God, in whom I trust."

So many people were in the room that their noise made it hard for Roselia to concentrate. These people really did think they were at a *fiesta.* Only the *lechón,* the roast pig, was missing.

Roselia tried to pray louder:

You will not fear the terror of the night,
nor the arrow that flies by day,
nor the pestilence that stalks in darkness,
nor the destruction that wastes at noonday.

More noise came from the loudspeaker. Roselia realized that names were being called and she strained to hear. She wished for yerba buena in her mouth and kept reading. For two hours, while she listened for their names, she read all her favorite psalms. Then she began to read them again.

"'You will not fear the terror of night . . . ,'" Roselia recited.

"*Señora Almonte y familia, casilla uno.*"
Elizabeth poked Mauricio.
"*Señora Almonte y familia, casilla uno.*"

* * *

They sat in a small office. Roselia gave the visa officer a half smile. Later she would remember him as being tall and wearing glasses and a suit.

"Does your husband have a car?" the visa officer asked.

"No," Roselia replied. She wondered if that was good or bad.

PHIL SIGIN-LAVDANSKI

"Who does he live with?"

"With one of his brothers."

There was a pause. The officer looked down at his papers.

"Now, which one is Elizabeth?"

Roselia pointed to her eldest daughter.

"What do you do?" the officer asked Elizabeth.

"I am a student."

"Where do you go to school, Elizabeth?"

"*Liceo* José DuBeau of Puerto Plata."

"What grade?"

"I am in the fourth year of secondary school."

Cristian will be next, Roselia thought. There was air-conditioning, but it was hot anyway. She could smell her daughters' lavender perfume.

"*Señora* Almonte," the officer said.

Why was the consul speaking to her again?

"*Señora* Almonte, I can only give the visas to you and your eldest daughter. A wife and three children would be too much for your husband to support."

Roselia was not sure she understood this man's Spanish. This could not be what he was saying.

She looked at her daughters. Elizabeth was shaking her head. Cristian was expressionless.

"In three months you can ask again for your other children," the officer said.

Roselia's head began to pound. She could not find the top or the bottom of her pain. The officer kept talking at her, giving her instructions she would not remember. She tried to focus on the letters of his name. M-u-e-l-l-e-r. She would try to never forget it.

"But with these two it would be too much. You can ask for the others in three months, if your husband's financial situation changes—or if you get a job."

Javier had never said this might happen.

"Is that okay, *Señora* Almonte?"

Roselia felt tears stinging her cheeks.

"*Señora* Almonte?"

"*Sí.*" Roselia was crying and could not find anything else to say.

"*Mami!*" Elizabeth was angry. "*Mami.* Are you crazy?"

Roselia sent her children to buy lunch from the vendors outside the consulate. She wanted peace when she filled out the forms the visa officer had given her. She wrote her name and Elizabeth's. Roselia knew what Elizabeth had meant. She should not have shown that *yanqui* visa officer—Roselia did not know how to pronounce his name, but she had memorized the letters, M-u-e-l-l-e-r—how bad he made her feel.

She wondered if she was crazy. She hadn't slept for three nights. Maybe she imagined all of this.

She had all the papers they had asked for on the sign outside the building. She knew exactly what Javier, his brothers, and sister had done to get their visas, and she had done the same thing. She had read all the advice Marta had sent in her letters from *Nieu Yersey*. She had answered all the questions. She told the truth. Except for one little lie.

She had said they lived in Puerto Plata at her nieces' house instead of in Camú. The mail delivery was better in the city. They had a real mailman there. They weren't going to deny her a visa for that!

She wasn't crazy. The *yanquis* were crazy. You don't separate a mother from her baby, from the boy, the shy, delicate boy who sleeps next to her every night. You don't tell a mother to leave without a pretty fourteen-year-old daughter. ✿

CHRISTINE GONSALVES

Nieu Yersey: New Jersey
Ronald Reagan: president of the United States from 1981 to 1989
Liceo José DuBeau: José DuBeau high school
Señora Almonte y familia, casilla uno: Mrs. Almonte and family, booth one
yanquis: Yankees
yerba buena: peppermint

LA CADENA

Patricia R. Pessar

ASHLEY JOHNSON

When Dominicans describe emigration to the United States, they speak about la cadena—*"the chain." Scholars who study immigration also use the term* chain migration *to describe the series of links in which each immigrant who settles in the adopted country reaches back to help another follow the same path.*

According to anthropologist Patricia R. Pessar, members of a cadena *are usually linked by kinship ties. Immigrants who are legal U.S. residents or naturalized citizens can petition to have their family members join them in the United States. This legal provision applies mainly to immediate kin: spouses, parents, children, and siblings. But the Dominican concept of family is much broader than the narrow definition contained in U.S. immigration regulations. For Dominicans, "family" also includes more distant blood relatives (such as cousins, aunts, and uncles) as well as nonrelatives known as fictive kin. The latter, called* compadres *in Spanish, are individuals who are chosen to witness rites of passage, such as baptisms and marriages; they become godparents to the children, but also maintain a special relationship with the parents. This broad extended family is one of the strongest institutions in the Dominican Republic, marked by bonds of trust, cooperation, and affection. Dominicans who have migrated make every possible effort to help their extended family members join them.*

In this excerpt, Pessar traces the history of one migration chain, that of the Ramírez family (a pseudonym). Their story shows how legal, extra-legal, and illegal migration practices are used, often in highly creative ways, to reunite a Dominican family in New York.

From Patricia R. Pessar, *A Visa for a Dream* © 1995. (Boston: Allyn and Bacon). © 1995 by Pearson Education. Reprinted by permission of the publisher.

All *cadenas* begin with a pioneer, and with the Ramírez family it was Willy, the owner of a furniture store in the city of Santiago. In 1975, at the age of forty-five, he was experiencing problems meeting both the demands of his creditors and mortgage payments on a recently purchased home in an affluent middle-class neighborhood. Having no immediate kin in the United States, Willy contacted a creditor who was also a *buscón*. In order to obtain a fraudulent visa from the broker, Willy transferred all the assets from his business, estimated to be approximately 3,000 pesos (US$2,200), to the *buscón*.

"I knew I was taking a big risk," Willy told me. "If I had not made it in New York, perhaps all would have been lost. I wasn't doing this just for my own advancement though, or even that of my wife and children. I was doing it for all my family. Many of us had needs, but no one was yet in New York to give us a helping hand."

Willy's fraudulent visa got him through U.S. customs. Once in New York, he easily secured a job and housing with the help of a *compadre* who had emigrated a few years earlier. Next, he had to find a way to regularize his legal status so that he might begin petitioning for the admission of his other family members. He decided that his best alternative was to arrange what Dominicans call a *matrimonio de negocio,* a "business marriage." This is a method whereby an individual pays a legal immigrant or citizen a fee to enter into marriage and then uses the family unification provision to acquire a permanent resident visa. Although sealed by a civil ceremony back in the Dominican Republic, such business marriages are meant to be undone.[1]

It took Willy three years of grueling work at two full-time jobs to save the $2,000 necessary to enter into a "business marriage" with a Dominican co-worker. Willy returned to the Dominican Republic and

remained there briefly while his "business wife" requested a visa for her "husband," which he soon received. During his short return home, Willy was visited by a first cousin who desperately wanted to migrate abroad. Willy promised to approach his boss in the United States for work authorization for the cousin, a promise Willy fulfilled soon after returning to New York.

Willy now had to wait several years, first to divorce his "business wife" and then to remarry his true spouse, Lidia. As is common in the Dominican countryside, Willy and Lidia had married for the first time in a religious ceremony. The second time around, they were married in a civil ceremony and Lidia presented only this marriage certificate when she was called sometime later for an interview at the U.S. consulate in Santo Domingo.[2] She immediately joined Willy in the United States, leaving her youngest children with her mother.

While Willy and Lidia planned to save money to sponsor the migration of their youngest children first, unexpected events intervened. In 1985 the husband of Carmen, their twenty-four-year-old daughter, was badly injured at work and she was left with the responsibility of maintaining her immediate family. Unable to find suitable employment, Carmen implored her parents to help her acquire a tourist visa. They sent her funds to contact a local lawyer and money for plane fare. For a fee of several hundred U.S. dollars the lawyer was able to produce sufficient documentation for Carmen (such as bank statements and a deed to her home) to convince a consulate official that she was traveling for recreational purposes and would likely return. With visa in hand, Carmen departed for New York, where she moved in with her parents. She easily found employment and, as planned, remained after her tourist visa had expired. Carmen understood that her financial responsibilities encompassed a wide group of kin: her husband and young children back in the Dominican Republic, who had moved in with her mother-in-law, as well as her brothers and sisters, who also sought visas. Her wages were apportioned to meet all these obligations and to contribute to the operating expenses of the Ramírez household in New York.

By 1988, some thirteen years after Willy's initial arrival in New York, he and Lidia were reunited with their three unmarried children. The petitions for these three were comparatively easy and inexpensive since unmarried children of temporary resident aliens are accorded preference under the family unification proviso. Willy also began to fulfill his pledge to help his own siblings. In 1990 he arranged for a poor, widowed sister to come to the United States. He paid $1,000 to a permanent returnee to the Dominican Republic who lent her green card to the widowed sister.

The final step will be for Willy to become a U.S. citizen. As a citizen, Willy will have the right to legally sponsor the emigration of his remaining married children, siblings, and elderly parents. Willy is unhappy about the prospect of denouncing his Dominican citizenship.[3] "I love my country and its flag," he told me, "but in the end my family comes first. I am doing it for them, so they can have the same chance I have been given."

The multiple ways that Dominicans like the Ramírezes manage to emigrate to the United States are by no means particular to this immigrant population. They represent strategies that are available to, and used by, members of all immigrant-sending societies whose populations view the United States as an economic mecca. ❁

buscón: visa broker

cadena: chain

compadre: person who is chosen to witness rites of passage, such as baptisms and marriages, becoming a godparent to the child, but also maintaining a special relationship with the parents

green card: identifies a legal permanent resident of the United States

resident alien: a citizen of another country who has legal authorization to reside permanently in the United States

Santiago: second-largest city in the Dominican Republic

tourist visa: permission to enter the United States as a tourist for a limited time only

NOTES:

1. Eugenia Georges, *The Making of a Transnational Community: Migration, Development, and Cultural Change in the Dominican Republic* (New York: Columbia University Press, 1990).

2. Persons seeking visas to enter the United States usually must apply at the U.S. consular office that is attached to the U.S. embassy in their home country.

3. The Dominican constitution was amended in 1994 to allow for dual citizenship. If Willy were becoming a naturalized U.S. citizen today, he would not have to give up his Dominican citizenship, but could remain a citizen of both countries.

NOS VAMOS

USE WITH: Units 15, 19, 20

DURATION: 1–2 classes

STANDARDS:

English Language Arts: 1, 2, 3, 9, 10

Social Studies: 1a, 1b, 1d, 1g, 3h, 5a, 7a, 7d, 9b

Foreign Language: 1, 2.1, 3, 4.2

GOAL: To gain insight into the experience of migration from first-hand accounts.

OBJECTIVE:

To demonstrate an understanding of the factors that lead people to migrate.

ACTIVITIES:

1. Students write a journal entry answering the following prompt: You have to leave your home and head to a new country. Where would you go? Why? Do you know anything about this place? Where did you get your information? What will you do when you get there? How do you know you will do this?

2. Students share highlights from their journal entries. This activity can be supplemented by showing an excerpt from the film "Nueba Yol," which illustrates an immigrant's misconceptions about his future life in the United States.

3. The teacher summarizes "Roots of Dominican Migration" (unit 15) and then assigns students to read either "At the Consulate"(unit 19) or "La Cadena" (unit 20).

4. As a class students answer the follow questions:

   • What is a visa? Why is it important in the immigration process?

   • Why do Dominicans such as the Almontes wait in long lines at the U.S. consulate to get a visa?

   • Why might officials sometimes deny visas to certain family members?

   Listen to "Visa para un Sueño" by Juan Luis Guerra and follow along with the lyrics.

ASSESSMENT:

Students list three factors contributing to Dominican emigration to the United States and explain what would need to change, in each case, to enable more Dominicans to remain in their home country.

MATERIALS:

• "Nueba Yol" (directed by Ángel Muñiz, Ideal Enterprises, 1996)

• "Visa para un Sueño" by Juan Luis Guerra (track 4 on *Grandes Exitos de Juan Luis Guerra y 440,* compact disc, Karen Publishing Co., 2000)

Lesson plan prepared by Rebecca Ford.

DEMOGRAPHIC EXPLOSION: DOMINICAN IMMIGRATION TO THE UNITED STATES

Ramona Hernández and Francisco Rivera-Batiz

Before the 1960s, the Dominican community in the United States was small. Relatively few people managed to escape the country during Trujillo's repressive regime; those who did were mainly professionals and political figures who had been persecuted by the dictator. That changed abruptly after Trujillo's death and the U.S. invasion in 1965. These events, combined with changes in U.S. immigration law, led to a massive emigration that cut across all sectors of Dominican society. Farmers, factory workers, teachers, students, domestic workers—people from every walk of life packed their bags and left, with hopes for a better future outside their homeland.

For many Dominicans in the United States, the path to that better life has not been easy. Poverty rates among Dominican Americans remain high, although average income is growing. In a 2003 report for the CUNY Dominican Studies Institute, sociologist Ramona Hernández and economist Francisco Rivera-Batiz describe the problems and progress of Dominicans in the United States today.

The two researchers used data from the 2000 U.S. census as a basis for calculating the Dominican population of the United States and of various localities. However, it is widely recognized that the census undercounts minority groups, and there is particular concern that the 2000 census substantially undercounted Dominicans. A key reason is that the census form failed to offer a check box that people could use to identify themselves as Dominican. The form offered check boxes for "Mexican," "Puerto Rican," and "Cuban," the three largest Latino groups in the country. Latinos of other backgrounds had to check "Other Hispanic or Latino" and could write in a nationality if they chose. This cumbersome process likely resulted in inaccurate data for various groups, including Dominicans.

Hernández and Rivera-Batiz therefore use supplementary sources of information in combination with the census figures to more accurately estimate the size of the U.S. Dominican population. For example,

Adapted from Ramona Hernández and Francisco Rivera-Batiz, "Demographic Explosion: Dominicans Will Become Third Largest Hispanic Population in the United States by 2010, New Report Says" (CCNY News, City College of New York, October 9, 2003). The article is a summary of the authors' study "Dominicans in the United States: A Socioeconomic Profile, 2000" (New York: CUNY Dominican Studies Institute, 2003). Used by permission of the publisher.

the census counted 764,945 Dominicans in the United States; Hernández and Rivera-Batiz calculate the true number at over 1 million. The census found 455,061 Dominicans in New York, while Hernández and Rivera-Batiz estimate 554,637. Other independent researchers have also produced estimates that are well above the official census figures. All agree, however, that Dominicans are currently the fourth-largest national group among U.S. Hispanics and that the community is growing rapidly.

The Dominican population in the United States almost doubled in the 1990s, from 520,121 in 1990 to 1,041,910 in 2000. By the turn of the millennium, Dominicans were the fourth-largest Hispanic group in the country, following Mexicans, Puerto Ricans, and Cubans.

The major source of Dominican growth has been immigration, with close to 300,000 Dominicans migrating to the United States on a net basis during the decade. (Net migration takes into account the fact that people move back and forth between the Dominican Republic and the United States and counts the overall increase in population.) But the Dominican population born in the United States also rose sharply in the 1990s. By the year 2000, one out of every three Dominicans in the United States was born here.

The largest concentration of Dominicans is still located in the state of New York, especially in New York City, where their numbers rose over the decade from 332,713 to 554,637. Dominicans are currently the second-largest Hispanic/Latino population in New York City, following Puerto Ricans. And if trends continue, Dominicans will overtake Puerto Ricans as the largest Latino population in the city within the next ten years.

Although New York City remains the premier Dominican destination, significant numbers have settled in other states during the last decade, including New Jersey, Florida, Massachusetts, Rhode Island, Pennsylvania, and Connecticut. Some of the largest numbers have settled close to New York City in towns such as Jersey City, Passaic, Perth Amboy, and Union City in New Jersey and Yonkers in New York. Others have moved farther afield; there are now large and growing Dominican communities in Lawrence and Boston, Massachusetts, in Providence, Rhode Island, and in Miami, Florida.

Irse a los países

Jorge Duany

In the 1990s, the Dominican Republic became one of the top five countries sending migrants to the United States, following Mexico, the Philippines, Vietnam, and China. In 1997, the U.S. Bureau of the Census found that nearly one out of ten persons of Dominican origin was living on the U.S. mainland. Of these, 24 percent were born in the United States, a figure that reflects a growing "second generation" of U.S.-born Dominican Americans.

In addition, substantial Dominican communities have emerged since the 1980s in Puerto Rico, Venezuela, Spain, Curaçao, and the U.S. Virgin Islands. During the 1990s, the Dominican exodus continued unabated and broadened to new places such as Italy, Switzerland, the Netherlands, Canada, Panama, Aruba, and Martinique. The massive displacement of people to the United States and elsewhere is popularly known in the Dominican Republic as *irse a los países*—literally, "moving to the countries." ✿

Adapted from "Los países: Transnational Migration from the Dominican Republic to the United States," in *Dominican Migration: Transnational Perspectives,* eds. Ernesto Sagás and Sintia E. Molina (Gainesville: University Press of Florida). © 2004 by Jorge Duany. Reprinted with permission of the University Press of Florida.

Dominicans in U.S. States and Territories, According to the 2000 Census

State or territory	Number of Dominicans	Total Population	Percentage Dominican
New York	455,061	18,976,457	2.39
New Jersey	102,630	8,414,350	1.22
Massachusetts	49,913	6,349,097	0.79
Florida	70,968	15,982,378	0.44
Puerto Rico	56,146	3,808,610	1.47
Rhode Island	17,894	1,048,319	1.71
Pennsylvania	12,186	12,281,054	0.10
Connecticut	9,546	3,405,565	0.28
Maryland	5,596	5,296,486	0.11
Washington, DC metropolitan area	1,496	572,059	0.26

Note: Official census figures are believed to underestimate the number of Dominicans, especially the undocumented.

Low Income and High Poverty

Dominicans currently have one of the lowest average income levels in the country. The mean annual per capita household income of the Dominican population in the United States in 1999 was $11,065. This was about half the per capita income of the average U.S. household. It was also significantly lower than the per capita income of the African American and overall Hispanic populations.

But the socioeconomic status of Dominicans also varies by region. Dominicans in Florida had the highest per capita household income, averaging $12,886 in 1999. Dominicans in Rhode Island had the lowest, at $8,500.

In New York City, the average per capita income of Dominicans was $10,032, less than half the average income of city residents and below the average for Dominicans in the United States as a whole. Dominican New Yorkers have a poverty rate of 32 percent, the highest of any major racial-ethnic group in the city. A high proportion of Dominican families in poverty are headed by women, with no spouse present. Close to half of Dominican female-headed families in New York City are poor. This is three times the poverty rate of white non-Hispanic female-headed households, and substantially higher than that of black female-headed households.

Labor market conditions help explain these discouraging numbers. The labor force participation rate of Dominicans—that is, the percentage of adults who are actively employed—is lower than that for the rest of the population. In 2000, it was approximately 64 percent for men and 53.1 percent for women. The figures for the overall U.S.

ERICK JONES

workforce are 72.7 percent for men and 58.5 percent for women. The unemployment rate of Dominican women and men is also high. In 2000, 7.8 percent of Dominican men were unemployed, compared to 3.9 percent of all men in the country. Among women, the Dominican unemployment rate was 10.7 percent, compared to 4.1 percent in the country overall.

Demographics and education lie behind the social and labor market challenges facing Dominicans. The Dominican labor force is very young and mostly unskilled. The overall educational attainment of Dominicans in the United States is among the lowest in the country. In 2000, 49 percent of Dominicans twenty-five years of age or older had not completed high school and only 10.6 percent had completed college. By contrast, less than 20 percent of the overall U.S. population had not completed high school and 24.4 percent had finished college.

Educational Transformation on the Way

But there are grounds for optimism regarding the economic future of Dominicans. Their per capita income showed significant growth in the 1990s. Education rates have also improved dramatically. The numbers are even better for those born here. For U.S.-born Dominicans in New York, the proportion that attained some college education rose from 31.7 percent in 1980 to 42.8 percent in 1990 and to 55.1 percent in 2000. Dominicans also have high school and college enrollment rates that exceed those of other minority groups. In New York City, Dominican high school retention rates (the rate at which students stay in school until graduation) are substantially higher than for other Latinos. For Dominican women, they approach the overall New York City school and college retention rates. Hopefully, these improvements in education will bring about corresponding improvements in the economic situation of Dominicans during the next decade. ⚙

DOMINICANS IN PUERTO RICO: A LOOK AT BARRIO GANDUL

Jorge Duany

Adapted from "Counting the Uncountable: Undocumented Immigrants and Informal Workers in Puerto Rico," *Latino Studies Journal 7*, no. 2: 69–106. © 1996 by Jorge Duany. Used by permission of the author.

After New York, the city with the largest percentage of Dominican immigrants is a closer Caribbean neighbor: San Juan, Puerto Rico. It's a short trip by air from Santo Domingo, or, for migrants without entry papers, a perilous boat ride across the rough waters of the Mona Passage that separates Puerto Rico from eastern Hispaniola.

Dominicans have been migrating to Puerto Rico in significant numbers since the 1960s, although most immigrants have arrived since 1980. Many come from rural areas of the Dominican Republic and moved to Dominican cities such as Santo Domingo and Santiago before emigrating to Puerto Rico. For many Dominicans, the island is a way station en route to the continental United States. A U.S. "commonwealth," Puerto Rico is

A young man relaxes outside of his house on a Sunday morning in Santurce, Puerto Rico.

legally considered U.S. territory and is subject to U.S. immigration laws. Domestic flights link San Juan to the U.S. mainland.

For some Dominican immigrants, however, Puerto Rico is a final destination. Although some perform agricultural labor such as picking coffee, the majority have settled in the urban San Juan area. Anthropologist Jorge Duany and his research team studied Barrio Gandul, a neighborhood of San Juan. In this article Duany reports on what his team saw as they interviewed people, ate in local cafeterias, and watched the street life taking place around them.

Barrio Gandul is located in the southwestern portion of Santurce, Puerto Rico. The neighborhood is primarily a residential enclave within a commercial part of the capital, San Juan.

Barrio Gandul bustles with activity during the day and part of the night. Old men, women, and children constantly walk in the streets, especially along the main avenues, lined by small businesses, cafeterias, corner bars, grocery stores, barber shops, tailor shops, beauty parlors, and repair shops. Large stores and office buildings are also located along the main avenues. The neighborhood contains several public and private schools and churches, mostly Protestant, such as Baptist, Pentecostal, and Assembly of God. Perhaps the most distinctive characteristic of the neighborhood is the perennial aroma from a nearby coffee factory.

Some people say the name of the neighborhood derives from the large number of gandul plants that once grew there. The area's original inhabitants were former slaves who leased the land of a wealthy Spaniard whose heirs still own much of the property. One elderly man recalls the dirt roads and wooden shacks that dominated

Outside of Latin Paradise Restaurant in Santurce, Puerto Rico, a sign advertises sancocho, *a typical Dominican stew of meats and root vegetables.*

the landscape at the turn of the century. A woman who arrived as a child in 1918 remembers that "Gandul was then an area of swamps and mangroves, surrounded by ditches to drain the water from the swamps."[1]

A number of the older residents are themselves migrants from other parts of Puerto Rico. Many came from the Island's central highlands to the city during the 1930s and 1940s. They are a portion of the thousands of Puerto Rican peasants, particularly from the coffee-growing areas of the interior, who moved to Santurce seeking better employment opportunities during the first half of the twentieth century.

Since the 1960s Barrio Gandul has received a new migrant stream, from outside Puerto Rico. It now has one of the highest proportions of foreign immigrants in Santurce and probably in all Puerto Rico. The 1990 census found that almost 27 percent of the residents had been born outside of the Island.[2] Our 1987 survey showed that about 25 percent of the population of Barrio Gandul was born in the Dominican Republic. Other immigrants came from St. Kitts, Anguilla, Dominica, Cuba, and Colombia.

Most of the Dominicans in the site were born outside the four largest cities of the Dominican Republic (Santo Domingo, Santiago, La Romana, and San Pedro de Macorís). Miches and Higuey on the east coast are also major senders of undocumented migrants from the Dominican Republic to Puerto Rico. We estimated that one-third of the

Dominicans in Santurce were undocumented immigrants, and two-thirds had arrived in Puerto Rico after 1980.

Work and Life in Barrio Gandul

Most households in Barrio Gandul lie outside the formal economy, surviving mainly on temporary, occasional, or seasonal labor. People clean houses, repair cars, collect aluminum cans and bottles, mend clothes, maintain gardens and lawns, paint commercial signs for small businesses, and peddle fruits and vegetables from small trucks. Others sell homemade *limberes* and *pasteles.* Such activities often supplement income from formal employment and public assistance. Contrary to popular stereotypes of working-class neighborhoods, welfare payments are a secondary source of household income.

Seen close up, the Dominican residents of Barrio Gandul do not belong to a single class, but rather occupy different positions within the social structure. At the summit of the occupational pyramid is a small entrepreneurial elite. They include the owners

Dominicans in Puerto Rico, According to the 2000 Census

City	Number of Dominicans	Percentage Dominican
San Juan	30,472	7.2
Carolina	6,227	3.7
Bayamón	4,128	2.0
Caguas	1,076	1.2
Trujillo Alto	1,032	2.0
Guaynabo	1,471	1.8
Ponce	496	0.3
Mayagüez	546	0.7
Arecibo	262	0.5
Cataño	439	1.5

Note: Official census figures are believed to underestimate the number of Dominicans, especially the undocumented.

Homes in the Dominican community of Santurce, where Barrio Gandul is located.

of small businesses such as cafeterias, *colmados*, bars, liquor stores, beauty salons, tailor shops, and auto repair shops. Such businesses are almost entirely in the hands of legal immigrants from the Dominican Republic, many

Waiting for a colmado to open.

of whom came to Puerto Rico during the 1960s.

Below this group are the "middle-income" sectors, such as the small merchants who travel frequently between Santo Domingo and San Juan. Many of them fly regularly to Puerto Rico to buy items such as women's clothing, automobile parts, and electric appliances, which they then resell in the Dominican Republic. Indeed, hundreds of Dominican men and women earn a living with "one foot here and one foot there." The majority of them have temporary visas to travel to the United States or a "green card" identifying them as permanent U.S. residents—documents that give them rights of travel and residency in Puerto Rico as well.

The vast majority of Dominican immigrants in Puerto Rico are members of the working class. Even within this group, however, there are social and economic divisions. Domestic service is the principal occupation of the great majority of Dominican women in Barrio Gandul, as thousands of Dominican women have come to lighten the domestic burdens of Puerto Rican middle- and upper-class

Immigrant Stories

Héctor came to Puerto Rico because in the Dominican Republic "what they paid me didn't go far." In Santo Domingo, he sold pigs and did painting jobs. In Santurce, he has worked as a waiter in a restaurant, a security guard, a hotel painter, and a pizza deliverer, but he didn't like those jobs because "they deducted too much and paid too little." Now Héctor buys ice cream at a local factory and sells it from a truck in the town of Loíza, an occupation that he finds more satisfactory.

Carmen came in a *yola* from Santo Domingo a year before the study. She was in her third year of university when she decided to move with her husband to Puerto Rico. In Santurce she earns between $30 and $45 per day cleaning houses. She prefers to work in different houses because she earns more money that way. On weekends she takes care of an elderly Cuban couple. In order to get an immigrant visa, she would have had to be employed as a sleep-in domestic. Carmen would like to return to Santo Domingo to see her two children, who stayed there with their grandmother.

Ricardo is one of the few Dominicans who have succeeded in becoming business owners in the informal sector. He has several trucks for moving furniture and other jobs and employs several Dominicans as helpers. He picks up trash, cuts trees, and does informal carpentry and "whatever other *chiripa* comes my way." He works more than eight hours a day. Before establishing this business, Ricardo worked for a painting company, but they didn't pay him well and always owed him money. He pays taxes to the government, but not social security for himself or his employees, and the government has never intervened in his business. Ricardo wants to earn enough money to enable him to return to live in the Dominican Republic and add a second floor to a house he has bought there.[5] ❁

5. The immigrants' stories are based on interviews in Spanish in Jorge Duany, Luisa Hernández Angueira, and César A. Rey, *El Barrio Gandul: Economía subterránea y migración indocumentada en Puerto Rico* (Puerto Rico: Universidad del Sagrado Corazón; Caracas: Editorial Nueva Sociedad, 1995).

housewives. Although some domestics work in only one house for the entire week, the majority work six days a week in different houses. Some jobs are stable, like that of a woman who had cooked for an elderly couple for three years. But the majority of domestic workers do not have access to a steady income, minimum wage, regular shifts, or even minimal benefits, and female domestic workers, especially the undocumented, are probably on the lowest rung of the occupational ladder. Because of the scarcity of formal job opportunities in Santurce, many Dominican women work below their occupational and educational skill levels.

Dominican men are a strong

One of the Partido de la Revolución (PLD) buildings in San Juan.

presence in the construction industry, especially as masons, plumbers, carpenters, electricians, and handymen. These Dominican workers form part of a reserve army of labor that flows into Puerto Rico with the ups and downs of the Island's economy. Others work in a variety of skilled trades, as mechanics, tailors, and musicians, and in unskilled service jobs, as waiters, security guards, and attendants at gasoline stations and parking lots. Many of them work for the business owners who make up the most privileged sector of the Dominican community in Santurce.

A large core group in Barrio Gandul consists of self-employed informal workers, especially street vendors. Vending is part of daily life in the barrio. Our field notes are full of references to residents who sold different items on the street, such as pocketbooks, slippers, sandals, pillows, radios, beauty products, ice cream, beans, and dietetic shakes.

Dominican-Puerto Rican Relations

Dominican immigrants are one of the most stigmatized ethnic groups within Puerto Rican society. Since many have rural origins, they are often stereotyped as impoverished and illiterate. However, the majority of the Dominican residents of Barrio Gandul actually come from the most prosperous region of the Dominican Republic—the Cibao. Many have a middle-class urban background and a higher level of schooling than many of their compatriots.

The prejudice against Dominicans in Puerto Rico comes mainly from the association between national origin and low-prestige manual labor. In contrast to many Cuban immigrants, Dominicans in Puerto Rico tend to perform the least prestigious and most poorly paid jobs on the Island. Moreover, high levels of unemployment and poverty have sharpened the economic competition between foreign workers and those born in Puerto Rico. Unfortunately, a great deal of the hostility toward foreigners is displaced from the realm of work to other aspects of daily life.

In Barrio Gandul, the dividing lines between Puerto Ricans and Dominicans are expressed in various ways. Almost invariably, Dominicans play merengue in their houses while Puerto Ricans prefer salsa or rock. Visual symbols, food, and speech patterns also mark differences. During our field work, for example, we frequented a Dominican cafeteria in the neighborhood where merengue or bachata were usually played. The walls were decorated with Dominican cultural symbols such as a tambora and a traditional carnival mask. Both the employees and the clientele had Dominican accents. The physical configuration of Barrio Gandul tends to reinforce these social divisions, as the two groups are practically segregated by streets and housing. While Dominicans are concentrated in the busiest and most commercial streets of the neighborhood, Puerto Ricans are concentrated on the less-traveled and more residential streets.

The two principal neighborhood organizations, one of residents and one of business owners, exclude foreigners. As a result, Dominicans are frequently forced to turn to their compatriots for work and housing. The bonds of solidarity with the Dominican community extend through a chain of social contacts

A police officer inspects a yola, *or wooden boat, used by Dominicans to cross the Mona Passage to Puerto Rico, February 2004.*

AP/WIDE WORLD PHOTOS

A Dominican migrant is arrested by police officers in Dorado, Puerto Rico, February, 2004.

that link New York, Santurce, Santo Domingo, and the more remote rural areas of the Dominican Republic.[3] The immigrants' interpersonal relations tend to be limited to relatives, *compadres*, and friends of their own nationality, especially if they are undocumented.

The undocumented population has a strong ideology of return. They frequently consider migration as a temporary strategy, whose primary purpose is to accumulate the necessary capital to improve their family situation and return to the Dominican Republic. Work instability, lack of job security, and poor earnings reinforce the transient mentality of many undocumented immigrants.[4] ❁

barrio: neighborhood
chiripa: odd job
Cibao: central region of the Dominican Republic
colmado: small grocery store
compadre: person who is chosen to witness rites of passage, such as baptisms and marriages, becoming a godparent to the child, but also maintaining a special relationship with the parents
gandul: pigeon pea
limberes: flavored ice cones
pasteles: pastries of steamed plantain, banana, and cassava filled with pork or chicken
tambora: double-headed drum played with sticks
yola: small wooden boat

NOTES:

1. Aida Iris Cruz Rodríguez, Nicolás García Trinidad, Vivian E. Díaz Vázquez, and Nora I. Ortiz Navarro, "Perfil sub-barrio Gandul: Santurce, Puerto Rico" (unpublished manuscript, Escuela Graduada de Trabajo Social, Universidad de Puerto Rico, Río Piedras, 1990).

2. U.S. Department of Commerce, "1990 Census of Population and Housing: Population and Housing Characteristics of Census Tracts and Block Numbering Areas. San Juan Caguas, PR CMSA" (Washington, DC: U.S. Government Printing Office, 1994). The 2000 census found that 26.5 percent of all residents of Barrio Gandul were of Dominican origin.

3. Patricia R. Pessar, "The Role of Households in International Migration and the Case of U.S.-Bound Migration from the Dominican Republic," *International Migration Review 16*, no. 2 (1982): 359.

4. In an earlier study of the Dominican community in Santurce, about 60 percent of the interviewees said they planned to remain in Puerto Rico.

A BLOCK STUDY IN YOUR COMMUNITY

USE WITH: Unit 23 (can also be used with unit 25)

DURATION: 1–2 classes

STANDARDS:

English Language Arts: 1, 3, 4, 5, 7, 9, 10

Social Studies: 1b, 1d, 2e, 3g, 3h, 4b, 4e, 4g, 4h, 5a

Foreign Language: 1, 2, 3, 4.2

GOAL: To analyze a city block in the students' community.

OBJECTIVE:

To create a micro-study of a city block.

ACTIVITIES:

1. Students read "Dominicans in Puerto Rico: A Look at Barrio Gandul" (unit 23).

2. In small groups, students create a micro-study of a block in their own community or a nearby community, modeling their analysis on that of Duany and his team. Students answer the following questions, building them into a report:

   • What types of buildings are found on the block? (What do they look like, how tall are they, etc.?)

   • What kinds of institutions are found on the block? (schools, stores, churches, government agencies, single-family homes, apartment buildings, etc.)

   • What visual or audible signs are there that people from particular ethnic groups live on the block?

   • What kinds of activities take place on the street at different times of the day? On different days? At different times of the year? Students may want to ask a community member or store owner.

ASSESSMENT:

In groups, students create reports based on their findings and present them to the class in a creative manner: poster, PowerPoint presentation, slide show, etc. Teacher assesses report.

MATERIALS:

• Paper for recording observations
• Access to computer, Internet, PowerPoint
• Art supplies for posters
• Camera

Lesson plan prepared by Ruth Glasser.

DOMINICANS IN NEW YORK: QUISQUEYA ON THE HUDSON

Jorge Duany

ARCHIVES, THE CITY COLLEGE OF NEW YORK, CUNY

New York City remains the destination of a large majority of Dominicans who immigrate to the United States. Although Dominicans have settled in every part of the city, they are concentrated in the Washington Heights–Inwood section of northern Manhattan, where 80 percent of new immigrants are from the Dominican Republic.

How do Dominican New Yorkers live? How do they maintain ties to their homeland while making new lives in New York? To answer these questions, anthropologist Jorge Duany and researchers from the CUNY Dominican Studies Institute at City College of New York took a close look at a single block in Washington Heights. Seven researchers—five of them Dominican college students living in Washington Heights—took a census of households on the block. They visited homes, interviewed residents and observed the rhythms of daily life.

In Washington Heights, they found, people speak Spanish, buy Dominican newspapers, eat Dominican food, and surround themselves with reminders of home. There is constant back-and-forth movement between New York and the Dominican Republic, and networks of family and friends span the two countries. Washington Heights, the study concludes, is a "transnational" neighborhood—one with ties to two countries and two cultures at the same time.

O n our block, street vendors sell oranges, corn, flowers, music cassettes, and the tropical ice cones that Dominicans call *frío fríos*. On hot summer days, small carts selling *frío fríos* appear on street corners. Children open fire hydrants and play with water on the sidewalks.

Speaking Spanish, the men listen to merengue, call out *piropos* to young women passing by, play dominoes, and drink Pres- idente beer. They play the lottery, talk about Dominican politics, and read Dominican newspapers such as *El Nacional, El Siglo,* and *Listín Diario.* Women take their children out in strollers, shop at the bodegas, and talk with neighbors in front of their buildings. Teenagers walk in groups to the local public school, bathe in the area's swimming pools, or listen to rap music on huge cassette players. Some people in the

Adapted from *Quisqueya on the Hudson: The Transnational Identity of Dominicans in Washington Heights* (New York: CUNY Dominican Studies Institute). © 1994 by Jorge Duany. Used by permission of the publisher.

streets look and sound Mexican or Central American, but most of the area's residents are Dominican immigrants.

181st Street Scene

With easy access to the George Washington Bridge, 181st Street is the neighborhood's transportation and commercial center. The old subway tunnel and elevators at the 181st Street station are badly rundown, and have been the object of recent protests by local residents. In the mornings, most residents take the subway to work in downtown Manhattan, returning uptown in the afternoons. Others ride the bus to factories across the Hudson River in New Jersey.

Near the subway station, many businesses specialize in sending remittances to the Dominican Republic, such as the Banco Dominicano. Gypsy cabs from the Dominican-owned Riverside Taxi Agency criss-cross the streets looking for customers. A newsstand at the corner of 181st Street and Saint Nicholas Avenue carries ten Dominican newspapers flown in daily from the island.

Small businesses offering private telephone services to the Dominican Republic have proliferated. A single Dominican entrepreneur from the town of San Francisco de Macorís owns twelve of these places, and plans to open fifty more in the near future.

Many cafeterias and restaurants sell typical food from the Dominican Republic. Traditional items include main courses like *mangú, carne guisada, sancocho, mondongo, cocido,* and *cabeza de cerdo;* side orders like *arroz*

Businesses like La Nacional *that facilitate remittances back home are common in Washington Heights.*

con habichuelas, empanada de yuca, and *tostones;* drinks like *jugo de caña* and *batida de fruta;* and desserts like *pastelillos de guayaba, yaniqueque, dulce de coco,* and *pan dulce relleno.* Grocery stores offer tropical staples ranging from plantains to *mamey,* and Dominican drinks like Cola Quisqueya, Refrescos Nacionales, and Cerveza Presidente.

Although primarily residential, our block has ten stores on the ground floor: two *bodegas,* two beauty salons, two bars, a restaurant, a bakery, a liquor store, and a hardware store. Dominicans own seven of these businesses. The immediate vicinity also has other bodegas, convenience stores, *botánicas,* travel agencies, car shops, and other small stores. Several business owners complained about the stiff economic competition in such a reduced space. "People aren't buying now because they have no money," said an ice cone seller. In addition, rising rents threaten to force many store owners out of the

market. In our block, merchants pay between $1,700 and $2,315 a month to lease very small commercial spaces.

Most employees of Dominican businesses are Dominican, although many stores employ other Hispanics as well, especially Ecuadorans, Mexicans, and Salvadorans. Many store owners display their ethnic origin by blasting music to the street, usually merengue and salsa, sometimes bachata and bolero. Some businesses are local subsidiaries of enterprises in the Dominican Republic, such as Nitín Bakery.

Commercial signs attest to the strong presence of immigrants from the Cibao region, such as Acogedor Cibao Supermarket, Cibao Vision Center, Cibao Meat Products, and Hielo Cibao. A Dominican immigrant who planted corn and black beans on Broadway Avenue and 153rd Street longed to have his "own little Cibao" in Washington Heights. During our fieldwork, a young man walked down the street with two roosters, a common sight in the Dominican countryside. Some Dominicans refer to their neighborhood as "El Cibao" or "La Platanera," much as Puerto Ricans call Spanish Harlem "El Barrio" or the Lower East Side "Loisaida."

Private social clubs from the Dominican Republic abound in Washington Heights. Dozens of recreational associations are based on hometown origins, such as those from the towns of Esperanza, Tamboril, Moca, and Baní. Club members dance merengue, play dominoes and baseball, watch Spanish soap operas, exchange information about jobs and housing, and raise funds to send back to their country. Some groups select a beauty queen and participate in New York's Dominican Day Parade. Although most clubs are still oriented primarily toward the Dominican Republic, they are increasingly concerned with the day-to-day problems of the immigrant community. The clubs help to receive newly arrived immigrants as well as to reaffirm the cultural roots of the established ones.

Despite its large Dominican population, Washington Heights is a multiethnic, multiracial, and multilingual neighborhood. Near Yeshiva University on 186th Street, middle-class Jews have occupied newly renovated buildings. Hasidic Jews occasionally walk by the neighborhood on Saturdays on their way to the synagogue. Jewish-Dominican relations have often been tense.

Dominican contacts with other Hispanics have mainly been cordial. On several buildings, Puerto Rican flags hang from the windows days before and after the Puerto Rican Day parade in June. This symbolic gesture suggests that some residents are Puerto Rican and that Dominicans also

Open air market in Washington Heights selling typical Dominican root vegetables and medicinal plants.

celebrate the parade with their Puerto Rican friends and neighbors. Physical traces of a large Cuban immigration remain in the neighborhood, especially businesses with Cuban names such as Restaurante Caridad, Cafetería El Mambí, Havana Bar, and Restaurante Sagua. But many Cubans have left the neighborhood for New Jersey and Florida. Our block also has Greeks, Chinese, Italians, Nicaraguans, Peruvians, African Americans, and other ethnic groups among its merchants and tenants.

Behind Closed Doors

Tenants keep their doors tightly closed and rarely meet in the hallways, except for a few newly arrived Dominican immigrants. Interethnic contacts are limited, especially among people of different physical appearance. The buildings' physical layout does not foster social interaction, lacking the open, public spaces to which Dominicans are accustomed in their home country. The block lacks a common meeting area, except perhaps for the bodegas and nearby parks.

When they are not at work, the tenants' daily life takes place mostly behind closed doors, in the privacy of their apartments. Many express fears of crime and a few are afraid of being deported by immigration authorities. "Neighborly relations don't exist here as in Santo Domingo," complained Freddy. "My neighbors are Anglos and in four years I haven't talked to them." Only once did we see children playing in the hallways.

Dominicans in New York, According to the 2000 Census

City	Number of Dominicans	Percentage Dominican
New York City	406,806	5.0
Yonkers	7,838	4.0
Freeport	3,226	7.4
Brentwood	2,744	5.0
Haverstraw	2,727	27.0
Copiague	1,440	6.6
Sleepy Hollow	1,167	12.7
Hempstead	887	1.6
West Haverstraw	841	8.2
Rochester	808	0.4

Note: Official census figures are believed to underestimate the number of Dominicans, especially the undocumented.

Nonetheless, some residents have managed to forge a small community by means of a frequent exchange of favors, mutual aid, and emotional support. In one building, tenants take care of their neighbors' children, take their trash down to the basement, share food, or buy them plantains at the marketplace. Each building has several major networks of social interaction, giving the place a sense of a self-enclosed little town. Long-time residents tend to know most people on their floors and some on other floors as well.

Most immigrants maintain their cultural traditions at home.

Some tenants place Spanish stickers on their apartment doors, especially with religious messages like "Jesús Cristo única esperanza," "Cristo cambiará tu vida," and "Construyamos la paz con Cristo." Inside their homes, Dominicans often hang religious prints on the walls with images such as the Sacred Heart and the Last Supper.

Some families hang calendars with a painting of the Virgin Mary, obtained in a local bodega. Others stick a Dominican flag or coat-of-arms in a visible place in the living room. Many Dominican homes have plastic-covered furniture, plastic tablecloths, and plastic flowers as their main

decoration. Some display the faceless ceramic dolls typical of the Dominican Republic, as well as plates painted in bright colors with folk themes from their country, usually a rural landscape, a peasant scene, the Cathedral of Santo Domingo, or a tropical beach. Such objects graphically recreate a Dominican atmosphere in Washington Heights. Decorating homes with folk items from their country is common among Puerto Ricans and other transnational groups in New York as well.

Many Dominican homes and businesses have small shrines with images of Catholic saints

A baseball game in Inwood Park, north of Washington Heights.

and the Virgin Mary in a corner of the hall or a private room. These humble altars are usually surrounded by flowers, lighted candles, food, and glasses filled with fresh water, wine, and other alcoholic beverages. Although the most popular figures are the Virgin of Altagracia and Saint Lazarus, the altars represent a wide range of religious images: Saint Claire, Saint Anthony of Padua, Saint Barbara, the Holy Child of Atocha, the Sacred Heart, the Holy Family, and the Virgin of Fatima, among others.

Even an Irish-American woman had dressed an altar in typical Dominican fashion with the help of an immigrant friend.

Like other Hispanic Catholics, many Dominicans believe that the saints will protect them from misfortune and help them to advance economically. One Dominican woman who wore a necklace with a medallion of the Virgin of Altagracia explained: "When you're away from your country, you need protection. And your country needs it too." ❁

MENA TROTT

arroz con habichuelas: rice and beans

bachata: Dominican popular music

batida de fruta: fruit "smoothie"

bodega: small grocery store

bolero: ballad-style music

botánica: store selling religious and medicinal items

cabeza de cerdo: pig's head

carne guisada: stewed meat

cerveza Presidente: brand of Dominican beer

Cibao: central region of the Dominican Republic

cocido: stew of meat and potatoes

construyamos la paz con Cristo: let us build peace with Christ.

Cristo cambiará tu vida: Christ will change your life

dulce de coco: coconut pastry

empanada de yuca: patty made from cassava

Jesús Cristo única esperanza: Jesus Christ is our only hope

jugo de caña: sugarcane juice

mamey: a tropical fruit

mangú: dish made with boiled and mashed green plantains

merengue: Dominican popular music

mondongo: tripe stew

pan dulce relleno: sweet bread with a filling

pastelillos de guayaba: guava pastries

piropos: suggestive remarks or compliments

platanera: Dominican (nickname)

Refrescos Nacionales: brand of soft drink

salsa: a music developed in New York City and the Caribbean by musicians of various Latin American and Caribbean backgrounds

sancocho: stew of meat and root vegetables

tostones: green plantain, sliced and fried

Virgin of Altagracia: patron saint of the Dominican Republic

yaniqueque: cornmeal fritter

A VISUAL COMPARE AND CONTRAST: DAILY LIFE IN BARRIO GANDUL AND WASHINGTON HEIGHTS

USE WITH: Units 23, 25

DURATION: 1–2 classes

STANDARDS:

English Language Arts: 1, 3, 9, 10

Social Studies: 1a, 1b, 1d, 1g, 3h, 4b, 4e, 5a, 9b

Foreign Language: 1, 2, 3, 4.2

GOAL: To explore living conditions and daily life in Barrio Gandul and Washington Heights.

OBJECTIVE:

To compare and contrast aspects of daily life in two Dominican immigrant communities: Barrio Gandul in San Juan, Puerto Rico, and Washington Heights in New York City.

ACTIVITIES:

1. To introduce the activity, students watch a clip from "Washington Heights."

2. Divide students into two groups and assign one of the following articles to each group: "Dominicans in Puerto Rico: A Look at Barrio Gandul" (unit 23) or "Dominicans in New York: Quisqueya on the Hudson" (unit 25).

3. Review the following comprehension questions. In two separate columns, write answers on the chalkboard, overhead, or chart paper.

   • Why do Dominicans migrate?

   • When did Dominicans begin to migrate to San Juan? To New York City?

   • What were Barrio Gandul and Washington Heights like before Dominicans arrived?

   • How difficult or easy was it for Dominicans to build communities?

   • How has Dominican migration changed Barrio Gandul or Washington Heights?

   • Using answers to the questions, photographs, and visual descriptions in the articles, as a class brainstorm adjectives that describe what Barrio Gandul might look like. Record ideas

Lesson plan prepared by Rebecca Ford.

on the chalkboard, overhead, or chart paper. Do the same for
Washington Heights.

ASSESSMENT:

Students create a visual format to express their interpretation of the
two communities. Upon completion students present their work to
the class with a brief explanation as to why they designed their work
in the manner they chose, using the articles to back their decisions.
Teacher assesses students' ability to illustrate the comparative and
contrasting elements of the two communities.

MATERIALS:

- "Washington Heights" (directed by Alfredo De Villa, Lions Gate
  Home Entertainment, 2003)

- Overhead projector, blank overheads

- Chart paper and markers

- Art supplies for creating projects

"THE FACTORIES MOVED OUT..."

Interview with Victor Morisete-Romero

In the northern Manhattan neighborhood of Washington Heights, a variety of organizations cater to the needs of the Dominican community. They include social clubs and "hometown clubs," as well as organizations that provide social services and advocate on behalf of immigrants. Through their day-to-day work with residents, staff members of these organizations have come to know the community and the social issues it is facing.

Victor Morisete-Romero emigrated from the Dominican Republic to New York in 1982. He has lived in Washington Heights since then, and is executive director of the Asociación Comunal de Dominicanos Progresistas (Community Association of Progressive Dominicans). He was interviewed by Catherine Sunshine in New York City on July 29, 1996.

From *Caribbean Connections: Moving North,* eds. Catherine A. Sunshine and Keith Q. Warner (Washington, DC: Network of Educators on the Americas). © 1998 by Network of Educators on the Americas; © 2005 by Teaching for Change. Used by permission of Teaching for Change.

This has been an immigrant neighborhood since the 1800s. At first it was mostly Irish, Italian, Jewish, and Greek. By the mid-1960s these older immigrant groups began leaving. Many of them moved out of the city to New Jersey or Westchester County. Their kids went to college, improved their position in society, and moved out of Washington Heights.

African Americans were the largest group in the neighborhood for a while. After 1965, Dominicans began coming in. While the Dominican community has continued to grow, recently new ethnic groups have also been arriving, such as Mexicans and Russian Jews.

Why have so many Dominicans come here?

Two reasons: politics and economics. The Trujillo regime ruled the Dominican Republic for thirty-one years and completely blocked any democratic process. After Trujillo was overthrown, an elected government headed by Juan Bosch governed briefly. It was overthrown by a military coup. There was a civil uprising to restore Bosch to power, and the United States invaded the country.

That's when a large number of people began leaving the island. They left because of political instability and because of the economic problems they faced. The United States government encouraged them to go, in part to get rid of people who had supported the Bosch government.

Why did so many choose New York?

In some cases they already had ties here. Economically well-off Dominicans would travel back and forth between the island and New York for business. Another reason was the presence of an established Puerto Rican community, which offered a Latino cultural base in the city.

As to why they settled in Washington Heights, it's difficult to say. One reason, though, was that most of the garment factories were in midtown Manhattan. People could commute by subway and be at their factory jobs in 25 or 30 minutes. When we came to New York my brother, who was seventeen, worked in a garment factory. Entire families would come here and find employment in the garment industry.

MARTHA COOPER

Travel agencies, shippers and money-transfer offices line commercial streets of Washington Heights.

And although the wages were low by U.S. standards, it was much more than most people could earn in the Dominican Republic.

You've lived in Washington Heights since 1982. How has the neighborhood changed during that time?

In the late 1970s the garment industry started to move out of New York. By the mid-1980s it had almost disappeared. That was when we began seeing many of the problems that the immigrant community faces today.

Some of the factories closed down. Others moved to New Jersey, to the South, or overseas. New York had become a very expensive city in which to do business because of the conges-tion, the high taxes, the high cost of labor. So they moved their factories to places like Haiti, Mexico, the Dominican Republic, and some Asian countries. It was a major shift. In the past, indus-tries recruited people from other countries to work here for cheap wages. Now they have moved the actual production overseas to take advantage of even cheaper wages in those countries.

The immigrant community that had worked in the factories was stranded, more or less. Most didn't have the skills necessary to shift to other job opportunities. People began to fall into dependence on welfare and other government benefits. People who traditionally would have worked in a factory had to find another way to make a living.

Some turned to selling drugs. Many more found work in street vending, in the delivery industry, or driving gypsy cabs.

By the mid-1980s you saw the Dominican community making a major move into the small grocery business. Many of the bodegas used to be owned by Puerto Ricans or Cubans, but their children didn't necessarily want to continue in the grocery business. So many of the stores were bought by Dominicans.

Although there are fewer job opportunities, you still have many Dominicans coming in.

One reason is the chain migration. People want to reunite their families and so they petition to bring their family members here. But the single most important reason is economics. However difficult life is in New York, living conditions in the Dominican Republic are far worse for most people.

The Dominican economy used to depend on agriculture, especially sugarcane. But agriculture has declined and the country has moved toward an economy based on tourism, manufacturing, and services. Workers who have been working in the sugarcane for years or farming other crops don't always have the training to find jobs in the new industries.

In the 1970s and 1980s it was primarily an unskilled labor force coming to New York. By the late eighties you began to see more people immigrating with higher education and professional skills. These people also face limited opportunities in the Dominican Republic. They may graduate from a university and find no jobs are available unless they're connected to a political party or some other network that can help them. Many of these people migrate, only to find that opportunities are scarce here as well. Lack of English is often an issue. And good jobs are hard to find these days even for people born and raised here. So you find Dominican teachers, doctors, nurses, and engineers in New York who are working in grocery stores or driving taxis.

What is life like for young people in this area?

Young people growing up today in Washington Heights face very difficult circumstances. There is a lack of incentive for them to achieve. Sadly, many of our young people have come to believe that education might not be the best way for them to get ahead. They see somebody who grew up on their block and is a professional, working for a company on Wall Street, making $30,000 a year; while the guy next door is getting his money the wrong way and driving a Mercedes. They make the comparison and ask, "What kind of lifestyle do I want? Do I want to be a professional and not have these luxuries, or do I want to make a lot of money quickly?"

We are trying to convince young people that, yes, these are real problems, but the only solution for them is to get an education. Because that is the only everlasting thing that they can hold on to for the rest of their life. And some do.

There is a severe lack of employment opportunity. This

year we had five thousand kids from the immediate area who applied for summer jobs. We were only able to place 912. Only 912 out of 5,000 had a shot at seven weeks of employment in federally subsidized jobs. The economic base of the city doesn't support opportunities for youth and that is hurting all of us.

Are there kids who are making it in spite of everything?

Absolutely. We see examples every day among the young people who come to our center. They're focused on college, and they're making it through hard work and through community involvement and family involvement in their lives. I know one child who comes to the center every afternoon after school, and the first thing he does is his homework. We encourage that by giving kids a place to study.

Many of the Dominicans here who do go to college enroll in the City University of New York. It's the most accessible, in location as well as economically. A large number have to work part-time while they are going to school. That in itself is a challenge—to work and go to school. For example, I've worked since age sixteen. I had no choice, because my family didn't have enough money to support all the children in the family. I packed groceries in a supermarket while I went to college, and I continued working part-time until I graduated.

The kids who are making it are doing so despite their families' economic circumstances. They are highly motivated and have strong values.

Part of our mission is to train youth to become community leaders. We offer entrepreneurship seminars to help high school students develop self-esteem, leadership ability, and essential life skills. The goal is for them to go on to college and hopefully focus on a professional or a business career. Then they can come back to the community, understand its problems and needs, and give something back in a positive way. ✿

DOMINICANS AND LOCAL POLITICS

Patricia R. Pessar and Pamela M. Graham

In this article Patricia R. Pessar, an anthropologist, and Pamela Graham, a Latin American studies librarian and political scientist, describe the emergence of Dominican New Yorkers as an active force in New York City politics.

Many Dominicans who have migrated to the United States hope to some day return, and they remain actively involved in the politics of their homeland. All the major political parties of the Dominican Republic have branches in New York and raise campaign funds from Dominican Americans. In 1996 thousands of New York Dominicans flew home to vote in the Dominican Republic's presidential election or help run campaigns. U.S. Dominicans played a critical role in that election, which was won by Leonel Fernández, a Dominican raised in New York City. And in 2004, Dominican citizens living in New York were able to vote in the Dominican presidential election at polling stations set up in New York City.

As the years go by, however, there is a growing realization among U.S. Dominicans—especially those born in this country—that they are here to stay. Given this reality, they have no choice but to organize to improve their opportunities and address pressing local concerns like schools, housing, jobs, and crime. Dominican participation in U.S. elections is gradually increasing as more immigrants naturalize and their U.S.-born children reach voting age.

There was little in the early history of Dominican mass migration to New York City to predict the prominent political role that Dominicans have assumed in our times.[1] In the 1960s and 1970s, Dominicans received little attention in the media and were often mistaken for Puerto Ricans. As "invisible immigrants" rather than an identifiable group, they were ignored as a political constituency. Candidates believed that Dominicans were unlikely to become citizens, or if they did naturalize, were unlikely to vote.[2]

Though overlooked by officials and outsiders, Dominicans began to create an extensive organizational life within their own communities focusing at first on cultural, recreational, and professional activities. By the late 1970s, at least thirty-six such clubs and associations existed in Washington Heights alone.[3] Branches of Dominican parties, such as the Dominican Revolutionary Party (PRD) and the Dominican Liberation Party (PLD), were also located in New York City. The political parties did not focus on conditions or issues affecting Dominicans in New York, but they set an important precedent for organizing immigrants on the basis of Dominican national origin.

Adapted from Patricia R. Pessar and Pamela M. Graham, "Dominicans: Transnational Identities and Local Politics," in *New Immigrants in New York*, ed. Nancy Foner (New York: Columbia University Press). © 2001 by Columbia University Press. Reprinted with the permission of the publisher.

Santo Domingo mayor Johnny Ventura addresses the Dominicanos/Dominicans 2000 conference.

Beginning in the early 1980s, a group of Dominican-born and U.S.-educated leaders emerged who were intent on competing for power and resources within New York City politics. These new leaders spearheaded drives aimed at gaining representation for Dominicans on the community advisory boards that determined funding for local antipoverty programs and on neighborhood school boards.[4] The movement for empowerment and control of District 6 began in the 1980s when the Community Association of Progressive Dominicans confronted the school board and superintendent to demand bilingual education and programs for newly arrived immigrant families. Yolanda López, a longtime resident of Washington Heights, still speaks passionately about the campaign to make the schools more responsive to the needs and aspirations of their Dominican students:

Even in the early eighties, our kids made up the bulk of students in the schools. But at that time our schools were the most overcrowded in the city, and many of our children left school without knowing how to read. We realized no one would help our kids if we Dominican parents did not struggle to take control.

Since then, Dominicans have gained majority representation on the school board and have been able to shape programs to meet the community's changing needs. Their success has been the product of an aggressive program of voter registration; the creation of a parents' network throughout the district; and the formation of a coalition of parents, community organizations, churches, and educators.[5] Dominican-born educator Guillermo Linares was elected president of the District 6 school board in 1986.

No Longer Invisible

By the end of the 1980s Dominicans had ceased being "invisible" in public affairs. Their new visibility proved significant when in the late 1980s New York City and state governments embarked on a process of redistricting aimed, in large part, at maximizing chances for representation of previously underrepresented populations.[6] Dominican activists in northern Manhattan prepared proposals for a new district that would represent a predominantly Dominican constituency. They noted the great strides Dominicans had made in local school board elections. They argued that Dominicans led all other groups in investments in Washington Heights and thus deserved the rewards of fair representation.[7] Impressed by such arguments, the New York City Districting Commission created District 10 in northern Manhattan—with a much greater percentage of Dominican residents than previous districts covering the neighborhood.

In 1993, when Guillermo Linares campaigned in District 10 for a seat on the City Council, his efforts encompassed both the United States and the Dominican Republic, illustrating the binational nature of the emerging political community of Dominican New Yorkers. Linares was endorsed not only by powerful New Yorkers such as then-mayor David Dinkins but also by prominent island politicians. Between the primary and general elections, Linares returned briefly to the Dominican Republic, where he raised funds for his campaign and participated in rallies that were covered by Spanish-language newspapers in New York. He even enlisted his mother to write a letter in Spanish from her home in the Dominican Republic urging New Yorkers to vote for her son. The letter, deposited in scores of residential mailboxes throughout Washington Heights, read:

As a mother of 9 children and 10 grandchildren, I have had

many occasions to be proud in my life. But never have I felt as I do at this moment. Next Thursday, my son Guillermo Linares will have the opportunity to become the first Dominican to serve as a member of the New York City Council.

Unfortunately I cannot be there personally on Thursday to share this important moment in Guillermo's life (I will be in Cabrera, Dominican Republic, from where I am writing you this card).

I will be waiting for the phone call to hear the good news. Please remember to vote for Guillermo Linares... You will have a member of the City Council who will make you proud. And you are going to contribute to the phone call from Guillermo to his mother that will be very, very special!

The 1996 election of New York-raised lawyer Leonel Fernández to the presidency of the Dominican Republic was another example of binational

politics—going in the opposite direction. It also paved the way for further changes in the status of Dominicans living abroad. Electoral reform laws were passed in 1997 that permitted immigrant Dominicans—such as the hundreds of thousands in New York City—to vote in presidential elections in the year 2000. Polling places in New York and other locations were not set up until 2004, however.

Over the past few decades Dominicans have begun to disperse in large numbers away from New York City and toward other growing centers of Dominican settlement such as Union City, New Jersey; Providence, Rhode Island; Lawrence, Massachusetts; and Miami, Florida. Political agendas have shifted with the migrants, away from local and toward more national issues. Umbrella groups such as the Dominican American National Roundtable have sought the support of Dominicans in New York while trying to redirect the political resources in the city toward other locales in order to address broader challenges faced

by all Dominicans in the United States. Education, economic and business development, immigration reform, and political empowerment are critical issues for immigrant Dominicans that go far beyond the borders of New York City.

Though Dominican New Yorkers have proven successful in organizing around their Dominican identity, strategic alliances are also being forged around more expansive pan-Latino and African American identities. The willingness to form racially based alliances reflects the fact that, regardless of their own understandings, Dominicans are frequently perceived by North Americans as black and are thus subjected to biases and prejudices in this country. In their efforts to focus broader attention on racial problems in New York, some Dominicans have concluded that it would be hypocritical to do so without also pointing to the severe discrimination against Haitian workers and their Dominican-born offspring back in the Dominican Republic. In this we see early signs that Dominican immigrants are beginning to extend their struggles against racism and requests for racial tolerance across national boundaries.

We also see a transition in the wings as a new group of young Dominican-born and U.S.-born leaders comes of age. Many of these youthful leaders have participated in the Unión de Jovenes Dominicanos (Dominican Youth Union) and in the organization it helped produce, Dominicanos/Dominicans 2000. Formed as a nonprofit organization in 1997, the small network of young Dominican activists worked for

Santo Domingo Mayor Johnny Ventura surrounded by participants of the Dominicanos/Dominicans 2000 conference.

three years to sponsor a conference that would lead to the construction of "a national agenda for the advancement of the Dominican community in New York City and the United States." The conference, held at City College of New York in February 2000, attracted more than 1,500 registered participants to workshops on health care, youth, law, interethnic relations, politics, economic empowerment, women and social change, the "diaspora and the island," the media, and the arts. While other local Latino political figures were also in attendance, the emergence of a new and youthful Dominican leadership was the most noticeable feature of what was probably the largest nationally organized political meeting of Dominicans and Dominican Americans to date.

Over the years women have also demanded a more visible role in forging the destiny of the Dominican New York community. Women like Democratic district leader María Luna have been active in formal politics, while others have stepped forward to found social service agencies and community groups. The founders of early women's groups often focused their attention on issues of importance to women in both the Dominican Republic and the United States. A second wave of Dominican women's organizations, however, like Colectivo de Mujeres Dominicanos (Collective of Dominican Women), emerged in New York in the mid-1980s. Mirella Cruz, one of the founding members of that group, argued for focusing on Dominican women in the diaspora. She believed that in the Dominican Republic women were in the vanguard organizationally whereas in the United States, Dominican women were "still dealing with such basic issues as gaining acceptance as spokespersons for the Dominican community."[8] One hopeful sign that women are getting that acceptance is the active participation of young women leaders in the events of Dominicans/Dominicanos 2000.

The increasing visibility of Dominicans in local and state politics during the 1990s has led some observers to wonder whether immigrant interest in politics in the "home" country can be sustained as Dominicans continue to be integrated into the U.S. political system. Political actors on different sides of the border have tended to highlight the importance of participation in the United States as a strategy of engagement with *both* nations. At the closing session of the Dominicanos/Dominicans 2000 conference, one of the best-known participants, Santo Domingo mayor Johnny Ventura, called for the linking of participation in both national contexts.[9] In his speech, Mayor Ventura praised the accomplishments of Dominicans living abroad, expressed gratitude for their contributions to the Dominican Republic, and emphasized that Dominicans in the United States were an "indisputable part of us...we are two parts of one community." ❈

NOTES:

1. Pamela M. Graham, "Re-imagining the Nation and Defining the District: The Simultaneous Political Incorporation of Dominican Transnational Migrants" (Ph.D. diss., University of North Carolina at Chapel Hill, 1996); Sarah Aponte, *Dominican Migration to the United States, 1970–1997: An Annotated Bibliography* (New York: CUNY Dominican Studies Institute, 1999).

2. Only 7.8 percent of those Dominicans admitted as permanent residents between 1960 and 1970 elected to naturalize by 1980. This rate increased to 17.7 percent one decade later for all Dominicans and to 21.7 percent for those residing in New York City. By contrast, immigrants from many Asian countries had naturalization rates well above 50 percent during this same period.

3. Saskia Sassen-Koob, "Formal and Informal Associations: Dominicans and Colombians in New York," *International Migration Review* 13 (1979): 314–32; Rudy Anthony Sainz, "Dominican Ethnic Associations: Classification and Service Delivery Roles in Washington Heights" (Ph. D. diss., Columbia University School of Social Work, 1990).

4. Fernando Lescaille, *Dominican Political Empowerment* (New York: Dominican Public Policy Project, 1992); Howard Jordan, "Dominicans in New York: Getting a Slice of the Apple," *NACLA Report on the Americas* 30, no. 5 (1997): 37–42.

5. Guillermo Linares, "Dominicans in New York: The Struggle for Community Control in District 6," *Centro de Estudios Puertorriqueños Bulletin 2*, no. 5 (1989): 77–84.

6. Silvio Torres-Saillant and Ramona Hernández claim that Dominicans as a community became known to many Americans after Washington Heights broke out in three days of disturbances and civil disobedience just a few days before the scheduled Democratic National Convention. At that time many Dominicans protested the killing by New York City police of a young Dominican man who was accused of selling drugs. Fearing that the convention might be disrupted by the protests, the police commissioner, many elected officials, and the mayor himself managed to appease Dominican New Yorkers by promising a complete investigation into the incident and adopting such measures as offering classes in cross-cultural sensitivity training for New York City police officers. See Silvio Torres-Saillant and Ramona Hernández, *The Dominican Americans* (Westport, CT: Greenwood Press, 1998).

7. Julio Hernández and Fernando Lescaille, "A Proposal for a Dominican-Based District in Washington Heights and Inwood" (paper presented by the North Manhattan Committee for Fair Representation to the New York City Redistricting Commission, 1991).

8. Torres-Saillant and Hernández, *The Dominican Americans*, 84.

9. Merengue icon Johnny Ventura was mayor of Santo Domingo from 1998 to 2002.

"MY LIFE CHANGED FOR THE BETTER..."

Interview with Miguelina Sosa

Miguelina Sosa (left) observing two trainees using the Hoyer lift at Cooperative Home Care Associates.

Many Dominican women in New York and other U.S. cities have found jobs in the health care sector. Often these are nurse's aide or home attendant positions offering low pay and few if any benefits, yet they provide a fragile foothold in the service economy. Miguelina Sosa's experience is in some ways unusual, because the home health care firm that employs her is a worker-owned cooperative. But her determination to succeed and become self-reliant is shared by many other immigrant women.

Miguelina Sosa was interviewed by Ruth Glasser on February 23, 1996, in New York City. The interview was translated and edited by Catherine Sunshine.

Adapted from *Caribbean Connections: Moving North*, eds. Catherine A. Sunshine and Keith Q. Warner (Washington, DC: Network of Educators on the Americas). © 1998 by Network of Educators on the Americas; © 2005 by Teaching for Change. Used by permission of Teaching for Change.

I was born in 1955 in the Dominican Republic, in a small village called Esperanza—that means "hope." I was the oldest of eight, so I had to spend much of my time taking care of my brothers and sisters.

My father and mother were farmers. They grew a bit of everything—tobacco, cassava, plantains, pigeon peas—and also raised livestock. That kind of life was better back then than it is now. Nowadays it's not easy to make a living working the land. So people prefer to move to the city, or to emigrate.

When I was twenty we emigrated to New York—my mother, one brother, one sister, and me. An older brother who was already here petitioned to bring us in. We lived in his house in the Bronx. Since I was too old to attend high school, I studied and got my GED degree. We all had to work—my brother was supporting us, plus there were five more brothers and sisters back in the Dominican Republic who needed assistance. My other brother and I got jobs in an electronics factory in Queens and worked there for five years. But then the factory closed. The company went out of business or maybe moved to Japan, I don't know precisely.

By that time I had married a Dominican man who worked as a carpenter for a company in New Jersey. We had two small children. While I was out on leave after the second birth, my husband became critically ill with kidney disease.

When he came home from the hospital I had three people to take care of: my sick husband, a newborn, and a three-year-old. There was no way I could leave the house to go out to work. My husband eventually received disability benefits, and we got food stamps, welfare, and Medicaid for the children. He had to have dialysis three times a week. I learned to give his medicines and prepare a special diet.

Eventually he had a kidney transplant, and after that he went back to work. Soon, though, he lost the kidney through rejection and had other serious complications. Luckily, he was able to receive another transplant which was successful. But the doctor said he couldn't work any longer. He wants to but he can't, so he's retired.

I stayed home until my younger child was in kindergarten. Then I got to thinking, and I said to my husband: "Suppose I were to look for a job; you could pick up the children from school." And we came to an agreement.

We were concerned about what kind of example we were setting for our children. They needed to see their parents working, at least one of us, to learn the importance of work.

I began looking for a job, but without success. I went to offices, factories, and stores. I even went back to school and completed courses in English and business, but my English still wasn't good enough for a business-related job.

Since I had so much experience taking care of others, I began applying for positions as a home attendant. By chance I wound up at Cooperative Home Care, a worker-owned firm in the Bronx that employs home health aides. A home health aide is different from a home attendant. An attendant cleans the house, while a home health aide cares for the sick person directly.

I didn't think I was going to pass the training course. I've always been somewhat shy, and most of the other students had much better English than mine. My self-esteem was low. But when I took the examination, I passed with an 89! Another student who was born here got only 70-something. When I realized that, it encouraged me tremendously.

My first patient was a woman who had asthma and used a portable pump. The situation wasn't quite what I expected. The woman's apartment was a mess— she had two dogs—and I spent most of the time helping her cook for her grandchildren. My next assignment was a woman with emphysema who used an oxygen tank. I had to give her sponge baths, cook for her, do the laundry. I went with her to the hospital many times.

Little by little I became experienced. One of the most delicate aspects of the job is that you can't get involved in family disputes in the client's household. One difficult case was a ninety-two-year-old Puerto Rican woman. She had two sons and a married granddaughter who were always arguing with her. Whenever she became angry with them, she took it out on me, and she could be quite nasty. Then one day, as I was on my knees scrubbing the tub, I saw her staring at me. "You do everything for me," she said. "Without you I wouldn't be here. And I treat you so badly." We sat down and talked for a long time, and things were much easier after that. I stayed with her until she died, a year later.

After three and a half years working as a home health aide, I was asked to train to become an assistant instructor. At first I said no because of my shyness, my problems with English. But my husband encouraged me and the staff encouraged me, and finally I gave in and took the training course.

As an instructor, I give demonstrations and check to see whether the trainees are doing the procedures correctly. Teaching adults requires special skill. If a trainee is doing something incorrectly, you have to tell her in a way that isn't a put-down, but helps her to improve. You can't treat the person like a child. She is an adult like you, only she is learning something new to her.

Some of the trainees lack confidence. Sometimes they need to hear someone say, "You can do it." They relax when I tell them that I'm a home health aide, that I did the same training and took care of patients, and I probably will again.

When I came to Cooperative Home Care, my life changed for the better, and not only because I began working and earning money. Also because I've learned so much from the people I've cared for . . . You learn how to care for different illnesses and about people of all backgrounds. Almost all of the clients are older and have had many experiences, and they can teach you about life.

Now that I'm a trainer, I'm earning more money and learning things I never imagined I would learn, such as computer skills. I prepare my own lectures and demonstrations, with help from the training staff. I believe in myself much more than before.

Sometimes when I have to work late, my children don't understand; they want me to be home at five o'clock. But they've gotten used to it. Sometimes I cook the family's dinner in the morning before work and set it aside for them, or I might cook enough for two days in a row. Or my husband cooks; we share like that. He understands the situation because we have good communication between us, always have had.

To succeed in this work you have to have two things: patience and a desire to help. You have to have something inside to give. If you don't have plenty of patience and a little love, you won't get anywhere. ❀

"MY DREAM IS TO START MY OWN BUSINESS..."

Interview with Julie Guerrero

Julie Guerrero was interviewed by Anne Gallin on February 19, 2004 in Queens, New York. The interview was translated by Patricio Zambrano-Barragán.

While northern Manhattan and the Bronx were the core areas of Dominican settlement in New York City, Dominicans have also been moving outward to the boroughs of Queens, Brooklyn, and Staten Island. According to a recent study by the CUNY Dominican Studies Institute (see unit 22), more than 95,000 Dominicans—17 percent of Dominicans in New York City—live in Queens. The largest concentration is in the neighborhood of Corona.

Pattycakes, a cake decorating school and baking supply company, lies between Corona and Jackson Heights, another heavily Latino neighborhood. Pattycakes offers two unique classes: "Dominican Decoration" and "Dominican Cake." The instructor is Julie Guerrero, who moved from Hato Mayor del Rey, Dominican Republic to Corona, Queens in 1993. Since she began teaching nearly four years ago, her bilingual cake decorating classes have become extremely popular among Latinos and other immigrants, as well as among native New Yorkers.

I have taken many courses. I started with the basics—how to prepare the dough, the cake—and then moved on to decoration. Later I took an advanced course that helped me improve my skills. I started to teach after I took the course at Pattycakes. One day, the owner asked me to bring her a sample of one of my cakes. She liked it and proposed that I work with her. I taught my first class about four years ago. Teaching has been a wonderful experience. I've had the chance to work not only with Hispanics, but also with Chinese, Haitians, Italians, and Americans as well, even though my English is not perfect. I have taught people between the ages of twenty and seventy-eight.

There are many Dominicans and immigrants from other Hispanic countries in the neighborhood where I live. They're fascinated by Dominican cake. Every time I make one, I see how much people enjoy it. There is a big demand for it in this country. We eat Dominican cake at birthday parties, weddings, baptisms, and baby showers.

People always say that what makes our cake special is its rich flavor; it's not too sweet. They like the decoration, but really it's the flavor that makes our cake different. People say, "This cake is so good you can even eat it for breakfast with coffee!"

Every baker has a different recipe for Dominican cake. I will give you mine. I always tell my students, "If you want a real Dominican cake, you must follow my recipe exactly as I teach it." You can walk down the street and just about every grocery store will have a sign saying, "We sell Dominican cakes." But if you really know Dominican cake,

you'll notice the difference.

My dream is to start my own business. When customers come to my store, I want them to find everything they need for baking, cake decoration, and birthday parties. I also want to offer Dominican cakes for all occasions.

Many of my students say to me, "Maestra"—teacher—"when are you going to start your own school?" I tell them, "I don't know, I'd really like to." They tell me they love the way I teach. It's nice, when you come from a country where people have to

sacrifice for almost everything. When I look at the people who take my classes, who don't have much money, I empathize with them because I come from a similar background. It's not difficult to understand where they come from. You feel like you are working with people who are just like you. I would like to start a school where I would teach not only how to bake cakes, but also how to prepare bridal bouquets, and everything related to party decoration. I would like to do all this, but it is in God's hands. ✸

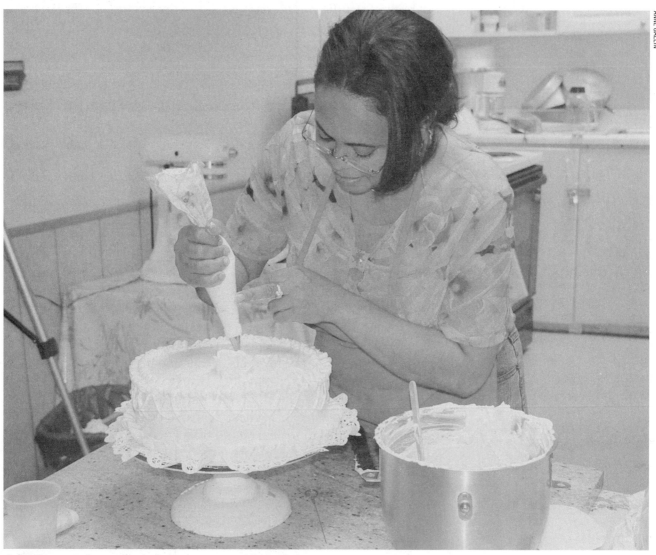

Julie Guerrero demonstrates how to create an icing rose.

Dominican Cake

Julie Guerrero

This cake serves 15 people. If they're American, it will serve 20, because Americans don't eat a lot of cake!

For the cake:

> 4 whole eggs
>
> 6 egg yolks (save the egg whites for frosting)
>
> 2 sticks unsalted butter
>
> 2 sticks margarine
>
> 2 cups sugar
>
> 3½ cups all-purpose flour
>
> 2 tablespoons baking powder
>
> ½ cup water
>
> ½ cup milk
>
> 1 tablespoon vanilla extract
>
> 1 tablespoon rum (optional)
>
> 1 teaspoon grated lime rind

Set out eggs, butter and margarine and bring to room temperature.

Preheat oven to 350°. Grease two 10-inch by 2-inch round cake pans with vegetable shortening. Or grease the sides and cover the bottom of the pan with wax paper.
Sift together the flour and baking powder and set aside.

In a separate bowl, mix the water, milk, vanilla, and rum and set aside.

In a mixer, cream the butter, margarine and sugar on the lowest setting until smooth. It should be thick and creamy.

Still on the lowest setting, add 6 egg yolks one at a time, then add 4 whole eggs one at a time.

Add the dry ingredients and the wet ingredients alternately to the butter-sugar mixture, mixing briefly after each addition. Add the lime rind. Do not continue mixing the batter after everything has been combined.

Pour batter into the cake pans, filling each pan only halfway. Sprinkle a few drops of cold water over the batter in each pan.

Bake at 350° for about 30 minutes. Do not open the oven for the first 20 minutes! To see if the cake is ready, stick a toothpick in the center of the cake. When the toothpick comes out clean, remove cake from oven, let stand one minute, then carefully flip the pans onto cooling racks and let cool completely. Do not remove cakes from pan until you are ready to frost them.

For the frosting:

> ⅓ cup water
>
> 2¼ cups sugar
>
> 7 oz. egg whites* (from 6 eggs used in batter)
>
> 1 teaspoon vanilla

In a medium sauce pan, stir the water and 2 cups of the sugar. Set on stove to boil.

In a separate bowl, using the mixer with the whisk attachment, beat the egg whites on high until they look like snow peaks. Add the remaining ¼ cup sugar to the egg whites.

When the boiling water-sugar mixture looks silver, remove from heat, but do not let it cool! Gradually add the dissolved sugar mixture to the beaten egg whites, continuing to beat well until the mixture is fluffy.

Before frosting the cakes, in a small sauce pan, combine a little bit of sugar and water, bring to a boil, and then brush mixture over cakes.

Remove one cake from pan and place on cake plate or similar surface, smooth side up. Cover top of cake with the filling of your choice. Then, place the other cake on top, smooth side up.

Cover the entire cake with a light coating of frosting to keep the crumbs in. Then, generously frost the entire cake using all but a little bit of frosting.

After frosting the cake, heat a little bit of water. Add a few drops of hot water to the remaining frosting in the bowl. Mix lightly. Use this heated frosting to smooth out the frosting on the cake.

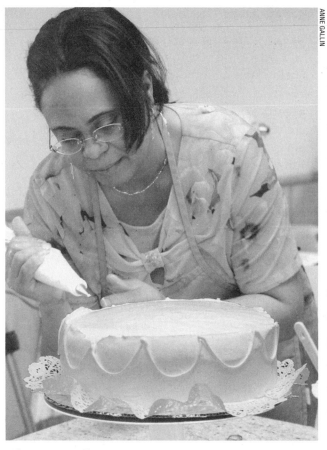

Julie Guerrero demonstrates an icing swag.

For the filling:

Use any one of the following fillings. Typical fillings from my country are made from pineapple, guava and condensed milk. They are very easy to make.

Pineapple filling:

1–20 oz. can unsweetened pineapple (or an equivalent amount of fresh pineapple)

2 cups sugar

Cut the pineapple into pieces and place in a blender. Add sugar. Blend until smooth. Pour the blended pineapple-sugar mixture into a medium saucepan. Cook over medium heat until thick enough to spread (about 35 minutes). Cool the mixture, then spread between layers of cake.

Guava filling:

1–14 oz. package guava paste (available at grocery stores that carry Latin American foods)

Place ½ of package of guava paste into a medium saucepan. Over low heat, add drops of water and stir until the paste is the right consistency to spread. Cool, then spread between layers of cake.

Condensed milk filling:

1–12 oz. can condensed milk

1 tablespoon rum (optional)

Put unopened can of condensed milk in medium saucepan and cover with water. Bring to a boil and then cook over medium heat for approximately 1 hour 45 minutes. Cool, add rum, then spread between layers of cake.

NOTE: Consumption of certain uncooked or undercooked foods such as raw egg whites put the consumer at a (slight) risk of food-bourne diseases such as salmonella. Use only properly refrigerated, clean, sound-shelled, fresh, grade AA or A eggs. Refrigerate broken-out eggs if you won't be using them within an hour. Or, you may prefer to substitute another white frosting for this recipe.

DOMINICANS IN NEW YORK CITY

USE WITH: Units 25, 27, 29

DURATION: 2–3 classes

STANDARDS:

English Language Arts: 1, 3, 9, 10

Social Studies: 1a, 1d, 3c, 3d, 3g, 3h, 4b, 4c, 4e, 4f, 4h

Foreign Language: 1, 2, 3, 4.2

GOAL: To research immigration experiences in New York City.

OBJECTIVE:

To interpret different Dominican immigration experiences in New York City.

ACTIVITIES:

1. Referring to the population table on Dominicans in New York (unit 25), mark the cities and towns with sizable Dominican populations on a map of New York State.

2. Discuss patterns of Dominican immigration and settlement. Where are most immigrants clustered?

3. Looking at a map of New York City and/or Manhattan, locate Washington Heights. If time permits, show a clip from the video "Washington Heights."

4. Students share what they know about Washington Heights.

5. In separate groups, students read one of the following articles while the teacher checks for comprehension:

   • "Dominicans in New York: Quisqueya on the Hudson" (unit 25)

   • "'The factories moved out . . .' Interview with Victor Morisete-Romero" (unit 27)

   • "'My life changed for the better . . .' Interview with Miguelina Sosa (unit 29)

6. The teacher puts students in groups of three. Each individual in the group will have read a different article. Students work together to answer one of the question groups below and then report back to class.

   • Why is Washington Heights such a predominantly Dominican neighborhood? What other types of people live in the area? What are the visual and audible signs that many Dominicans live here?

Lesson plan prepared by Ruth Glasser.

- How do Dominicans in Washington Heights maintain ties with their homeland? How do they "recreate" their homeland in Washington Heights?

- How is the "chain migration" from particular areas of the Dominican Republic visible in the names of the businesses mentioned in "Quisqueya on the Hudson?" What region of the Dominican Republic do many Washington Heights residents seem to come from?

- What are some of the social and economic problems of the neighborhood's residents and how are individuals and groups working to solve them? What are some of the advantages and disadvantages of focusing on problems in New York rather than on concerns back home in the Dominican Republic?

ASSESSMENT:

Students explore the growth of Dominican populations in their own and nearby communities using the following questions as a guide: Has there been chain migration from particular areas of the Dominican Republic to your community? If so, how did it start and why has it persisted? Each student should write a paragraph with findings and analysis. Teacher assesses student understanding of chain migration as described in the paragraph.

MATERIALS:

- Map of New York State

- Overhead projector

- "Dominicans in New York" population table copied onto transparency

- "Washington Heights" (directed by Alfredo De Villa, Lions Gate Home Entertainment, 2003)

"YOU'VE GOT TO BE CONNECTED..."

Interview with Francisco García-Quezada

The town of Haverstraw, New York, thirty miles north of New York City, wasn't always an immigrant mecca. But a stroll through downtown along Main Street and Broadway shows how much has changed. Dominican-owned businesses and social organizations such as El Clarín newspaper, Bueno Unisex barber shop, López-Cintrón travel agency, and Quisqueya[1] Sports Club impart a Caribbean flavor. Almost 60 percent of Haverstraw's 10,000 residents are Hispanic, the 2000 census found. More than a quarter of the town's population, 2,727 people, trace their roots to the Dominican Republic.

Francisco García-Quezada arrived in Haverstraw in 1979, at the age of thirteen. He graduated from North Rockland High School in neighboring Thiells and went on to pursue degrees in administration and counseling. In 1994 Francisco returned to North Rockland High to teach Spanish to native Spanish speakers. Seventy percent of the Latino students at the school are of Dominican or partially Dominican heritage.

Francisco García-Quezada was interviewed by Anne Gallin in Thiells, NY, on November 26, 2003.

It was the summer of 1979. We came directly to the village of Haverstraw because my mom had some relatives who had been here since the early sixties and late fifties. I remember the day we arrived. People we had never seen who were related to us and friends of my mom came to the house to bring presents—pillows, sheets for the beds, everyday practical things for four kids. That was a custom back then.

About two weeks after we came, a young man, Rumaldo Peralta, came to the door to invite us to a youth group that was run out of St. Peter's Church, which was very populated with Dominicans who had come

here. That young man later became a priest ordained in Haverstraw and he ended up marrying my wife and me.

St. Peter's had adult groups that promoted the faith and work of the church in the community. There was also a large youth group, with seventy-five or eighty young people who were very actively involved in the community. The youth group was a great experience. We were like a family; we met every week. We had outings: we went to all of the northeast beaches from Jersey all the way out to Connecticut. We also had fundraisers and retreats. We were able to bring Millie Quezada[2] and many other artists

Francisco García-Quezada (far right) with some of his North Rockland High School students.

Francisco García-Quezada with former student Sydney Valerio Candelaria. García-Quezada also mentored her as a new teacher (English) at North Rockland, where she is also co-advisor of the Aspira Club.

to perform. We would raise $2,500 in a single dance to run activities for the community. We used some of that money as hospitality money. When we knew people were moving into the town we would bring gifts to the house, just as people did for us.

Community Activism

Some of us also belonged to organizations like the Hispanic Coalition or Latinos Unidos. We promoted Latino culture but also raised questions of injustice, especially concerning the migrant workers in the area. We wanted to make sure that they were treated justly and given the right pay. So we worked with a group of young professionals, some of them attorneys, both Latinos and non-Latinos.

When I was a kid in the Dominican Republic, I remember one of our neighbors whose name was Dulce. Dulce lived across the street from my family and looked out for all of us little ones when our parents were working, or in the house or cooking. She would sit outside, tell on us all the time when we were doing the wrong thing. As a kid I didn't like her being around. But as a young adult I realized how important she was for my mom and for everybody's mom. We would have been in a lot of trouble if Dulce had not been there. Thank God I was able to say that to her before she passed away, because we saw each other often when I went back to visit.

I don't think we come even close to doing that here. It's not just because of the U.S. mentality. It's because of the time. People don't seem to have the time, or they don't give the time. So I

think we need to be able to say, "What is the time that I could give and to what cause?" And then pick a cause or service or project, or create one if you don't find one that fits you, and be involved that way.

I hear a great deal: "Oh, young people today…" Well, if we're not modeling it for the young people then why are we blaming them? I had models. Most of them were not in my family, but I saw people and I liked what I saw in them. I didn't have the father image that I would want to have had in my life but I saw older adult males and I saw the qualities. I think we need to be able to be that for each other. Dulce was not related to me by blood and I am not related by blood to many of the kids I help.

My wife and I, with our girls, do community service locally when we go to group homes and bring food and clothing and collect other things through the community. We're actively involved in various causes to keep ourselves grounded. I think that if people live in a place without really being part of what's going on, that's when they're beginning to die.

Much Work to Be Done

I would like to see the local agencies and politicians in Haverstraw be more inclusive in addressing the needs of newcomers. I think the folks who have been here for a while are capable of continuing to help themselves, but the newcomers need some help in adjusting and finding jobs and services. We have an influx now of people from Central America and Mexico in this area, which we have never had before. They

Melina Salvador, Chayane Galarce and Betsaida Pabon.

deserve assistance because they don't have the kind of connection that my family did. There is also a need for more affordable housing for folks so they can continue to live and work in this county.

I'd like to see the school district be more responsive to the needs of all students, which would include our newcomers. I would like to see representation of our Latino community on school boards in the county. I think among the seven or eight districts there's only one person on the board who is of Latino descent. And although our school district is 42 percent Latino, we don't have a Latino or Latina on the board yet. It can't be me because I work for the district, so I have to help find someone and train them to look at the issues. For example, bilingual education services have been eliminated in almost all the districts in the county, but because of the growing Spanish-speaking population, we need to continue those services. They're not perfect but we need them.

I'd like to see the Latino community become more cohesive. At the Quisqueya Sports Club in Haverstraw, I understand they have added all the flags of other

Latin American countries that have joined them.[1] They're very open so they're becoming like a welcoming center to the community, which I think is really nice. I'd like to see that happening more. Agencies like Latinos Unidos or Hispanic Coalition are working on that, too.

Involving the Next Generation

If you can get kids involved at any age, they will learn that they are connected to others. You say to a kid, "You know what? We need people at the community center after school to tutor or to help at the homework center. Who wants to go?" And you put up a list and say, "I'm going to be there from this time to this time. Who can be there with me?" And you get names! They'll volunteer. You cannot just say "Can you do it?" and send them out. You can do that once they've been doing it for a while, but the first time you've got to model it for them.

Once they begin to do community service, they are connected. For the rest of their life they'll know that when they help, they become connected to people. We need each other and if you want to live in a vacuum somewhere isolated from society, then that's really sad. If you're going to live in this society, in this life, you've got to be connected somehow. I think it's wonderful when people of any age say, "How can I help? What can I do?" ❀

NOTES:

1. Quisqueya is the indigenous name for the Dominican Republic, so the club's name indicates its original Dominican focus.

2. Female merengue performer and leader of the popular group, Millie y los Vecinos.

Astha Wadhwa and Ariel López.

DOMINICANS IN NEW JERSEY: THRIVING COMMUNITIES

Cid D. Wilson

After New York, New Jersey boasts the second-largest population of Dominicans in the United States. Unlike most other states where the great majority of Dominicans are concentrated in a single city, New Jersey has numerous separate Dominican communities in Paterson, Passaic, Newark, Jersey City, Union City, Trenton, Camden, Atlantic City, and Perth Amboy. According to the 2000 census, four of the ten cities in the country that had the largest population increases of Dominicans between 1990 and 2000 are in New Jersey.

In this brief sketch, Cid D. Wilson, president of the Dominican American National Roundtable, describes some of the Dominican political and cultural organizations that have developed in New Jersey over the past few decades.

Adapted from Cid D. Wilson, "Dominicans in New Jersey," in the *Dominican American Calendar 2003*, published jointly by the Dominican American National Roundtable and the CUNY Dominican Studies Institute. © 2003 by Dominican American National Roundtable. Used by permission of the publishers.

In the early years of Dominican migration to New Jersey, the community relied on New York for its needs, ranging from authentic Dominican food and merchandise to airline travel to the Dominican Republic. Today, virtually all of the communities in New Jersey are self-supporting with such goods and services. Newark Liberty International Airport now has nonstop flights to Santo Domingo, Puerto Plata, and Santiago.

New Jersey has three Dominican Day parades, in Jersey City, Union City/West New York, and Paterson. The New Jersey State Dominican Day Parade and Festival in Paterson is the second-largest Dominican parade in the United States, after New York City's.

There is a rich Dominican organizational life in New Jersey. Some of the more prominent Dominican organizations include Casa de la Cultura Dominicana

Dominicans in New Jersey, According to the 2000 Census

City	Number of Dominicans	Percentage Dominican
Paterson	15,331	10.3
Jersey City	9,186	3.8
Perth Amboy	8,897	18.8
Passaic	8,865	13.0
Union City	7,688	11.5
Newark	6,266	2.3
West New York	3,847	8.4
Elizabeth	3,629	3.0
New Brunswick	2,855	5.9
Camden	1,874	2.3
Clifton	1,853	2.4
Hackensack	1,573	3.7
Bayonne	1,072	1.7

Note: Official census figures are believed to underestimate the number of Dominicans, especially the undocumented.

in Paterson, Dominican Empowerment Political Action Committee in Union City, Congreso Domínico-Americano de Nueva Jersey in Hudson County, Alianza Domínico-Americana in Jersey City, Dominican Communitarian Association of New Jersey in Perth Amboy, Alianza para el Desarrollo Dominicano-Americano in Jersey City, and Asociación Médica Dominicana of New Jersey in Perth Amboy. Rutgers University has the largest Dominican student organization in the state.

The New Jersey State Conference on Dominican Affairs is the largest annual gathering of Dominican leaders in the state. The conference attracts elected officials from New Jersey and Dominican leaders from New Jersey, New York, and the Dominican Republic. As a result of this annual conference, the various Dominican communities within New Jersey have begun to function more like one large community.

Dominicans in New Jersey have followed the footsteps of their counterparts in New York and Rhode Island by increasing their political activism and running candidates for public office. In November 2001 Ramón "Tito" Rosario of Atlantic City became the first Dominican to be elected to a city council in New Jersey. Six months later Manuel Segura was elected to an at-large position on the Trenton City Council and Tilo Rivas was elected commissioner of Union City. In addition, Lizette Delgado was appointed assistant secretary of state in early 2002, making her the first Hispanic female ever to be named to the post and one of the highest-ranking Latinas in New Jersey state government. ❖

AGUANTANDO

Junot Díaz

Junot Díaz.

EDUARDO HOEPELMAN. COURTESY OF THE CUNY-DOMINICAN STUDIES INSTITUTE LIBRARY, CITY COLLEGE.

Dominican-born author Junot Díaz moved from Santo Domingo to the New Jersey suburb of London Terrace, near Perth Amboy, in 1975. His short story collection Drown *was published to wide acclaim in 1996. In this excerpt from the story titled "Aguantando," Díaz shows the estrangement between parent and child that sometimes results when a parent migrates, leaving family members behind.*

Díaz's work has appeared in Story *magazine,* The Paris Review, The New Yorker, *and* The Best American Short Stories of 1996. *He received a Guggenheim Fellowship in 1999. He is presently an associate professor at Massachusetts Institute of Technology.*

I lived without a father for the first nine years of my life. He was in the States, working, and the only way I knew him was through the photographs my moms kept in a plastic sandwich bag under her bed. Since our zinc roof leaked, almost everything we owned was water-stained: our clothes, Mami's Bible, her makeup, whatever food we had, Abuelo's tools, our cheap wooden furniture. It was only because of that plastic bag that any pictures of my father survived.

When I thought of Papi I thought of one shot specifically. Taken days before the U.S. invasion: 1965. I wasn't even alive then; Mami had been pregnant with my first never-born brother and Abuelo could still see well enough to hold a job. You know the sort of photograph I'm talking about. Scalloped edges, mostly brown in color. On the back my moms's cramped handwriting—the date, his name, even the street, one over from our house. He was dressed in his Guardia uniform, his tan cap at an angle on his shaved head, an unlit Constitución squeezed between his lips. His dark unsmiling eyes were my own.

I did not think of him often. He had left for Nueva York when I was four but since I couldn't remember a single moment with him I excused him from all nine years of my life. On the days I had to imagine him—not often, since Mami didn't much speak of him anymore—he was the soldier in the photo. He was a cloud of cigar smoke, the traces of which could still be found on the uniforms he'd left behind. He was pieces of my friends' fathers, of the domino players on the corner, pieces of Mami and Abuelo. I didn't know him at all. I didn't know that he'd abandoned us. That this waiting for him was all a sham.

...

When Yunior was nine, a letter arrived from his father, telling the family that he would be coming to take them back with him to the United States. Yunior's brother Rafa warns him that it's not the first time their father has made that promise.

The week after the letter came I watched her from my trees. She ironed cheese sandwiches in paper bags for our lunch, boiled plátanos for our dinner. Our dirty clothes were pounded clean in the concrete trough on the side of the outhouse. Every time she thought I was scrabbling too high in the branches she called me back to the ground. You ain't Spiderman, you know, she said, rapping the top of my head with her knuckles. On the afternoons that Wilfredo's father came over to play dominos and talk politics, she sat with him and Abuelo and laughed at their campo stories. She seemed more normal to me but I was careful not to provoke her. There was still something volcanic about the way she held herself.

On Saturday a late hurricane passed close to the Capital and the next day folks were talking about how high the waves were down by the Malecón. Some children had been lost, swept out to sea and Abuelo shook his head when he heard the news. You'd think the sea would be sick of us by now, he said.

That Sunday Mami gathered us on the back patio. We're taking a day off, she announced. A day for us as a family.

We don't need a day off, I said and Rafa hit me harder than normal.

Shut up, OK?

I tried to hit him back but Abuelo grabbed us both by the arm. Don't make me have to crack your heads open, he said.

She dressed and put her hair up and even paid for a concho instead of crowding us into an autobus. The driver actually wiped the seats down with a towel while we waited and I said to him, It don't look dirty, and he said, Believe me, muchacho, it is. Mami looked beautiful and many of the men she passed wanted to know where she was heading. We couldn't afford it but she paid for a movie anyway. *The Five Deadly Venoms.* Kung fu movies were the only ones the theaters played in those days. I sat between Mami and Abuelo. Rafa moved to the back, joining a group of boys who were smoking, and arguing with them about some baseball player on Licey.

After the show Mami bought us flavored ices and while we ate them we watched the salamanders crawling around on the sea rocks. The waves were tremendous and some parts of George Washington were flooded and cars were churning through the water slowly.

A man in a red guayabera stopped by us. He lit a cigarette and turned to my mother, his collar turned up by the wind. So where are you from?

Santiago, she answered.

Rafa snorted.

You must be visiting relatives then.

Yes, she said. My husband's family.

He nodded. He was dark-skinned, with light-colored spots about his neck and hands. His fingers trembled slightly as he worked the cigarette to his lips. I hoped he'd drop his cigarette, just so I could see what the ocean would do to it. We had to wait almost a full minute before he said buenos días and walked away.

What a crazy, Abuelo said.

Rafa lifted up his fist. You should have given me the signal. I would have kung-fu-punched him in the head.

Your father came at me better than that, Mami said.

Abuelo stared down at the back of his hands, at

MURAT BAYSAN

the long white hairs that covered them. He looked embarrassed.

Your father asked me if I wanted a cigarette and then he gave me the whole pack to show me that he was a big man.

I held on to the rail. Here?

Oh no, she said. She turned around and looked out over the traffic. That part of the city isn't here anymore.

...

Rafa used to think that he'd come in the night, like Jesus, that one morning we'd find him at our breakfast table, unshaven and smiling. Too real to be believed. He'll be taller, Rafa predicted. Northamerican food makes people that way. He'd surprise Mami on her way back from work, pick her up in a German car. Say nothing to the man walking her home. She would not know what to say and neither would he. They'd drive down to the Malecón and he'd take her to see a movie, because that's how they met and that's how he'd want to start it again.

I would see him coming from my trees. A man with swinging hands and eyes like mine. He'd have gold on his fingers, cologne on his neck, a silk shirt, good leather shoes. The whole barrio would come out to greet him. He'd kiss Mami and Rafa and shake Abuelo's reluctant hand and then he'd see me

behind everyone else. What's wrong with that one? he'd ask and Mami would say, He doesn't know you. Squatting down so that his pale yellow dress-socks showed, he'd trace the scars on my arms and on my head. Yunior, he'd finally say, his stubbled face in front of mine, his thumb tracing a circle on my cheek. ❀

Abuelo: Grandfather
aguantando: holding on
barrio: neighborhood
campo: countryside
concho: taxi
Constitución: brand of cigarette
Licey: baseball team from Santo Domingo
George Washington: seaside avenue in Santo Domingo, also called the Malecón
Guardia: the National Guard
guayabera: embroidered cotton shirt worn by men
malcriado: spoiled brat
muchacho: young man
Nueva York: New York
ojos: eyes
plátanos: plantains
tíos: uncles

DOMINICANS IN MASSACHUSETTS: THE BOSTON-MIRAFLORES CONNECTION

Peggy Levitt

Adapted from Peggy Levitt, *The Transnational Villagers* (Berkeley and Los Angeles: University of California Press). © 2001 by The Regents of the University of California. Used by permission of the publisher.

After New York and New Jersey, Massachusetts has the third-largest Dominican population outside the Dominican Republic. In Lawrence, Massachusetts, Dominicans make up over 22 percent of the city's population—a greater proportion than in any U.S. city except Haverstraw, New York. Boston has attracted nearly 13,000 Dominicans, and there are growing Dominican populations in surrounding cities such as Lynn, Lowell, and Worcester.

The Dominican community in Boston shows clearly how international migration establishes connections not only between countries, but also between individual cities and towns. Through chain migration, people from a particular town in the sending country will often cluster in a particular city, town, or neighborhood in the receiving country, creating little overseas satellites of the hometown. Since the 1960s, Dominicans from the town of Miraflores have been settling in Boston, and connections between the two communities run deep.

Sociologist Peggy Levitt studied Dominicans in Miraflores and

ANNE GALLIN

Street sign in Lawrence, Massachusetts.

Boston and the complex ties between them. Levitt shows that immigration is no longer necessarily a one-way process of leaving the homeland and staying away, or even the two-way trip of a sojourn in a new country followed by an eventual permanent return. Rather, we now see the development of "transnational" communities in which people, goods, and ideas move back and forth continuously, and migration's effects are felt on both sides. In addition to studying the lives of Mirafloreños in Boston, Levitt spent time in Miraflores examining the impact this immigration had on family members and friends who stayed behind.

The high-tech "Massachusetts Miracle" of recent decades failed to reach most Dominican immigrants. Nevertheless, even working at low-wage jobs, Boston's Dominicans have become a critical source of economic support to their families on the island. Millions of dollars flow annually from Boston to Miraflores. The following excerpt from Levitt's book The Transnational Villagers *shows the impact of economic remittances—wages earned in Boston and sent to the island. It also shows the effects of less tangible social and cultural remittances on one sphere of Dominican life: childrearing.*

Mimosa tree.

Dominicans in Massachusetts, According to the 2000 Census

City	Number of Dominicans	Percentage Dominican
Lawrence	16,186	22.5
Boston	12,981	2.2
Lynn	5,517	6.2
Salem	2,176	5.4
Worcester	1,611	0.9
Methuen	1,308	3.0
Haverhill	1,179	2.0
Lowell	1,024	0.9

Note: Official census figures are believed to underestimate the number of Dominicans, especially the undocumented.

The top part of the avenue leading from the Dominican city of Baní to the village of Miraflores is bordered by thick, leafy mimosa trees. Throughout the year, they are covered by orange blossoms and blanket the street with a delicious shade. On the way out of town, the sidewalks are busy with women shopping and children returning home from school. The streets grow quiet as the beauty parlors, small grocery stores, and lawyers' offices closest to the town square gradually give way to residential neighborhoods. On one corner is Mayor Carlos Peña's feed store, where he and his coworkers from the Partido Revolucionario Dominicano (PRD) meet to talk about politics every late afternoon. Farther down the street, members of the Partido Reformista Social Cristiano (PRSC) also sit in front of their party's headquarters, drinking sweet cups of coffee and discussing the current election campaign. At the edge of town, the buildings end abruptly in overgrown fields. The avenue goes silent except for a lone motorcycle driver. The countryside is overwhelmingly beautiful.

A few hundred yards ahead, two sights unexpectedly interrupt this peaceful landscape. On the right side of the road, four partially complete mansions stand behind large iron gates. Their crumbling marble pillars and large cracked windows, so out of character with the rest of the scene, mock onlookers from the street. A little farther down the avenue, at the edge of a large, uncultivated field, a billboard proclaims, "Viaje a Boston con Sierra Travel"—travel to Boston with Sierra Travel. Telephone numbers in Boston and Baní, coincidentally beginning with the same exchange, are hidden by grasses so tall they almost cover the sign completely.

Turning off the road into this village of close to four thousand residents reveals further discontinuities. While some of the homes resemble miniature, finished versions of the empty mansions along the avenue, one out of five families still live in small, two-room wooden houses. Four in ten use outdoor privies. Though the electricity goes off nightly for weeks at a stretch, nearly every household has a television, VCR, or compact-disc player. And although it takes months to get a phone installed in Santo Domingo, the Dominican capital, Mirafloreños can get phone service in their homes almost immediately after they request it.

What explains these sharp contrasts? Who is responsible for these half-finished homes that differ so completely in style and scale from the other houses in the area? Who is the audience for the billboards in the middle of fields that advertise international plane flights? How is it that people who must collect rainwater in barrels so they can wash when the water supply goes off are watching the latest videos in the comfort of their living rooms?

Transnational migration is at the root of these contradictions. The billboard speaks to the nearly two-thirds of Mirafloreño families who have relatives in the greater Boston metropolitan area. These migrants pay for the home improvements and buy the appliances. And some built the dream palaces on the avenue, which they completed only halfway before their money dried up.

Mirafloreños began migrating to Boston, Massachusetts, in the late 1960s. Most settled in and around Jamaica Plain, traditionally a white-ethnic neighborhood until Latinos and young white professionals replaced longtime

TOP: *Mozart Park, located on Center Street in the heart of the Dominican community in Jamaica Plain.* BOTTOM: *Mozart Market on Center Street.*

residents who began leaving the city in the 1960s. Over the years, migrants from the Dominican Republic and the friends and family they left behind have sustained such strong, frequent contacts with one another it is as if village life takes place in two settings. Fashion, food, and forms of speech, as well as appliances and home decorating styles, attest to these strong connections. In Miraflores, villagers often dress in T-shirts emblazoned with the names of businesses in Massachusetts, although they do not know what these words or logos mean. The local colmados stock SpaghettiOs and Frosted Flakes. Many of the benches in the Miraflores Park are inscribed with the names of villagers who moved to Boston years ago. And almost everyone, including older community members who can count on their fingers how many times they have visited Santo Domingo, can talk about "La Mozart" or "La Centre"—Mozart Street Park and Centre Street, two focal points of the Dominican community in Jamaica Plain.

In Boston, Mirafloreños have re-created their premigration lives to the extent that their new physical and cultural environment allows. Particularly during the early years of settlement, but even today, a large number of

Freddy's Market on Center Street in Jamaica Plain.

migrants lived within the same twenty-block radius. There are several streets where people from Miraflores live in almost every triple-decker house. Community members leave their apartment doors open so that the flow between households is as easy and uninhibited as it is in Miraflores. Women continue to hang curtains around the doorframes; these provide privacy without keeping in the heat in the Dominican Republic but are merely decorative in Boston. Because someone is always traveling between Boston and the island, there is a continuous, circular flow of goods, news, and information. As a result, when someone is ill, cheating on his or her spouse, or finally granted a visa, the news spreads as quickly in Jamaica Plain as it does on the streets of Miraflores.

Why They Came

Since 1970, migration from Miraflores to Boston has grown steadily. Unlike other country-of-origin groups, who move first to urban centers within their own country before migrating across borders, nearly all Miraloreños traveled directly to the United States (96 percent). More than three-quarters went to Boston.

More than 75 percent of the Miraloreños who migrated said they did so for economic reasons. The first to leave were the more educated, better-off members of the community. Social networks played an important role in migration's spread. Most Miraloreños trace their journey back to one individual who they say is responsible for setting the

network-building process in motion. Jaime Cárdenas first came to Baní when Trujillo was in power. In those days Trujillo controlled commercial shoe production on the island. To ensure a captive market, the dictator made it illegal to go barefoot and set the fine for doing so higher than the price of shoes. Don Jaime opened his own shoe factory in Baní to cater to the provincial market. Despite his success, he was ostracized by the city's elite. After his first marriage ended in scandal he moved to Miraflores, where he built a large home and began a new family. He became popular among his new neighbors and among young people in particular, because he generously supported the village baseball team. When his factory eventually went bankrupt, he migrated to Boston with his children and encouraged some of the young men he knew to follow him there.

Many of the first to go stayed at the Cárdenas apartment when they arrived. Jorge, a forty-one-year-old return migrant to Miraflores recalls:

When I first got to Boston in the early 1970s, there were four or five other people there. The first night I got there I went to Cárdenas's house. He was not there but his daughter, María del Carmen, said that I could stay there for a few days until I found a room. I did until I got a job

packing oranges and I rented a basement room there on Mozart Street. Then María del Carmen was supervisor for a cleaning company and she got me a job cleaning buildings downtown.

As more village members settled and found work in Boston, a network of connections between Miraflores and Jamaica Plain deepened and spread. Early migrants helped those who came later to find work.

Despite their incorporation into low-wage jobs, Miraloreños assumed increasing responsibility for supporting their nonmigrant family members. Almost 60 percent of the households in Miraflores received some of their monthly income from relatives in the United States. For nearly 40 percent of those households, remittances constituted between 75 and 100 percent of their income. In contrast, only 31 percent of the households earned their money entirely in the Dominican Republic.

When I asked the many Miraloreños I spoke with to describe how migration had transformed their community, they generally began by pointing out the homes, school, and health center that were built and renovated with money from Boston. They said that most people live better now, with enough money for food and clothing, though there are still families who

Button and medal depict Trujillo.

wait anxiously for their remittances each month. Further discussion, though, revealed the hidden costs of these gains to their community. Material progress came at a high price.

Though most villagers have more income and live better than they did before large-scale migration began, few have achieved this through their own labor. Instead, they have grown accustomed to greater comfort, and they covet it even more, even as their ability to accomplish this on their own grows weaker. They are more satisfied yet at the same time more restless. They see their village becoming the place they always dreamed it should be—and a place where they can no longer afford to stay. They cling to their old ways while they experiment with new ones, finding that neither works particularly well in the rapidly changing context in which they live.

Childrearing across Borders

Social remittances and cross-border parenting have transformed parent-child relations in Miraflores. Twenty-year-old Elena cannot remember a time when she actually lived with her mother, Nuria. For as long as she can recall, Nuria lived and worked in Boston, while Elena and her two siblings remained behind in Miraflores to be raised by their grandparents.

Elena's childhood memories are filled with vivid images of her mother's once-a-year visits. Every Christmas, Nuria would arrive home with a suitcase filled with new clothes and toys. Elena remembers nearly bursting with pride as she showed off the gifts

she received to her friends. Her mother always took everyone out for ice cream or for an afternoon outing to the swimming pool. The pride Elena felt almost made up for how deeply she missed her mother during the year.

Elena's experience of being brought up across borders is increasingly common. She was raised jointly by her mother in Boston and by relatives in Miraflores. By distributing the tasks of production and reproduction transnationally, Mirafloreños create and strengthen their transnational community. Migrant family members earn most of the household income, while nonmigrants remain behind to care for children.

Cheap telephone rates and airplane fares make it easy to believe that parenting across borders is possible. Instead of acting when a problem first comes up, an aunt might call the United States for instructions. When migrant parents admonish their children to change their behavior or order that they be punished, they are never sure whether their instructions will be carried out. Some children actively exploit this disparity between real and surrogate parental authority. They know their grandparents need the money their parents send. Because grandparents need their migrant children's support, they are reluctant to assert their authority. Consequently, a whole generation of young people, many Mirafloreños fear, is being brought up without proper discipline or guidance.

This is particularly true when children, like Eduardo,

are sent back and forth to live between Boston and Miraflores. Eduardo says he often feels unsure about where he belongs. His mother and father left him with his aunt and grandmother when he was less than a year old. By the time he joined them in Boston five years later, his parents had divorced. His mother soon remarried and started a new family. Since then, he has been back and forth between Boston and Miraflores, unable to feel completely comfortable in either place. When he has trouble in school in Boston, he is sent back to live with his grandmother in Miraflores. Things normally go well when he first arrives, but within months new problems always seem to crop up. A series of frantic phone calls to Boston about what should be done ensues.

Relations between migrant adults and children in Boston also have to be renegotiated because of the new demands of immigrant life. Parents have less control over their children because they have to work long hours away from home. Many parents only see their children briefly, when they come home to eat and bathe between their daytime and evening jobs.

These arrangements stand in stark contrast to Miraflores, where family members spend most of the day together. Even most of the men who farm come home to eat and relax for at least part of the afternoon. They can always be called home if a problem arises. Since there is a sharper separation between work and family life in Boston, and work schedules are more rigid, parents cannot move as seamlessly between these two worlds as they do at home.

Furthermore, in Miraflores, parents raise their children with help from the entire community. In Boston, they are on their own. Because they are working, most parents cannot watch their children as closely as they would like. Elisa has to leave the house at 5 a.m. to catch her ride to work. She thought her daughter and son were going to high school each day until she received a call from the truant officer telling her that her daughter had not been to school for weeks. Carmen, another return migrant to Miraflores, recalls that in Boston she had to hope that her kids could make it the five blocks home each day because she could not be home until an hour after school let out:

> I couldn't bring my kids up in the same way I would have in Miraflores. Our lives were so different. My husband left early to go to work. He didn't see the kids when he left in the morning because they were sleeping and he didn't see them when he came home at night because they were already in bed. We hardly knew our neighbors. When I had to go out in an emergency, I had no one I could ask to watch the children for me. They grew up quicker, but they were also more difficult to control.

Carmen liked how responsible her children became in Boston. She was pleased that her boys learned to cook and that they helped support the family. But these same gains made it more difficult for her to supervise them.

When migrant children visit Miraflores, or when they call their friends and relatives who stay behind, they introduce new ideas about how parents and kids should act toward one another. Nonmigrant youngsters like what they see and hear. To those who have not migrated, Boston begins to look like a mecca. They, too, want more say over what they do and when they do it. They want the independence their friends enjoy because they have jobs that put money in their pockets. Young women also want to be able to go out without a chaperone.

Migration transforms family and work in Miraflores in ways that heighten divisions and reinforce community at the same time. Nonmigrants need migrants' economic support. Migrants need those who remain behind to raise their children, manage their affairs, and show them the respect they are denied in Boston. Both parties accept changes in the balance of status and power, and negotiate new ways to define these, partly out of love and commitment to one another and partly because they have little choice. Heightened class and generational divisions are part and parcel of increasing social and economic interconnectedness across borders, making this strong but conflict-ridden community likely to endure. ❁

colmado: small grocery store
Mirafloreño: a person from Miraflores
Partido Reformista Social Cristiano: Christian Social Reformist Party
Partido Revolucionario Dominicano: Dominican Revolutionary Party
return migrant: someone who migrates to another country, then migrates back to the country of origin
triple-decker house: three-story wood-frame house providing apartments for three families, characteristic of New England
Trujillo: Dominican dictator

TRANSNATIONAL TIES: DOMINICANS IN BOSTON AND MIRAFLORES

USE WITH: Unit 35

DURATION: 1–2 classes

STANDARDS:

English Language Arts: 1, 2, 3, 4, 9, 10

Social Studies: 1a, 1d, 1f, 3c, 3d, 4b, 4c, 4h, 7d, 7f

Foreign Language: 1, 2, 3, 4.2

GOAL: To understand the concept of transnationalism by exploring the ongoing ties between Dominicans in Boston and Miraflores.

OBJECTIVES:

- To interpret tables that contextualize Dominican immigration to Massachusetts/Boston.

- To answer questions on concepts and conflicts discussed in "Dominicans in Massachusetts: The Boston-Miraflores Connection" (unit 35).

- To write a letter that demonstrates understanding of the above.

ACTIVITIES:

1. On a map of Massachusetts, students mark the towns where Dominicans have settled. Refer to the population table on Dominicans in Massachusetts (unit 35).

2. Ask: Is it fair to say that Dominican settlement in Massachusetts is mainly in the Boston area? Why or why not?

3. Students discuss the following pre-reading questions:

   - When and why do you think Dominicans began to migrate to Boston?

   - What do you think Jamaica Plain was like before Dominicans arrived?

   - Where do you think Dominicans in Boston live, work, and go to school?

4. Students read "Dominicans in Massachusetts: The Boston-Miraflores Connection" (unit 35).

5. In pairs, students answer one of the following comprehension questions and report back to the class:

   - What is transnationalism?

   - What are remittances? How do remittances both help and hinder Miraflores and its residents?

Lesson plan prepared by Claudia Bedoya-Rose.

- How has Dominican immigration to Boston changed the community of Miraflores? What are some signs of migration's impact?

- What does Levitt see as contradictions in the way Dominicans in Miraflores live?

- How has chain migration produced a very particular Dominican community in Boston?

- How does the Dominican world in Jamaica Plain reproduce that of Miraflores?

- How do Mirafloreños raise children across borders? How do they divide the labor of childrearing?

- What are the costs and benefits of transnational childrearing for (1) immigrant parents, (2) grandparents and others who stay behind, and (3) the children?

- Why and how do Dominican parents raise their children differently in Boston than they do in Miraflores?

- How do new ideas from Boston filter back to children in Miraflores?

ASSESSMENT:

Each student pretends to be one of the children or parents described in the article. He or she writes a letter to another person describing the family's situation, the problems they are having, and possible solutions. Teacher grades the letter. (Students dealing with sensitive family issues similar to those discussed in the article should be given the option of adapting the assignment. They can write the letter posing as a counselor or social worker helping the children or parents.)

MATERIALS:

- "Dominicans in Massachusetts" population table copied onto an overhead

- Map of Massachusetts

- Overhead projector

RAISING CHILDREN IN THE DOMINICAN REPUBLIC AND THE UNITED STATES

USE WITH: Unit 35

DURATION: 1-2 classes

STANDARDS:

English Language Arts: 1, 3, 4, 5, 9, 10

Social Studies: 1a, 1d, 1f, 4b, 4c

Foreign Language: 1, 2.1, 3, 4.2

GOAL: To explore the differences between childrearing in the Dominican Republic and the United States.

OBJECTIVES:

- To analyze the difficulties that Dominican families may encounter raising children in the Dominican Republic and Boston.

- To compare the benefits and disadvantages of raising children in both countries.

ACTIVITIES:

1. Students watch a clip from the video "Nueba Yol," which illustrates the troubles that Dominican parents (and their children) sometimes experience in the United States as a result of conflicting cultural norms and expectations.

2. Students read "Dominicans in Massachusetts: The Boston-Miraflores Connection" (unit 35).

3. In partners or small groups, students analyze one of the following concepts as discussed in the article:

   - Loss of control
   - Lack of respect from children
   - Language barrier
   - Parent/child relationship
   - Family support
   - Behavior of children whose families have migrated

4. Students report their findings to the class and discuss similar or different challenges they face with their parents.

Lesson plan prepared by Claudia Bedoya-Rose.

ASSESSMENT:

Students choose one of the concepts and write a short essay describing three ways to deal with this challenge.

MATERIALS:

"Nueba Yol" (directed by Ángel Muñiz, Ideal Enterprises, 1996)

RELIGIOUS LIFE ACROSS BORDERS

Peggy Levitt

While Dominicans at home and abroad have a variety of religious affiliations, the majority practice the Catholic faith. Centuries ago, the Spanish colonial government established Catholicism as the island's official religion and founded numerous churches. But priests were always in short supply, especially in small towns such as Miraflores. As a result, many rural Dominicans developed their own versions of Catholicism, blending the traditional faith with elements of indigenous and African religions.

In this article, sociologist Peggy Levitt focuses on the religious life of Dominican immigrants from Miraflores now living in Boston. She describes how the Mirafloreños joined Catholic parishes in Boston that had been shaped by immigrants from many Spanish-speaking countries. This multiethnic, pan-Latino religious culture, combined with the social and economic constraints of life in Boston, gradually transformed the Dominican-style Catholicism of the Miraflores migrants.

Adapted from Peggy Levitt, *The Transnational Villagers* (Berkeley and Los Angeles: University of California Press). © 2001 by The Regents of the University of California. Used by permission of the publisher.

Puerto Ricans and Cubans who came to Boston in the early 1960s filled the pews left empty by traditional white-ethnic parishioners, who were leaving the city in large numbers. The new Latino members created a vibrant, but separate, religious world of their own. They occasionally crossed paths with Anglos at Mass, at specially planned bilingual celebrations, or at the after-Mass coffee hour, but generally, they remained within a Latino environment.

Church leaders expected Mirafloreños to assimilate into this pan-Latino atmosphere. Latinos, in general, were the group that the wider society defined as their co-ethnics.[1] These migrants, however, came from all parts of Central America, South America, and the Caribbean. Each group brought different practices, preferences for particular saints, and distinct understandings of the relationship between religion and society.

Churchgoing Mirafloreños had to adapt to this least-common-denominator Catholicism and let go of their Dominican-specific one. They also had to adapt to the ways in which this Latino Catholic space had been customized to fit within Anglo structures.

La Virgen de la Altagracia.

COURTESY OF GLADYS MALDONADO

Certain home-based, informal folk practices, traditionally at the core of Mirafloreño religious life, transfer easily to Boston. It is as simple to create an altar, practice devotions, or light candles to a particular saint, make *promesas,* or say the rosary in Boston as it is in Miraflores. Local colmados in Jamaica Plain sell all the necessary religious supplies. Everyone knows about Marli, a woman who leads prayers in people's homes for a small fee. As a consequence, Mirafloreños can stay on the margins of the church when they migrate, and many do. It is only when they want or need to express their beliefs in more organized, institutionalized settings that the transformation of religious life begins.

Mirafloreños gravitated toward the church for a number of reasons. Some said they sought comfort and support. It was one of the few places where they found a community of like-minded individuals. For others, going to church, like participating in political and community groups, fulfilled a social function. They knew they would see people from home at Mass.

Others had to go to church to fulfill their religious obligations. They had to go to Mass if they wanted to officially baptize their infants. Children had to go to religious-school classes to receive their first communion. These prerequisites pushed Mirafloreños toward the formal church. Still others were drawn to the church for reasons of expedience. They said it was easier and more reliable to have a Mass said in honor of a deceased parent than to organize home-based prayer

sessions. You could never be sure if enough people would come so you could actually hold the ceremony.

When Mirafloreños did go to church, they had to adjust their beliefs and practices accordingly. The Catholic templates they shared with Anglos provided some common ground. They were already familiar with many of the prayers and rituals. The services offered by the Hispanic Apostolate lowered barriers to their entry. Some Anglo priests were bilingual and familiar with Dominican culture. But in many cases, different national worship styles, administrative requirements, and new lifestyle arrangements meant that Mirafloreños had to fundamentally change their religious practices.

For example, in order to be baptized in Boston, one had to belong to a particular parish. "People don't know what parish they belong to in the U.S. because there are so many of them," one priest said. "It is not like Miraflores, where there is only one

church." The archdiocese also required that to baptize a baby, its godparents must be married in the church, a practice that is fairly rare among Mirafloreños.

Basic stylistic differences also characterize the Mass in each country. In Miraflores, religious services go on for varied lengths of time. The Dominican church also has a strong tradition of lay participation and leadership. Lay people actively plan services, form choruses, organize readings, and take responsibility for the upkeep of the church. The worship includes many rhythmic songs. Father John, a priest in Boston explains:

> The Anglo Mass at our church is more reserved, private, individualistic. Mass in the Dominican Republic is more communal. There is more music, community participation, a sense of gathering people together. Children are brought to Mass at an early age. There is an emotion or drama that gets

acted out, like when we reenact the stations of the cross on Good Friday.

Confession was also more complicated for migrants in Boston. Unlike the predetermined baptismal ceremony or Mass, the priest-parishioner exchange is a matter of the heart. Meaningful encounters require a cultural as well as an organizational fit. Padre Nelson, a Dominican priest in Boston, explains:

> Banilejos are very hard workers and like to earn money. They don't have time to come to church. They might not be able to come during the hours set for confession. I understand how they are, and I listen to them. I can orient them in a different way than other priests who aren't Latinos because I know where they come from, what their strengths are, how they live their lives. I know how to help them better than other priests, and they understand me better because I speak to them in a language they can assimilate.

The changing character of Mirafloreño immigrants' lives further transformed their religious practices. As with politics, the climate, pace of life, and difference in the balance of work and leisure in Boston and Miraflores changed how faith was expressed. In Miraflores, most families finish work by midafternoon. They have the rest of the day free to participate in religious activities or to visit with priests.

COURTESY OF GLADYS MALDONADO

In Boston, since many Mirafloreños worked a second, part-time job in the evenings, in addition to their full-time day jobs, they had much less time to be active at church. It was normally too cold to organize events like religious processions during Holy Week. And since Mirafloreños lived farther away from one another than they did at home, it was not as easy for them to meet spontaneously to pray. One woman living in Miraflores said the following about what she had learned from her sister who was living in Boston:

> My sister said it is not like here where the priest walks down the street and everyone is inviting him to eat something, to have a cup of coffee. He is always visiting in our homes. There, you see the

priest once a week up on the fancy altar dressed in fancy robes. He is like a teacher you are afraid of rather than a family member or friend. And you can't organize prayer groups or lead services unless he says it's okay. Here we all take part in the planning. We form our own little groups to pray and study together. But there, it seems like you have to do what the priest says. I'm not sure I would like that so much. It sounds like it is well organized, but it also sounds like it is very cold.

Migration also resulted in the commercialization of the sacraments. Marriages consecrated solely to obtain visas became common. Dominicans who were legal residents in the United States were known to charge as much as $5,000 to "marry for business." The demand for baptismal classes increased when baptism became a requirement for migration. While most priests felt that "sacraments for visas" depreciated these rituals, some felt it offered them a unique outreach opportunity. "Once we get them to come to church," one priest said, "we can take advantage and bring them more firmly into the fold."

Selecting baptismal godparents also assumed economic overtones. Mirafloreños now tend to choose migrants rather than their closest friends and family members on the island as the *madrina* or *padrino* for their children. They feel that migrants will offer their children greater financial support. As a result, a new type of godparent has developed. One set stands in for *los ausentes* at the actual ceremony and takes care of the godchild's day-to-day needs. The other "real" godparents, who live in Boston, take care of "big ticket" items like special clothing for a first communion or a party to celebrate a fifteenth birthday.

By 1993 in Boston, there were thirty-three parishes staffed by thirty-four Spanish-speaking priests. Instead of promoting eventual assimilation, as earlier church officials had done, a Puerto Rican auxiliary bishop, Msgr. Roberto González, claimed that the goal was to integrate new parishioners into their new church while allowing them to maintain their unique identity, pray in their own language, and celebrate their homeland festivals. The Hispanic Apostolate coordinated a range of services, including Spanish-speaking Mass, Bible study, and prayer groups; Latino youth groups; and celebrations of country-of-origin holidays.

In sum, migration between Boston and Miraflores produced a series of religious ties that created a continued place for "Latino" Catholicism in the United States. The Catholic Church in Boston needed a new constituency after longtime parishioners left the inner city. It created an infrastructure that offered newly arriving Latinos a pan-ethnic style of worship. Migrants assimilated into this style, which offered them a generic religious experience rather than one specific to their country of origin. New migrants continued to join the U.S. church. ❁

Apostolate: devoted Catholic ministry network that assists priests in conducting parish activities
Banilejos: people from Baní
co-ethnics: members of the same ethnic group
colmado: small grocery store
los ausentes: those who have emigrated (literally, "the absent ones")
madrina: godmother
Mirafloreños: people from Miraflores
padrino: godfather
promesas: promises to abstain from something or engage in a particular behavior if something one requests in prayer comes true.

NOTE

1. David Mittleberg and Mary C. Waters, "The Process of Ethnogenesis among Haitian and Israeli Immigrants in the United States," *Ethnic and Racial Studies* 15 (1992): 412–35.

"THE FACE OF THE CITY IS CHANGING..."

Interview with César Sánchez Beras

César Sánchez Beras began to write when he was fourteen years old. He had been working as a lawyer for fifteen years in the Dominican Republic when his first book, Memorias del retorno, *was published in 1993. César moved to Lawrence, Massachusetts in 1995 and started teaching Spanish at Lawrence High School in 1996. In this interview, he reflects on his career as a poet and how he interests his students in writing.*

César Sánchez Beras was interviewed by Anne Gallin on November 22, 2003 at Casa Dominicana in Lawrence, Massachusetts. The interview was translated by Patricio Zambrano-Barragán.

César Sánchez Beras

I started to write early, but it was nonsense, basically things about my youth. Afterwards there was an interval during which I did not write, up until the age of twenty, when I entered the university. Then I started writing social poetry, not romantic poetry.

I deeply admire Pablo Neruda, and Federico García Lorca, and Robert Frost. And I admire a Dominican poet named Manuel de Cabral, who, because of political problems, lived for a long time in exile. He had to leave my country because of Trujillo's dictatorship. De Cabral was very socially committed, a very

critical poet. He wrote in three different styles: a poetry that spoke up for black culture, erotic poetry, and social poetry.

What I like about Frost is that he came from another state, and he made a life here in Lawrence and wrote for Lawrence, about the reality of Lawrence. I feel in a sense as if I have inherited his work because I also come from another place, and now I live in Lawrence and write about what happens here.

I usually write at night. I have a routine: I sit down in front of the computer at ten-thirty, eleven at night, every day. Whether I write or not, I sit nonetheless. I'm making outlines, planning my work... Occasionally I have a poem in my mind for a long time, and some of its pieces are missing, but when that piece comes along I go ahead and write.

I write in every style, but often I make a strategic choice of one style or form, one strophe or stanza. For example, my first book, *Memorias del retorno,* consisted entirely of free verse. My second book was a monograph composed of ten-line strophes called *décimas. Comenzó a llenarse de pájaros el sueño* was a book about the city, about the city as the house where everyone lives. My current book, *Historias*

COURTESY OF CÉSAR SÁNCHEZ BERAS

Sabor a Quisqueya (Taste of Quisqueya) Restaurant and Music and Arts School in downtown Lawrence.

del mar, deals with nostalgia for the sea and everything that has to do with the marine world.

The City of Lawrence

I wrote *Lawrence, una ciudad enamorada del tiempo,* a collection of poems about the city. There are many details that interest me, such as the old Lawrence and Methuen cemetery, and the clock tower that you can see no matter where you stand. The railroad, even though it's not here anymore, keeps whistling in the memory of those who came. The chimneys recall another past, that of the textile industry. Likewise, Robert Frost lived here, so I have poems about his house and about him. I also write about the workers' struggle, about the Bread and Roses movement here. All this makes the city of Lawrence distinctive: it's small, it has curious and historic elements tucked away inside, and these details intrigue me.

I like writing about the many immigrants who have come here—the Greeks, Italians, Dominicans, Puerto Ricans, and recently, Central Americans. All these people make the city theirs, and then, sometimes, move on. The city welcomes the people; they progress and then they return to their home countries, or they settle here to stay. And so the city changes its outlook; the face of the city is changing… For instance, forty years ago there were no signs in Spanish. Now, next to the Trípoli Bakery, there's one for Daisy G.'s Restaurant, owned by Rafael and Daisy Gómez. Little by little we have changed this city's face, and that is a process we need to explore.

In my poem about Lawrence the city itself is seen as a metaphor for the human being, because man is a city. When you walk the street at night, you see homeless people, empty streets, mannequins behind store windows… You see the clock in the tower standing tall and alone… It's a different world.

Why Teach?

Teaching Spanish allows me to work in the language with young people who will keep on speaking it. Language dies when there is no one to speak it, and it deteriorates as children mix it with other languages. For instance, many talk half in English, half in Spanish, in Spanglish… They lose part of both languages. I try to have them learn the basics of their native language as well as possible, so that when they learn another one, they won't forget their first language.

Every year or two, I bring two or three writers to the school. They see these writers as models: if students want to write poetry or fiction, they know they can do it because someone else has done it too. For instance, the students were thrilled listening to Junot Díaz, Rhina Espaillat, Juan Matos. They liked how these writers describe their reality using a language that's close to the way they speak.

The fundamental thing for students to understand is that a poet does not have superior mental qualities, but is a human being with a different sensibility. If forty of my students look out the window on a snowy day, each one of them will see something different. The one with more sensitivity will see the snow in a more sensitive manner. When they understand that, you can explain to them that poetry can have a social function, an educational function, an informative function, and that it is an art to work with language and with words… When they know that, and when they believe they can do it, then I encourage them to write about their own reality as only they can do, to communicate their unique vision of the world. ✤

Clock tower in downtown Lawrence.

Lawrence City

César Sánchez Beras

Yo amo esta ciudad
que anochece al filo de la desesperanza
que derrumba sus torres en recodos de angustias
y desoye sus pasos en un vals de nostalgia

Yo amo esta ciudad

que se acuesta ella misma
y amanece de todos

y entre luces y gritos y bocinas ruidosas
desordena el milagro de mantenerse en vida
reconstruye el milagro de encontrar siempre rosas
yo amo estos caminos

que se cruzan se pierden
que se achican se vuelcan
y se llenan de gente

estas calles pequeñas que se van entre sombras
estas calles distintas que entre sueños regresan

yo amo todos los rostros que en tránsfugas sonrisas
se descubren un día a mitad de estas calles
y no saben decir donde nacen sus pasos

ni hacia donde se marchan sus voces siderales

amo su flor de junio
su nieve de noviembre
sus cometas de agosto que parecen marcharse
y sus lluvias de otoño que hacen de los ensueños
un refugio común para enterrar la tarde

yo amo esta ciudad como si fuese mía

con sus calles estrechas con recodos de olvidos
con sus parques repletos de ardillas y quimeras
esta ciudad que nace con todos los viajeros.

Lawrence City

César Sánchez Beras

I love this city
that darkens at the stroke of despair
that tumbles its towers in twists of anguish
and is deaf to its steps in a waltz of nostalgia

I love this city

that lies down for itself
and dawns for all of us

among lights and cries and noisy horns
it undoes the miracle of keeping itself alive
reworks the miracle of forever finding itself roses

I love these roads

that crisscross and are lost,
that narrow and turn,
that fill with people

these sidestreets that move away through shadows
these separate streets that return through dreams

I love all the faces whose fleeting smiles
appear one day down these streets
and cannot say where their travels began
or where their starry voices are wending

I love its flowers in June
its snow in November
its birds in August that feign departure
and its autumn rains that fashion from daydreams
a common refuge to bury the afternoon

I love this city as if it were mine

with its narrow streets of forgettings and crannies
its squares full of squirrels and fantasies
city reborn in all its transients.

❁

Reprinted from *Trovas del mar/Troves of the Sea* (Santo Domingo: Editora Búho).
© 2002 by César Sánchez Beras. Used by permission of the author. English translation by
Rhina P. Espaillat.

Comenzó a llenarse de pájaros el sueño: The Dream Began to be Filled by Birds
Historias del mar: Stories of the Sea
Lawrence, una ciudad enamorada del tiempo: Lawrence, a City in Love with Time
Memorias del retorno: Memories of Return

A sandwich board outside Sabor a Quisqueya (Taste of Quisqueya) Restaurant in downtown Lawrence.

DOMINICANS IN CONNECTICUT: THREE *PIONERAS*

Ruth Glasser

Dominicans are a relatively recent presence in Connecticut. A trickle of immigration began in the late 1950s, but the largest numbers have arrived since 1980. Sandwiched between the Dominican communities of New York City, Providence, and Boston, Connecticut's Dominican settlements are growing quietly but steadily in all of the state's major urban areas, as well as in smaller towns such as Torrington and Winsted. Many Dominicans in Connecticut have come from larger cities—New York, Boston, Miami—looking for a quieter and safer place to live.

In some communities such as Danbury, Dominicans have surpassed the long-established Puerto Ricans in numbers. In others, such as Waterbury, Dominicans are a community still in the making. In this article, Connecticut historian Ruth Glasser explores the lives of Dominicans in Waterbury and the story of three pioneering women who used their skills to create the largest Hispanic day care association in the state.

"My sister emigrated in 1973. She was the first and she brought my mother and our seven brothers and sisters. She worked in a factory in the Bronx. The factory moved to Connecticut so she decided to come here to live."
—*Felicia Díaz*

"We have a cousin named Carmen Peña. Her husband was a tailor. He worked in New York and his company moved here. So Carmen told us that Waterbury was a very peaceful city, especially to raise children, better than New York. So we came here in 1973."
—*Gladys Maldonado*

"It so happened that members of the church that I went to in the Bronx had family in Waterbury. They brought me to visit and I liked it because it was a good city to raise children. I decided it was a place where I could find more support and peace in my life. So this group of family members who were in New York and who were here got together and helped me to move to Waterbury."
—*Adelaida García*

When Felicia Díaz, Gladys Maldonado, and Adelaida García arrived in Waterbury in the 1970s, the industrial area known as the Naugatuck Valley was still relatively prosperous. The center of the country's brass industry, the area also had many smaller metalwork, rubber, and apparel shops. Dominicans settled near those factories, in areas already populated by Puerto Ricans. Like their fellow Spanish-speakers, Dominicans worked in the Anaconda and Century Brass factories downtown, in the Uniroyal rubber plant in nearby Naugatuck, and in the clusters of coat, glove, pocketbook, and suit workshops in Waterbury's North End.

Women were often the *pioneras*—the pioneers—of these overseas Dominican communities. Immigration laws sometimes made migration easier for women than for men, and many young unattached women and single mothers saw moving overseas as a strategy for beginning a new life. For Felicia, Gladys, and Adelaida, their children's needs played a large part in their decision to locate in Waterbury. In other ways, their role as nurturers and members of large extended families would condition the life choices of these Dominican *pioneras* in Waterbury.

Felicia Díaz came from Santiago with a small daughter and another baby on the way. The daughter of storeowners, she had hoped to advance her education once she got to Connecticut. But the need to support her family obliged her to juggle several jobs.

"I always had a full-time job and a part-time job," she remembers. She worked weekdays at a factory packing lipstick cases, cleaned houses and offices at night, and did manicures and pedicures on the weekends. Occasionally she drew upon her skills as a baker to make cakes for birthdays, weddings, and other celebrations.

Adelaida García, from the town of Salcedo, had worked from the time she was a young girl to help support her family of thirteen, picking coffee, selling homemade candy, and hiring out as a servant. After several years on public assistance when her children were small, she also balanced several jobs:

> I lived at 26 Maple Street and I worked across the street at Hilda Dress [factory]. Then I went to work at Waterbury Garment. From Waterbury Garment I went to PM Sportswear. After that I became independent. I began to work selling clothing, I had my license for a small business based in the house. I'm a beautician also, I do hair.

These women labored diligently not just to survive, but also to bring other family members from the Dominican Republic. They were part of an ongoing chain of migration and did not question their role as links in that chain. Felicia Díaz described the genealogy of migration in her family:

> First my sister came. She brought my mother, my mother brought her children, they brought their children and their spouses. Those spouses were then able to bring their mothers, their brothers and sisters. So over time you could bring a cousin, a friend. Someone always lent a hand to those who were doing badly in Santo Domingo and brought them over.

Just as important as bringing people over was helping the newcomers. Felicia's son Victor never had his own room until he was an adult, recalling, "I always shared my room with three or four people." His mother says, "What happened is that there were

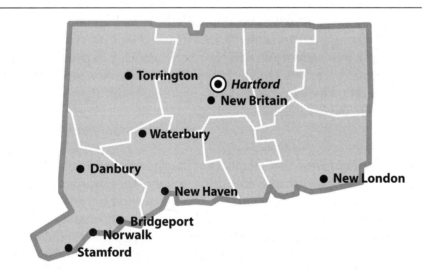

Dominicans in Connecticut, According to the 2000 Census

City	Number of Dominicans	Percentage Dominican
Danbury	2,033	2.7
Waterbury	1,336	1.2
Hartford	1,013	0.8
Bridgeport	886	0.6
Stamford	656	0.6
New Haven	460	0.4
New Britain	326	0.5
New London	280	1.0
Norwalk	216	0.3
Torrington	162	0.5

Note: Official census figures are believed to underestimate the number of Dominicans, especially the undocumented.

Felicia Díaz opened a day care center and helped form the Hispanic Professional Day Care Association.

always people who came and had nowhere to live. And if you're humanitarian you say, 'Come, stay with me until you get a job.' Then they would go, but when they went someone else would arrive."

This community spirit fostered mutual aid among the small number of Dominican families living in Waterbury. "The way we helped each other," Díaz recalls…

…is if one person didn't have a car and had to get to work, another person would pick him up at his house, give him a ride. If someone needed an interpreter at the hospital, the same thing. We helped them to find work and if a person came from Santo Domingo or New York we showed them where they sold the most inexpensive clothing, where they could find Hispanic food.

Dominican women were community activists in more formal ways as well, carving out Dominican cultural spaces

within a larger Spanish-speaking culture. For many, the church was an important social and cultural center from early on. Adelaida García found support and sustenance in Pentecostal churches, while Felicia Díaz and Gladys Maldonado found their home in the Catholic Church. Puerto Rican migrants had, with Father John Blackall, founded a Spanish-speaking parish called St. Cecilia's in the late 1950s. The Dominicans who subsequently settled in Waterbury were warmly welcomed into the church. By the late 1980s, when Dominicans began arriving in larger numbers, Maldonado and Díaz decided it was time for the church to commemorate the Dominican Republic's patron saint. They organized a celebration and now every February, Dominicans at St. Cecilia's (now merged with the SacredHeart/ Sagrado Corazón parish) and their fellow parishioners worship La Virgen de la Altagracia, patron saint of the Dominican

Republic, with a special Mass.

Dominican women have also been instrumental in the founding of a local social and cultural club. Other Connecticut cities with more established Dominican communities such as Danbury, Bridgeport, and Hartford have had Dominican clubs for years. A group of Dominicans in Waterbury began meeting in a local restaurant owned by a woman named Ycelsa Díaz. Out of those informal get-togethers emerged a Dominican club sponsoring baseball teams, domino competitions, and celebrations of national holidays. The group now gathers in a small building once occupied by the Cape Verdean community club, near the site of the North End factories where dozens of Dominicans used to work.

An Economic Niche

The family feelings, community spirit, and entrepreneurial energy of Waterbury's Dominican women have also been poured into a remarkable local organization: La Asociación de Proveedoras Profesionales Hispanas, or Hispanic Professional Day Care Association. Founded in 1996, the group is the largest Hispanic day care association in the state and has trained dozens of women (and a few men) to become family day care providers. These providers get to run a business from their homes, while offering a special service to Spanish-speaking parents looking for affordable, culturally compatible child care. In addition to attending classes and monthly mutual support meetings, members visit convalescent homes, participate in neighborhood cleanups, and put on Halloween and Christmas parties for their young charges.

The association was founded by a woman from Puerto Rico named Luz Lebrón, herself a single mother trained as a child care provider. After starting a group for women transitioning off welfare, Lebrón took inventory of the women's skills and found that the majority were most confident at what they'd been doing a good part of their lives—child care. Those who were looking for outside employment, moreover, found getting a reliable and trustworthy child care provider to be one of the biggest hurdles in their quest to enter the workforce.

Felicia Díaz and Adelaida García were early members of this group. For Díaz, it was the fulfillment of a long-held desire:

I always wanted to find a way to have my own business. And I was always interested in children. One day I read in the newspaper that Luz Lebrón was giving a training class to open a "day care." I went quickly and got my first orientation, and I never missed a class. There were about seven of us who got our licenses. We formed the association, and now we have fifty-five women.

Adelaida García saw the welfare-to-work trend as both a threat to her current livelihood and a new opportunity:

Since I sold clothes, the majority of my customers were people on welfare. When they began to take away welfare, my customers disappeared on me. Luz Lebrón was my daughter's friend and my daughter said, "Take advantage of these classes." And I did it because I come from a big family, so I said to myself, "Why not keep working with children since I like it?" Now I've spent about seven years in day care.

These entrepreneurs have found an economic niche, and are now helping other women advance as well. The community-minded Díaz explains how and why it works:

Now this is the big source of business for Dominican women. Maybe because they see this as a way to be able to work and stay home. In fact today a Dominican woman called and I said to her, "It's a great business, where do you live? ...That area, fantastic, we don't have providers in that area." I go to where my Dominican women friends are and I tell them, "Look, things are going well for me, why don't you come with me?" So I bring her in, and this one brings in another, and that one brings another, and I think that's one of the ways that Dominican women keep coming. ✿

Co-editor Ruth Glasser, in carnival costume, poses with Felicia Díaz, who models a folkloric dress.

COMPARING IMMIGRATION STORIES: DOMINICANS IN CONNECTICUT AND YOUR TOWN

USE WITH: Unit 40

DURATION: 5 classes

STANDARDS:

English Language Arts: 1, 3, 4, 7, 8, 9, 10

Social Studies: 1c, 1d, 2b, 4a, 4b, 4c, 4h

Foreign Language: 1, 2, 3, 4.2

GOAL: To discern and analyze various immigration problems and possible solutions.

OBJECTIVES:

- To compare and contrast two distinct immigration histories.
- To analyze immigration issues.
- To conduct historical research and collect oral history.

ACTIVITIES:

1. Students read "Dominicans in Connecticut: Three *Pioneras*" (unit 40).

2. As a class, discuss and collaborate on developing an outline of the article by answering the following questions:

   - Who did most of the initial migrating, either from the Dominican Republic or from bigger cities?

   - What were their motivations for moving?

   - What was the time frame of this history and what economic developments during this period shaped the migrants' experiences?

   - What were some of the problems encountered by the early migrants?

   - How did they cope with these problems?

3. Divide the class into groups of two or three. Student groups research the history of a family member, or of a particular ethnic group in their town. Students might want to keep a journal of their research and a catalog of any tapes or videos. (The teacher can set up the interviews in advance with certain individuals or groups.)

4. Set up a time frame: research handed in and approved, journals checked regularly for progress, final date for finished project.

Lesson plan prepared by Lola Lopes.

5. Finished project should consist of (1) an oral history presentation (see unit 45—Oral Histories of Immigration) by the group supplemented by photos, videotapes, audiotapes, a PowerPoint presentation, or any other audiovisual support, or (2) a written paper answering the questions in activity 2 above.

ASSESSMENT:

Written or oral evaluation of students' comparison between Dominicans and their target group.

DOMINICANS IN RHODE ISLAND: DOÑA FEFA'S STORY

Marta V. Martínez

Doña Josefina "Fefa" Rosario.

Doña Fefa was interviewed by Marta V. Martínez, founder of the Hispanic Heritage Committee of Rhode Island, in Warwick, RI in 1991.

The following article based on the interview is adapted from "Nuestras Raíces: The History of Hispanics in Rhode Island," unpublished personal interviews and research housed at the Latino Archives of Rhode Island. © 2004 by Marta V. Martínez. Used by permission of the author.

The first Dominicans to settle in Rhode Island, in the mid-twentieth century, were drawn by the promise of abundant jobs in the state's thriving jewelry factories and textile mills. Many had started off in New York City, and came to Rhode Island to find work and a quieter and safer way of life for themselves and their children. "During that time," writes historian Marta V. Martínez, "it was said that jobs were so abundant that factory owners took to the streets to look for workers. And the Dominicans who found these jobs sent home word of the employment opportunities with money tucked inside their letters."

Over the past thirty years, Providence, Rhode Island has become an increasingly popular destination for Dominican immigrants. According to the 2000 census, 14,683 Dominicans live in Providence, where they are the largest Latino group and make up 8.4 percent of the city's population. A walk along Broad Street and other parts of the south side of Providence shows the entrepreneurial endeavors of Dominicans in the form of bodegas, restaurants, and beauty salons.

Dominicans are also becoming active in the state's political life. In 2000, the Dominican community helped elect León Tejada, the second Hispanic legislator in the history of Rhode Island, to a state House seat.[1] Local elections in 2002 brought two more Dominicans to office—Miguel Luna to a seat on the Providence City Council, and Juan Pichardo to a state Senate seat, making him the first Latino state senator in Rhode Island.

This emerging activism builds on the energy and vision of early Dominican residents of the state. One of the founders of Providence's Dominican community was Josefina "Fefa" Rosario. A pionera, or pioneer, who arrived in Providence in the 1950s, she helped many Dominicans who came later to set down roots in Rhode Island. She also became known for her work in educating Latino residents on their voting rights.

I first met Josefina Rosario, affectionately known as "Doña Fefa," at a gathering in a friend's home in 1991. Doña Fefa and her family, my friend Juanita told me, had opened the first Hispanic restaurant in Rhode Island in the late 1950s. I also learned that she was one of the first women to become involved in educating the Puerto Ricans living in Rhode Island in the 1960s about the importance of registering to vote. She and her husband, Tony, would offer to drive people to and from the polls on election night.

I left the party feeling that I wanted to get to know more about Fefa. A few months later, I called and asked if I could pay her a visit. Armed with a tape recorder, I drove to her house with a reporter from the *Providence Journal,* whom I had invited because I thought there was something special about Fefa and I wanted the newspaper to honor her for Mother's Day that year. As we talked through the night, I discovered that there was indeed more to Fefa's story than even she and her family had realized.

Josefina was born in the Dominican Republic when Rafael Trujillo came to power and established one of the longest-lasting dictatorships in Latin America. It was during Trujillo's reign of terror that many Dominicans, fearing they would be killed by his men, began to flee to the United States.

Fefa was personally affected by Trujillo's power in 1937 when secret service men murdered her father while he was in a hospital recovering from gunshot wounds. Her mother was left alone to raise ten children. Fefa, the youngest, eventually made her way to New York City. "I was twenty-one years old when I came to the United States," Fefa told me. "My sister Minerva del Rio lived in New York and I came to live with her for what I thought would be a brief visit."

She remembers that it was cold when she arrived, not like Santo Domingo, where she had left behind warm tropical

weather. It was September 8, 1949. Her "brief" visit turned into months, then years. She met and married Antonio Rosario, a Puerto Rican man who also was living in New York.

After eight years in the city, Fefa and her husband moved to New Haven, where they found jobs working for the owner of a Greek restaurant.

I started out there washing silverware. After a few years, [the restaurant owner] and his wife decided to open a new place over here, in Rhode Island. A restaurant called Les Shaw, located right across from the airport in Warwick... My husband was hired as the cook, and I was the salad lady.

This was 1957, a time when Hispanics were rare in Rhode Island, and the Rosarios felt the isolation keenly.

I strongly believe that my family and I were the first Dominican family to live in Providence, and maybe Rhode Island... I believe that because in 1959, when we moved from Warwick to Providence—I

was pregnant with a baby girl at the time—my husband decided he wanted to open his own Spanish-food restaurant. So, he went up to a policeman on the street and asked him: *"Dónde está la comunidad Hispana? Dónde viven los Hispanos?"*—"Where do the Hispanic people live over here?"

The policeman said, "I don't know where [the Spanish-speaking people] live in Providence, but I know of one Hispanic family in East Providence." We went over there and asked around, and finally someone there told us

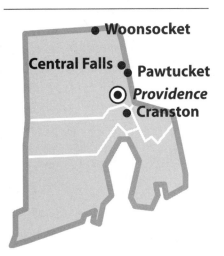

Dominicans in Rhode Island, According to the 2000 Census

City	Number of Dominicans	Percentage Dominican
Providence	14,638	8.4
Pawtucket	804	1.1
Cranston	734	0.9
Central Falls	575	0.3
Woonsocket	343	0.8

Note: Official census figures are believed to underestimate the number of Dominicans, especially the undocumented.

The Dominican Festival at Roger Williams Park in Providence, Rhode Island, 1998.

and Puerto Ricans who were looking for work or a quieter place to live soon began hopping a one-way ride back with them to Providence.

I also had a lot of people living with me in my house, people my husband and I brought or sponsored from Santo Domingo. They stayed with us until they could find their own apartment or house. The Dominicans really got their start right there, on Chester Avenue. We had a sort-of boarding house for people who also wrote to us from Santo Domingo who wanted to come to the United States.

To this day, people who remember Rosario from those days call her "Doña Fefa." The first Dominican families, their children and relatives, and other Hispanics who came later to Rhode Island see her today and remember how Fefa brought them here.

Fefa remembers how small the community was in the 1960s:

By the mid-sixties, there were around ten of us... well, very few of us. After that, between '66 and '69, that's when more and more Hispanics started buying houses. Then they started writing to their families and friends, asking them to come join them in the United States. The Dominican community started slowly growing then, and they began to settle in homes off of Broad Street, and people started to open a few businesses then, too.

Today, I feel like many Hispanic people treat me like

about two Puerto Ricans who lived there. I asked about any Dominican people or more Puerto Rican people, and they said that there were no other Puerto Ricans over there, no other Hispanics anywhere.

Stayed in Rhode Island

Soon after the Rosarios moved to Providence, the restaurant in Warwick closed and the owners moved back to Connecticut. "When that happened," said Fefa, "they asked me and my family to go back with them to Connecticut, and my husband said: 'I don't want to depend on you all the time. I have a family now and I want to stay here.'"

But how to make a living?

We got the idea of opening a market soon after we moved to Providence, because we would often—almost every weekend—drive to Connecticut in our blue

station wagon to buy food for ourselves. Things like *plátanos, yuca, café,* cilantro... We would do that because they didn't have Spanish products here at all. We would drive to New Haven and sometimes to New York and bring back food and sell it door-to-door, *como de domicilio,* right on Chester Avenue.

In 1959, with the Hispanic community growing in Providence, the Rosarios opened a market on Broad Street, calling it Fefa's Market. Not long after, they opened a restaurant next to the market. It soon became a popular place to eat in South Providence, especially as the community became more ethnically diverse.

Brought Back More than Food

Eventually, food was not the only thing the Rosarios would bring back with them from their journeys to Connecticut and New York. Many Dominicans

I am somebody special. I guess I brought an awful lot of people together. See, we were such a small community here back then, and we took care of each other. In those days, when people needed something, they would come to us. They knew we would help them. And we never felt we could ever turn anybody down.

About her role in educating Hispanics on their voting rights, she remembers:

There was a time when I worked hard to help Hispanic people register to vote. Especially many of the Puerto Ricans who had already been living here for a few years. They had never registered before, so my husband and I went out and helped them register.

I remember when [Mayor] Buddy Cianci was running for office, my husband went out and got a school bus. And if you could see the people that he put in that bus to go and register to vote… Wow! There were lots of them. Many of them had no idea about politics or who to vote for, and we helped with that, too.

Now "Retired" from Activism

Doña Fefa tells me that she is now "retired" from her active life in the 1960s and 70s. She knows that many people still remember her from those days. And she is aware of how the younger generation of Hispanics look up to her, children and grandchildren of the first wave of Dominicans who settled in Providence.

So many young people from this generation that I don't really know personally know who I am. Sometimes, when I am sitting in my car waiting at a stop light, I will hear a car honk and somebody says "Fefa!" And when I look up, you know, I don't know who that person is! Then they will say, "I'm related to this person or that person." It seems everybody knows me, but I don't know everybody else.

Doña Fefa and her family planted a seed back in the 1950s, one that has now grown and turned into a proud group of individuals: immigrants who are now citizens, who have earned their place in the history and growth of Rhode Island. ❁

bodega: small grocery store
café: coffee
como de domicilio: just like homemade
Doña: title of respect for an older woman
Nuestras Raíces: Our Roots
plátanos: plantains
yuca: a starchy tuber

NOTE

1. In 2004, Grace Díaz, of Dominican heritage, unseated León Tejada as State Representative.

COMMUNITY ACTIVISM IN RHODE ISLAND

USE WITH: Unit 42

DURATION: 1–2 classes

STANDARDS:

English Language Arts: 1, 4, 5, 10

Social Studies: 1a, 1b, 1c, 1d, 1e, 1f, 1g, 3g, 3h, 4c, 4f, 4h

Foreign Language: 1, 2, 3, 4.2

GOAL: To explore the Dominican migration experience in Providence, Rhode Island.

OBJECTIVE:

To examine the effects of Dominican community activism.

ACTIVITIES:

1. Students read "Dominicans in Rhode Island: Doña Fefa's Story" (unit 42).

2. In small groups students answer the following questions:

   • Why have Dominicans moved to Providence? List at least 3 factors.

   • What impact, if any, did the Rosario businesses have on the community?

   • How were Doña Fefa's volunteer activities important for the Hispanic community in Providence?

ASSESSMENT:

Students imagine that they have migrated to a different country; after a few years, they are joined by relatives or friends. How would the students—now more experienced immigrants—go about helping the new arrivals to establish themselves? Teacher assesses the students' ability to extract information from the reading and apply it to this hypothetical situation.

Lesson plan prepared by Lola Lopes.

EUGENIA KIM

EUGENIA KIM

A sign announces the schedule of various services at Church of the Sacred Heart, a cultural center of the Washington, DC Latino community.

"'BLACK BEHIND THE EARS'—AND UP FRONT TOO? DOMINICANS IN THE BLACK MOSAIC:" DOMINICANS IN WASHINGTON, DC

Ginetta E. B. Candelario

Dominicans began arriving in the nation's capital during the early 1940s as part of diplomatic legations to Washington, DC. The dictator Trujillo allowed the diplomats and their families a certain freedom of migration that was denied to other Dominicans, including the privilege of bringing domestic servants with them to their overseas posts. These women who arrived as service workers, most of them Afro-Dominicans, routinely married into the African-American community in Washington. As a result, they and their children participated in the political, economic, and social mobility of African Americans in the city. At the same time, as sociologist Ginetta E. B. Candelario shows, they helped to create and sustain a vibrant Dominican and multicultural Afro-Latin community.

Adapted from "'Black Behind the Ears'—and Up Front Too? Dominicans in the Black Mosaic," *Public Historian* 23, no. 4: 55–72. © 2001 by the Regents of the University of California and the National Council on Public History. All rights reserved. Reprinted from *The Public Historian.*

The Dominican community in the nation's capital is small, particularly compared to the more than 450,000 Dominicans in New York City. But Washington, DC's Dominican community is mature and sociologically complete: it has established leaders, community organizations, cultural events, social networks, and local entrepreneurs. It also has a unique identity and history of its own, shaped by interaction with both the local African-American community and the broader Latin American community in Washington.

In the Dominican Republic, the vast majority of Dominicans with some degree of visible African ancestry are referred to as *indio,* with qualifiers such as *oscuro* and *claro.* This practice is rooted in the Trujillo regime's racist philosophy, which glorified the country's indigenous past while disregarding or denigrating the population's African heritage. Racial classifications such as indio were printed on the identification cards that every Dominican had to carry, and were institutionalized through the educational system and in official histories of the country.[1] The last Dominican census that recorded racial identification was taken in 1960 and claimed that only 10 percent of the nation's inhabitants were "black."

Dominicans migrating to the United States largely continued these patterns of racial self-identification. In the 1990 U.S. census, Dominicans in New York primarily chose the racial category called "other;" only about 28 percent identified themselves as "black."[2] However, nearly half of Washington, DC's 1,500 Dominican residents identified themselves as black in the 1990 census.[3] The identification of DC Dominicans with African Americans has its roots in the overlapping histories of the two groups.

By the turn of the twentieth century, the District of Columbia "hosted the largest urban concentration of African Americans in the entire nation."[4] During the 1930s and 1940s, the great labor migration of African Americans from the southern United States to northern cities further expanded and consolidated the black community in Washington. International migration also made its mark, bringing in black immigrants from various countries in Central and South America and the Caribbean.[5]

The influx of African Americans coincided with the arrival of a Latin American diplomatic community in Washington. Members of that community often relied upon the domestic labor of Afro-Latin women from their countries. Many of the domestics who accompanied Dominican diplomatic families came from regions of the Dominican Republic that had traditionally been subject to African-American and West Indian influences.[6] Some 5,000 African-American colonists settled in the Samaná region during the early nineteenth century, while laborers from the British West Indies settled around the large sugar factories of the southeast in the late nineteenth and early twentieth centuries.

Unlike their counterparts in New York, who had access to a large community of Dominicans and other Latinos, black Dominican women in Washington married into the African-American community right from the start. The earliest known

Dominican to settle in Washington, DC is "Mamá" Corina Saillant, who arrived in 1921. She married into a local African-American family and became the informal "welcome wagon" for subsequent Latin American arrivals. Her home was often the first stop that Dominican newcomers made, and with her guidance they learned to negotiate life in DC.

The vast social distance between African Americans and whites in the United States perplexed Juana Campos when she arrived in 1940. An astute reader of the social landscape, Doña Campos recalled more than fifty years later that "people here were separated like tuberculosis patients, black and white apart."[7] Neither in New York City, where her boat from the Dominican Republic had docked, nor in her hometown of Pelmar had she experienced the kind of visibly entrenched Jim Crow

segregation that characterized the U.S. capital. Indeed, it was a new Puerto Rican friend who "instructed" the recently arrived Campos on the rules of Jim Crow. A brown-skinned woman, Juana Campos appeared to U.S. observers to be clearly of African descent, and her friend warned her that she was likely to experience discrimination. From the first, Juana Campos was determined that neither she nor her Washington-born children, Ramberto and Carmen Toruella, would be constrained by Jim Crow. The circumstances of her work as a housekeeper, their residential location, and the timing of her children's growing up helped shield them from the worst of this institutionalized racism.

In the 1940s and 1950s, Latin American service workers lived alongside African Americans south of Columbia Road NW. That thoroughfare was then the racial dividing line of the Adams Morgan neighborhood, where much of the international community had settled because of its proximity to the newly established embassies. At the same time, because of their status as Spanish-speaking immigrants and their work connections to Latin American legations and embassies, the domestic workers socialized primarily with other Latin American immigrants. Although regular daily or weekly socializing was organized along class lines, service staff had fairly regular social contact with elite embassy and legation families because the Latino community was so small. Ramberto Toruella, Juana Campos's son, who grew up in DC during the 1950s and 1960s, recalled:

EUGENIA KIM

The Embassy of the Dominican Republic in Washington, DC.

The only Latinos in this town were embassy personnel [and their] support staff. So we grew up with all the embassies. If the Embassy of Venezuela would have a celebration to celebrate their Independence Day, all the Latinos were invited. And we'd go to the Venezuelan Embassy, eat Venezuelan food, and dance Venezuelan dances. And the same with the Mexican Embassy, the Dominican Embassy. There was a handful: within a fifty-mile radius there must have been a hundred Latinos. We knew every Latino in DC. Every Latino in DC knew each other.[8]

Working and social relationships with Latin Americans, and with whites who lived in the neighborhoods where the embassies and legations were located, protected early Dominicans from the sort of Jim Crow policies and practices their African-American neighbors and co-workers were experiencing.[9] It also enabled them to retain a Latin American identity in the first generation, and to develop a generalized Latino identity in the second generation through shared cultural practices—particularly foodways, dance, and religion—and through the continued use of Spanish.

Children of early immigrants like Doña Juana, whether born here or brought here by their mothers, came of age in the 1950s and 1960s in the midst of the most publicly active civil rights movement to date. Dominican women and their children participated in this movement and benefited from the expanding political, economic, and social roles

and increased opportunities for African Americans in the Washington area. At the same time, they created and sustained a small multicultural Afro-Latin community that reached out to welcome new arrivals from the Dominican Republic and other parts of Latin America. In 1954 Juana Campos initiated the first Mass to La Virgen de la Altagracia at Sacred Heart Church, which was and remains a cultural center of the DC Latino community.

Beyond Race

Although Washington's Spanish-speaking community is now large and diverse, there continues to be an incentive to black self-identification for Dominicans in the city. African Americans are a numerical majority in the nation's capital. They dominated the city's political life for the last quarter of the twentieth century, and although this dominance is eroding somewhat, they still hold the vast majority of local government posts and jobs. As former Howard University professor and historian Maricela Medina put it:

In my case I didn't have to go the Dominican route. I could go the African-American route. [Contrary to the notion that] there are only disadvantages to being African American, [I found] there were a lot of advantages when I went to school because this was the time of the civil rights movement. The black power movement. The militancy on campus. A lot of things were changing and there were a lot of opportunities offered to

African Americans. Puerto Ricans were always included and Mexican Americans, but if you were Hispanic of any other origin, unless you qualified as African American, you weren't able to participate.[10]

Dr. Medina attended Howard University as an undergraduate and went on to obtain a graduate degree in Latin American history from the University of Michigan with financial and institutional support received because she self-identified as black, if not African-American. She subsequently taught Latin American history at Howard and continuously challenged her students to reconsider their notions of blackness and Hispanicity.

The class structure of the African-American community in Washington, DC also serves as an incentive to adopt a black racial identity. A significant portion of the local black community is middle-class; Prince George's County, a Maryland suburb of Washington, has the highest percentage of affluent blacks of any county in the United States. In New York, by contrast, the political and economic disempowerment of most African Americans—particularly those with whom Dominicans live, work, and go to school—reinforces the prevailing Dominican association of blackness with low socioeconomic standing. As Carmen Toruella Quander explained:

The Dominican blacks that come [to DC] or the mixed blacks, like myself, that come here, we get involved in the African-American community. We see that there is a very, very deep class consciousness and that there is a place for us, a positive place. In New York City, although there are affluent African Americans, they are not in a mass concentration the way you have in DC.[11]

Many Dominicans who currently live and work in Washington acknowledge their African-American connections but see their identities as going far beyond the category of race. Toruella Quander continued:

I know my roots. I took my family to the grave of all of my ancestors. Why is it that you want to take my heart and soul just because you see the color of my skin? Toruella is my last name. That's from the south of Spain. I say, I'm Dominican. I am a person of color. I am of the African diaspora but you know what, you talk to me about other things. We came here knowingly. I am a person of color and very proud of it but you cannot stay in that box.[12]

The "box" Toruella Quander refers to is the one that gives racial identity primacy over national or ethnic identity. Francia Almarante, a Dominican hairdresser, put it succinctly: "I am black, but that's not all I am."[13]

⚛

claro: light
diplomatic legation: diplomatic mission smaller than an embassy
Doña: title of respect for an older woman
Hispanicity: ideology affirming Spanish heritage and culture
indio: Indian
La Virgin de la Altagracia: patron saint of the Dominican Republic
oscuro: dark

NOTES

1. See Silvio Torres-Saillant, "Introduction to Dominican Blackness" (Dominican Studies Working Papers Series, CUNY Dominican Studies Institute, City College of New York, 1999); and David Howard, "Colouring the Nation: Race and Ethnicity in the Dominican Republic" (Ph.D. diss., Jesus College, Oxford University, 1997).

2. Peggy Levitt and Christina Gómez, "The Intersection of Race and Gender among Dominicans in the U.S." (paper presented at the ASA Conference, Toronto, August 8–13, 1997); and Carlos Dore-Cabral and Jose Itzigsohn, "La formación de la identidad hispana entre los inmigrantes dominicanos en Nueva York" (paper presented at Congreso Internacional: La República Dominicana en el Umbral del Siglo XXI, Pontífica Universidad Católica Madre y Maestra, Santo Domingo, July 24–26, 1997).

3. The 1990 census is used because it corresponds to the period in which the Black Mosaic exhibit and the interviews conducted for this article took place.

4. Robert D. Manning, "Multicultural Change in Washington, DC: The Contested Social Terrain of the Urban Odyssey" (Report 91–3, Institutional Studies Office, Smithsonian Institution, April 1991), vi.

5. "The Black Mosaic: Community, Race, and Ethnicity among Black Immigrants in Washington, DC" (exhibit text, Anacostia Museum, Washington, DC, 1994).

6. See Alfonso Aguilar, "Leyendas de nuestra historia: Juanita A. Campos, 54 años de vida en DC," Foro Newspaper, April 28, 1994; Juana Campos, interview by Hector Corporán, Black Mosaic archives, Anacostia Museum, Washington, DC; Juana Campos, interview by author, August 1998, Washington, DC.

7. Juana Campos, interview by Hector Corporán, 1994, Black Mosaic archives, Anacostia Museum, Washington, DC. Black Mosaic files were not systematically archived when this research was undertaken in 1998. Instead, Black Mosaic materials were stored in various offices, file cabinets, and boxes throughout the Research Department of the Anacostia Museum. As a result, data source citations are descriptive rather than archival.

8. Ramberto Toruella, interview by author, Washington, DC, August 1998.

9. América Paredes, for example, was a Dominican domestic in the Georgetown townhouse of John F. Kennedy during his terms as representative and senator. She continued to work for the Kennedy family after Kennedy's assassination until her retirement in the early 1990s, and still vacations at the family's Hyannisport home. Hector Corporán, interview by author, August 1998, Washington, DC.

10. Maricela Medina, interview by author, Washington, DC, August 1998.

11. Carmen Toruella Quander, interview by author, Washington, DC, August 1998.

12. Carmen Toruella Quander, interview by author, Washington, DC, August 1998.

13. Francia Almarante, interview by author, Washington, DC, July 1998.

ORAL HISTORIES OF IMMIGRATION

USE WITH: Units 27, 29, 30, 32, 39, 42, 58, 69

DURATION: 3–4 classes

STANDARDS:

English Language Arts: 1, 2, 3, 4, 6, 7, 9, 10

Social Studies: 1b, 1d, 4a, 4b, 4c, 4f

Foreign Language: 1, 2.1, 3, 4.2

GOAL: To explore immigration experiences by developing oral histories of family and community members.

OBJECTIVES:

- To interpret and analyze oral histories of Dominican immigrants.
- To document experiences of immigration.
- To practice interviewing techniques.
- To write narratives based on oral histories.

ACTIVITIES:

1. Students read two or more of the following oral history narratives: Miguelina Sosa (unit 29), Julie Guerrero (unit 30), Francisco García-Quezada (unit 32), César Sánchez Beras (unit 39), Josefina "Fefa" Rosario (unit 42), Silvio Torres-Saillant (unit 58), Pedro Tavarez (unit 69).

2. Students define oral history and discuss the differences between an oral history interview and other kinds of interviews. The teacher can facilitate the discussion by asking students what other kinds of interviews they have seen on television, in magazines, etc.

3. As a class, students list criteria of a good oral history narrative and then judge the extent to which those in the book match their criteria.

4. Students identify an individual from their family or community who has immigrated to their area from the Dominican Republic or another country.

5. Distribute "Oral History Assessment Sheet." Review with students; then compile a list of possible interview questions. The point scale can be assigned at the discretion of the teacher or by both students and teacher.

The lesson plan, oral history assessment sheet, and interviewing tips are adapted from Connecticut Teacher's Guide, *Aquí Me Quedo: Puerto Ricans in Connecticut: Interdisciplinary Teacher's Guides for Elementary, Middle and High School Classrooms* (Middletown: Connecticut Humanities Council, 1998).

6. Students interview their subjects and transcribe the interviews (if tape-recorded). See "Tips for Interviewing."

7. In small groups, students read each other's histories-in-progress and provide feedback. Stress readability and interest.

8. Students edit their interviews (i.e., decide which parts of the interview to include and which to cut).

9. Students write short introductions to their narratives, giving basic information such as the date and place of the interview and the reason why the subject was chosen.

10. Students print the finished documents for display. They may wish to collect artifacts such as photographs, articles of clothing, birth certificates, and so forth, to make their displays more interesting.

11. Students display their oral histories in the classroom or in a public space at school or in the community.

ASSESSMENT:

Teachers and students complete Oral History Assessment Sheet.

MATERIALS:

- Oral History Assessment Sheet
- Tips for Interviewing

Oral History Assessment Sheet

Questions	Student points	Teacher points	Total points
1. How well did you complete your interview? Do you have useful responses from your subject?			
2. How well did you tell the story of the migration experience in your oral history? Was who, what, when, where, why, and how covered? Were significant events identified?			
3. How well written is your oral history? (grammar, spelling, punctuation)			
4. How well did you research additional information and collect artifacts to make your story more interesting?			
5. How good are the artifacts of the first oral history? Do they relate to the oral history narrative and are they meaningfully labeled?			
6. How neat and presentable is your finished product?			
7. How timely was your project? Was it in class the day it was due?			

Comments:

Tips for Interviewing

1. Ask questions that require more of an answer than "yes" or "no."

2. Ask one question at a time.

3. Ask brief questions.

4. Don't let periods of silence fluster you.

5. Don't worry if your questions or answers are not as beautifully phrased as you would like them to be.

6. Don't interrupt a good story.

7. Interviews usually work out better if there is no one else present except the narrator and the interviewer.

8. Don't use the interview to show off your own knowledge, vocabulary, charm, or other abilities. Good interviewers do not shine; their interviews do.

9. Keep the interview time short (no more than an hour and a half).

DOMINICANS IN SOUTH FLORIDA: SUBURBAN SUNSHINE

Carol Hoffman-Guzmán

While Florida's huge Latino population is dominated by Cubans and Puerto Ricans, increasing numbers of Dominicans along with Colombians, Nicaraguans, Mexicans, Venezuelans, and Brazilians are coming to the Sunshine State. Sociologist Carol Hoffman-Guzmán's research on a segment of South Florida's Dominican population, which is largely middle- and upper-class, breaks the common stereotype of the poverty-stricken Quisqueyan newcomer. Nevertheless, she contends, being affluent does not necessarily mean giving up one's culture and becoming 100 percent "Americanized."

Gerardo and Viviana Pérez, both born in the Dominican Republic, recently moved from Miami-Dade County into a secure, tranquil, gated community in western Broward County. Gerardo, who comes from an extended family of Dominican professionals, brought his family to Miami in the 1960s, after years of higher education in New York City. The couple go on American cruises, delight in Disney World, and shop in big American malls. Their even more assimilated adult children, who grew up in Florida, have graduate degrees, married non-Dominicans, and maintain social networks that are decidedly multicultural American. Gerardo Pérez and his wife rarely travel back to the Dominican Republic, except to attend funerals. Their main contact today with family "over there" is by phone and e-mail.

But still they are Dominican in their food, music, and family relationships. Late on Christmas Eve in 2000, a *rondalla* comes strolling through the streets of the Pérezes' gated neighborhood. The doors and garages of the $300,000-plus homes are flung open to welcome the singers and enjoy their *aguinaldos.* Adults sit outside on lawn chairs, teenagers lean against expensive cars and SUV's, and children play with their new and latest toys. Food and drink from many different cultures are shared all around.

The sounds and smells and traditions are largely Caribbean, but the homes are ultra-modern, with tiled roofs, swimming pools, and twinkling holiday icicle lights from Walgreen's. Gerardo and Viviana don't need to return to the Dominican Republic—the best and most cosmopolitan of Caribbean life is available right here in South Florida.

Dominicans are one of many immigrant groups who are transforming South Florida into a new frontier of multicultural America. The old image of immigrant America has been one of disadvantaged people living in inner-city ghettoes, dusty border towns, and migrant camps. But in Florida, as in similar communities in California, Texas, and along the East Coast, many immigrants from throughout the world are joining the American middle class and enjoying the suburban lifestyle, with a slightly different flavor. Although the Dominican communities in Miami-Dade and Broward counties have poverty rates similar to the general population in South Florida, families are spread across all income levels, including the most affluent.

Dominicans are currently the sixth-largest Hispanic community in Miami-Dade County. Although there is one inner-city Dominican neighborhood, Allapattah, only 8 percent of the Dominicans in Miami-Dade County now live there, according to the 2000 census. Nearly 65 percent of Dominicans in South Florida live in neighborhoods that can be described as lower middle, middle, or upper middle class. In order to find these middle-class Dominicans of South Florida, one heads west into the Fontainebleau, West Hialeah, and Doral Country Club areas; north to Miami Lakes, or further north into Broward County and Pembroke Pines, Plantation, and Davie; or south into Kendale Lakes, The Crossings, or Cutler Ridge. Nearly 50 percent of Dominicans in South Florida live in newer areas in the western and northeastern suburbs of Miami-Dade and Broward counties. Nearly half of the Dominicans in Miami-Dade live in census tracts that did not exist in 1999; these areas are either new or their population has increased greatly because of new housing developments. In these communities, many Dominican families own their own homes, townhouses, or condominiums (48 percent in Miami-Dade and 62 percent in Broward, according to the 2000 census).

Living in suburban America does have its down side. Francisco Alvarez says that he misses the friendliness and *calor humano* of life in the Dominican Republic. There, he recalls, "The windows are open. People are selling avocados. The smell of burning coal, oregano, the maids cooking in the middle of the street." Here in Florida the neighbors are less friendly, less visible. But immigrants compensate by spending a lot of time with their families, with friends, and in their comfortable homes.

How They Came

Dominicans living in South Florida represent two main types of immigrant journeys. One, the less common, is emigration from the Caribbean directly to Florida. At the time of the 1990 census, only 38 percent of South Florida's Dominicans had come there directly from the Dominican Republic or Puerto Rico.[1] Those who did were typically members of the middle and upper classes who arrived with a college education, a background in business, some English, and connections that helped them easily blend into the local population.

José Facundo, who relocated from Santiago to Miami with his family, reflects on the relative ease of his move: "The fact that my father was here [meant] that I wasn't starting from zero." Still, even relatively privileged immigrants often have to struggle. Danilo Gascue's family was "rather affluent" in the Dominican Republic and had many live-in servants. Although his mother had an apartment and a job waiting for her when she arrived in Florida, Danilo, with few English skills, had to start off working as a janitor in a shopping mall. It took him seven years and continuous study to move up into the executive job he now holds in an international firm.

More commonly, Dominicans arrive in South Florida after a short or long sojourn in another state. According to the 1990 census, 62 percent of the Dominicans then living in Miami-Dade had relocated from different areas of the United States, often from New York City.[2] This group is drawn primarily from the lower classes in the Dominican Republic. One primary reason that fewer lower-income Dominicans come initially to South Florida is because of the region's poor job market for low-skilled workers. In Florida they are relegated to service or agricultural jobs, whereas they can do much better in the urban areas of the Northeast.

Most of these families struggled and suffered through years of poverty, discrimination, and personal stress. Eventually, however, their members learned English, obtained college degrees, and through hard work became economically successful enough that they were able to relocate to South Florida, where the climate and culture were more agreeable and familiar.

Antonio Gil was born in Santiago into a lower-class family—"the lowest of the low," he says. Gil's family came to the United States through chain migration: his uncle, the first link in the chain, moved to Boston, and then sought entry visas for Antonio's mother and sister. In Santiago Antonio attended college, paid through financial assistance for gifted students. But with Antonio's mother struggling financially in the United States, his uncle requested that Antonio quit the university after two years and come to help her pay the rent and other expenses. "I was responsible, the paterfamilias, at eighteen. I got a job in a factory and one in the evening too. I was cleaning bathrooms at first. But I was happy, supporting my family. It came naturally." Then they began sending for the rest of the children.

In Boston Antonio was eventually accepted at a technical school and graduated with honors. He was hired by an established corporation and later by a start-up technology firm that transferred him to Miami to open a branch office. Now he owns his own international technology firm. He knows that a young man from his poor background could never have done this in the Dominican Republic. Antonio believes that in the United States you are judged more for your ability. He feels very proud of his fellow Dominicans and believes that once they are given education and opportunity, they will strive and achieve financial success.

Several years ago Antonio moved his family out of Miami into Broward County, where he has lots of land so that his children can play safely. His new home in Weston is not quite like the Dominican countryside, where he remembers "the wide open spaces… You could go to the pool, ride a bike. I'd 'shower' in the river"—but it's close enough. Antonio likes to cook, so he has barbecues, invites all his friends and family, and plays the congenial Dominican host. In a small way, he is imitating the hospitality of his Dominican hometown, though in a more affluent American style. Antonio hasn't forgotten his roots, however, and when you ask him his identity, he says, "Dominican. But I'm an American by convenience."

Today the Dominican population in South Florida is spread thinly over many different neighborhoods, towns, cities, and counties. Many Dominicans do not belong to Dominican organizations or participate in Dominican activities such as church or baseball. Surprisingly, though, many still feel strongly "Dominican." In a study of 66 middle-class Dominicans living in South Florida, respondents were asked about their identity, and 60 percent gave two or more answers: Dominican, Dominican-American, American, Hispanic, Latino/a, and Afro-Caribbean (as well as more individual answers such as "artist," "human being," or "me.") When asked where their "home" was, 42 of the 66 interviewees (67 percent) called Miami "home" and 31 (47 percent) called the Dominican Republic "home." But 38 percent of the immigrants gave multiple responses, claiming at least two homes—the United States and the Dominican Republic.[3]

Perhaps because South Florida has a large population of Hispanics (56 percent of the population in Miami-Dade), Dominicans do not seem to experience the same degree of discrimination that is found in other regions. In the above-mentioned study, about one-fourth of all the interviewees said that they had experienced some discrimination in South Florida (often by other Hispanics), but most did not consider it a major barrier. These Dominicans, even those with darker skin, had other

Miami, Florida.

Dominicans in Florida, According to the 2000 Census

City	Number of Dominicans	Percentage Dominican
Miami	6,370	1.8
Hialeah	4,106	1.8
Carol City	1,785	3.0
Fontainebleau	1,779	3.0
Hollywood	1,681	1.2
Orlando	1,191	0.6
Pembroke Pines	1,637	1.2
Miramar	1,439	2.0
Tampa	1,397	0.5
Country Club	1,309	3.6
The Hammocks	1,167	2.5
Miami Beach	1,084	1.2
North Miami City	1,032	1.7

Note: Official census figures are believed to underestimate the number of Dominicans, especially the undocumented.

assets that helped them in the job and housing market, such as a college education, good English skills, and professional dress.

In South Florida today, many Dominicans are enjoying the advantages of living in two cultures, having several identities, and viewing more than one place as "home." They have a middle-class American lifestyle with all its amenities; yet they can live and work with other Hispanics, talk in Spanish freely, buy their favorite Dominican foods in suburban supermarkets, and travel easily back and forth between the Dominican Republic and the United States.

Barbara Martínez, who has made this move several times, believes that "Miami is the home where you have been searching for new opportunities, finding the things that you need to live with more dignity and more comfortably." Pedro Espaillat, who works with an international technology corporation, comments: "Look at Miami today. It's a mecca. It's huge, as far as international commerce, business relationships." Bilingual and bicultural skills have become an asset for living and working in Miami, where Latinos dominate local county and city governments. Second-generation immigrants mix with and marry people of many different cultures and nationalities. Although many white Anglo-Americans (and even some Hispanics) have relocated elsewhere because of the immigrant influx, those who remain are becoming comfortable with being part of a cosmopolitan, globalized population. ❈

aguinaldos: Christmas songs
calor humano: human warmth
chain migration: series of links in which each immigrant who settles in a new country reaches back to help another follow the same path
Quisqueyan: Dominican
rondalla: group of wandering singers
Santiago: second-largest city of the Dominican Republic

NOTES:
1. Author's calculation from the 1990 Miami-Dade PUMS census data.
2. Author's calculation from the 1990 Miami-Dade PUMS census data.
3. This research was carried out for the author's doctoral dissertation in 2002.

DOMINICANS IN SOUTH FLORIDA

USE WITH: Unit 46

DURATION: 1 class

STANDARDS:

English Language Arts: 1, 3, 4, 5, 10

Social Studies: 1c, 1d, 1e, 3b, 3c, 3g, 3h, 4c, 4e, 4g, 4h

Foreign Language: 1, 2.1, 3, 4.2

GOAL: To examine the Dominican experience in Florida.

OBJECTIVE:

To analyze the relationship between class, geography, and ethnic identity.

ACTIVITIES:

1. Ask students: How would you define ethnic identity? How would you describe your own ethnic identity?

2. Referring to the population table on Dominicans in Florida (unit 46), students mark the towns with Dominican populations of 1,000 or more on a map of Florida.

3. The class discusses the following questions:

   - Which city or town in Florida has the largest number of Dominicans?

   - Which city or town has the highest percentage of Dominicans?

   - Is there any pattern to the clustering of Dominicans in Florida?

   - Why might there be more Dominicans in one area of Florida than another?

4. Students read "Dominicans in South Florida: Suburban Sunshine" (unit 46) and answer the following questions:

   - When and why have Dominicans migrated to Florida?

   - Where do Dominicans live, work, shop, and celebrate in South Florida?

   - How difficult or easy was it for Dominicans to build communities in South Florida? Why?

   - What stereotype do Dominicans in this article defy, and how?

   - Do you think this article is representative of all Dominicans in South Florida? Why or why not?

Lesson plan prepared by Ruth Glasser.

5. In pairs, students discuss their feelings about their own ethnicity. Do they have a strong ethnic identity? Is it related to where they live, work, shop, or celebrate, or are there other practices (such as food, religion, family relationships) that contribute to their ethnic identity?

ASSESSMENT:

Students write a journal entry explaining what ethnic identity means to them and comparing this to what it seems to mean to the Florida Dominicans described in the article.

MATERIALS:

- "Dominicans in Florida" population table, copied onto a transparency
- Overhead projector
- Map of Florida

IMMIGRATION BY THE NUMBERS

USE WITH: Any of the units in part 2, "Migration and the Dominican Diaspora." This lesson plan makes use of the population tables in the units (reproduced below).

DURATION: 1–2 classes

STANDARDS:

Math: Data Analysis and Probability

Social Studies: 3d, 3h

GOAL: To become familiar with the quantitative aspects of Dominican immigration.

OBJECTIVES:

- To identify patterns of settlement among Dominican immigrants.

- To differentiate between population measurements in absolute numbers (how many?) and proportions (what percentage or what fraction?).

ACTIVITIES:

1. STATES. Referring to the population tables at the end of this lesson plan, students should:

   - Identify two U.S. states (or one state and Puerto Rico) that have the largest absolute numbers of Dominicans. For each of these two, write the total population, the number of Dominicans, and the percentage of the population that is Dominican on a sheet of paper.

   - Identify two U.S. states (or one state and Puerto Rico) that have the largest percentages of Dominicans (Dominicans as a percentage of total population). For each of these two, write the total population, the number of Dominicans, and the percentage of the population that is Dominican.

   - Compare the two lists. Are the results the same? Why or why not?

2. CITIES. Referring to the population tables at the end of this lesson plan, students answer the following questions:

   - Which city in these states or territory has the largest number of Dominicans? The second-largest number?

   - Which city in these states or territory has the largest percentage of Dominicans? The second-largest percentage?

   - Would you expect Dominicans to have more impact on communities where they are high in number or high in proportion? Why?

Lesson plan prepared by Ruth Glasser.

3. Changes over time.

- Each student selects a city from the population tables, goes to the Census Bureau website (www.census.gov), and finds the number of Dominicans in that city in both 1990 and 2000.

- As a class, create a new table with four columns. The first column lists the cities selected by the students. The second column gives the Dominican population of each city in 1990, and the third column gives the Dominican population of the city in 2000. The fourth column, for percentage change, is blank.

- Students calculate the percentage growth or decline of the Dominican population in each city between 1990 and 2000, and enter the figures in the fourth column.

ASSESSMENT:

Students estimate the likely number of Dominicans in the selected cities for 2005 and 2010, based on the trend between 1990 and 2000. If possible, they should check their estimates against current population projections available on the Census website. If projections are available for Hispanics but not broken down by nationality, students can speculate what percentage and number of that total might be Dominican based on previous growth trends.

MATERIALS:

- Map of U.S. states, including Puerto Rico

- Copies or overheads of population tables

- Access to the Internet

These population tables present data from the 2000 census. Further information for the different localities may be available on the Census Bureau website (www.census.gov). It should be kept in mind that the 2000 census is believed to have undercounted Dominicans, and that independent researchers have produced estimates significantly higher than the figures presented here (see unit 22).

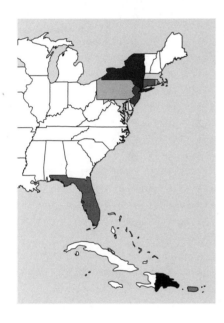

POPULATION TABLES

Dominicans in U.S. States and Territories, According to the 2000 Census

State or Territory	Number of Dominicans	Total Population	Percentage Dominican
New York	455,061	18,976,457	2.39
New Jersey	102,630	8,414,350	1.22
Massachusetts	49,913	6,349,097	0.79
Florida	70,968	15,982,378	0.44
Puerto Rico	56,146	3,808,610	1.47
Rhode Island	17,894	1,048,319	1.71
Pennsylvania	12,186	12,281,054	0.10
Connecticut	9,546	3,405,565	0.28
Maryland	5,596	5,296,486	0.11
Washington, DC metropolitan area	1,496	572,059	0.26

Dominicans in Connecticut, According to the 2000 Census

City	Number of Dominicans	Percentage Dominican
Danbury	2,033	2.7
Waterbury	1,336	1.2
Hartford	1,013	0.8
Bridgeport	886	0.6
Stamford	656	0.6
New Haven	460	0.4
New Britain	326	0.5
New London	280	1.0
Norwalk	216	0.3
Torrington	162	0.5

Dominicans in Florida, According to the 2000 Census

City	Number of Dominicans	Percentage Dominican
Miami	6,370	1.8
Hialeah	4,106	1.8
Carol City	1,785	3.0
Fontainebleau	1,779	3.0
Hollywood	1,681	1.2
Orlando	1,191	0.6
Pembroke Pines	1,637	1.2
Miramar	1,439	2.0
Tampa	1,397	0.5
Country Club	1,309	3.6
The Hammocks	1,167	2.5
Miami Beach	1,084	1.2
North Miami City	1,032	1.7

Dominicans in Massachusetts, According to the 2000 Census

City	Number of Dominicans	Percentage Dominican
Lawrence	16,186	22.5
Boston	12,981	2.2
Lynn	5,517	6.2
Salem	2,176	5.4
Worcester	1,611	0.9
Methuen	1,308	3.0
Haverhill	1,179	2.0
Lowell	1,024	0.9

Note: Official census figures are believed to underestimate the number of Dominicans, especially the undocumented.

Dominicans in New Jersey, According to the 2000 Census

City	Number of Dominicans	Percentage Dominican
Paterson	15,331	10.3
Jersey City	9,186	3.8
Perth Amboy	8,897	18.8
Passaic	8,865	13.0
Union City	7,688	11.5
Newark	6,266	2.3
West New York	3,847	8.4
Elizabeth	3,629	3.0
New Brunswick	2,855	5.9
Camden	1,874	2.3
Clifton	1,853	2.4
Hacksensack	1,573	3.7
Bayonne	1,072	1.7

Dominicans in New York, According to the 2000 Census

City	Number of Dominicans	Percentage Dominican
New York City	406,806	5.0
Yonkers	7,838	4.0
Freeport	3,226	7.4
Brentwood	2,744	5.0
Haverstraw	2,727	27.0
Copiague	1,440	6.6
Sleepy Hollow	1,167	12.7
Hempstead	887	1.6
West Haverstraw	841	8.2
Rochester	808	0.4

Dominicans in Puerto Rico, According to the 2000 Census

City	Number of Dominicans	Percentage Dominican
San Juan	30,472	7.2
Carolina	6,227	3.7
Bayamón	4,128	2.0
Caguas	1,076	1.2
Trujillo Alto	1,032	2.0
Guaynabo	1,471	1.8
Ponce	496	0.3
Mayagüez	546	0.7
Arecibo	262	0.5
Cataño	439	1.5

Dominicans in Rhode Island, According to the 2000 Census

City	Number of Dominicans	Percentage Dominican
Providence	14,638	8.4
Pawtucket	804	1.1
Cranston	734	0.9
Central Falls	575	0.3
Woonsocket	343	0.8

Caribbean Connections

THE DOMINICAN REPUBLIC

PART THREE

SHAPING A DOMINICAN IDENTITY: LANGUAGE, RACE, AND GENDER

North Rockland High School students (l-r) Eduardo Llanos and Kenny Rodríguez.

YOU CALL ME BY OLD NAMES

Rhina P. Espaillat

Rhina P. Espaillat was born in Santo Domingo and grew up in the town of La Vega, in the central Cibao region of the Dominican Republic. She immigrated to the United States in 1939, at the age of seven. Espaillat writes poetry and prose in both English and Spanish, and her work has won many awards. She has published seven poetry collections: Lapsing to Grace, Where Horizons Go, Rehearsing Absence, Mundo y Palabra/The World and the Word, Rhina P. Espaillat: Greatest Hits, 1942–2001, The Shadow I Dress In, *and* The Story-teller's Hour.

You call me by old names: how strange
to think of "family" and "blood,"
walking through the flakes, up to the knees
in cold and democratic mud.

And suddenly I think of people
dead many centuries ago:
my ancestors, who never knew
the dubious miracle of snow...

Don't say my names, you seem to mock
their charming, foolish, Old World touch.
Call me "immigrant," or Social
Security card such-and-such,

or future citizen, who boasts
two eyes, two ears, a nose, a mouth,
but no names from another life,
a long time back, a long way south.

CON NOMBRES VIEJOS ME LLAMAS

Rhina P. Espaillat

Con nombres viejos me llamas: y que extraño
honrar "la alcurnia" y "la sangre," si nos cala
el frío de esta nieve en que luchamos,
el lodo blanco que a todos nos iguala.

Y de repente se me ocurren los ausentes,
los que fundaron mi estirpe en el pasado,
para quienes el milagro de la nieve—
si es milagro—fué espectáculo vedado…

No pronuncies mis nombres, que te burlas
de su dulzura, su absurda antigüedad.
Dime "inmigrante," aplícame la cifra
que porta mi carnet de identidad,

o "ciudadano futuro," que hace alarde
sólo de ojos, nariz, boca y oído,
y no de nombres que vivieron otra vida
en otro tiempo, allá en un sur perdido.

Rhina P. Espaillat at the door of her father's childhood home, where she lived as a child with her paternal grandmother in La Vega.

ALFRED MOSKOWITZ

IMAGE AND IDENTITY

Jorge Duany

As Dominican immigrants in the United States set down roots, they and their U.S.-born children are seeking new ways to define themselves. Increasingly seen as part of a broader U.S. "Latino" community, they nonetheless retain a strong sense of being Dominican. In this article, anthropologist Jorge Duany discusses how Dominicans in the United States are gradually forging new cultural and racial identities.

Since the 1960s, leading politicians in the Dominican Republic have seen migration to the United States as a safety valve for rising unemployment, overpopulation, and political dissidence on the island. Since the 1980s, however, Dominican authorities have been concerned with growing return migration from the United States, blaming it for many social ills including crime and drug addiction. Popular terms referring to return migrants include *Dominican-york* and *cadenú.*

Dominicans in the United States have often rejected negative stereotypes and sought alternative ways of represent-ing their identity. For years, they considered themselves *dominicanos ausentes,* but their descendants are slowly embracing the Dominican-American label. An increasing number of Dominicans in the United States are second-generation—the children of immigrants. The gradual shift from the first to the second generation has been accompanied not just by significant changes in language, food, music, and other cultural preferences, but also by new ways of looking at identity. Like other migrants from the Hispanic Caribbean, Dominicans continue to assert their national origin at the same time that they have begun to claim membership

Adapted from "Los países: Transnational Migration from the Dominican Republic to the United States," in *Dominican Migration: Transnational Perspectives,* eds. Ernesto Sagás and Sintia E. Molina (Gainesville: University Press of Florida). © 2004 by Jorge Duany. Reprinted with permission of the University Press of Florida.

LUIS J. POMALES

North Rockland High School students strike a pose.

in a pan-ethnic category such as Latino. They rarely describe themselves solely as American.

Dominicans and other Latinos have become a "middle race" between whites and blacks in the United States. Many avoid the bipolar model of racial classification into white or black, which still prevails in the United States. Most Dominican migrants do not align themselves with African Americans when describing themselves. Instead, they tend to make common cause with other Spanish-speaking groups. They have also been artificially separated from non-Spanish-speaking Afro-Caribbean migrants, such as Jamaicans and Haitians, with whom they share much culture and history. This is partly because Dominican government officials have long defined Haitian immigration to the Dominican Republic as a national security problem as well as a threat to the country's cultural identity. ❀

bipolar: offering two opposing choices

cadenú: literally, someone who wears gold chains—the implication is of association with drug trafficking

dominicanos ausentes: "absent" Dominicans, those living outside the Dominican Republic

Dominican-york: Dominican resident of New York City

pan-ethnic: spanning multiple ethnic groups (in this case, multiple Spanish-speaking nationalities)

return migration: migration from the adopted country back to the country of origin

WHERE HAS MY SPANISH GONE?

Jocelyn Santana

In this essay, adapted from her forthcoming memoir Dominican Dream, American Reality, *educator and writer Jocelyn Santana explores the role of her native Spanish language in the development of her identity. For her, the process of becoming a Dominican American has been about linguistic and cultural gains and losses.*

During the oral defense of my dissertation in 1999, one of the outside readers asked me to explain my decision to translate Spanish interviews into English. The dissertation was an autobiographical study of a Dominican immigrant being Americanized, and I had interviewed my teachers and relatives in Spanish. I admitted that I had not thought of having the Spanish and English texts appear together on the same page. I had not been too concerned with my Spanish in the dissertation, except to acknowledge that my native language skills had facilitated my acquisition of English.

As I mulled over the reader's question, I realized for the first time that my Americanization had involved making Spanish an afterthought. Though I still possessed a high level of literacy in Spanish (sufficient to write curriculum materials, read, and interpret literary texts), I had not invested much effort in maintaining my Spanish.

Until recently, I thought of learning English as part of the process of adapting to a new culture. I failed to notice that much more was going on. I had unconsciously bought into the linguistic power structure of this country, which denigrates Spanish and sends the message that English is superior. My immersion in English and in United States culture has involved a subtle shame toward my Spanish language and Dominican culture. The process of Americanization has been about losses as well as gains for me.

Making It, at a Cost

It has taken me a long time to realize this. When I came to this country in 1980, upward mobility meant throwing myself into the study of English and embracing American culture. Even before emigrating here, I had developed an exalted idea of the United States. As a little girl in the Dominican Republic, I had seen white American doctors at the Dominican private clinics I was sometimes taken to, and yes, they looked smart, bold, and sharp. *"Los americanos son inteligentes,"* I heard. They spoke louder than Dominicans did; their English words took over the

Dominican air. They filled my Dominican mind and made me imagine the American I would one day become.

After I moved to New York, my Dominican upbringing and family values, my adolescent immaturity, and my lack of awareness of the power struggles and inequality in U.S. society all prevented me from anticipating the pain and loss I would experience. For years I focused on "making it" by learning English and "becoming an American." I believed that by following this path I would eventually be accepted into North American society. I chose to assimilate because I thought that Americanization through education would save me from poverty, discrimination, sexism, and even my own limitations.

What I did not know was that no amount of American cultural knowledge or English acquisition was going to make me an American. Education does not confer the right to equality. After years of total immersion, I ended up with a fragile Dominican-American identity. I am not American enough for the United States even after a Ph.D. in English and twenty-five American years. I am not Dominican enough for the Dominican Republic even though I lived in my native land for the first fourteen years of my life.

My cousin Benny, who was my research assistant, was also born in the Dominican Republic and has lived in Spain for many years. Spanish is our shared native language. However, she noticed that when we visited our homeland in 1997, I chose to speak English to her in public. At the time, I chose to ignore her observation, thinking that my

behavior was an isolated occurrence. However, other experiences have shown me that in immersing myself in North American culture and the English language, I have distanced myself from a Spanish-speaking, Dominican identity.

How far I have internalized the mainstream media's negative stereotypes of Latinas and Latinos was brought home to me in a recent incident. On this day Addison, my stepson, was wearing a head covering resembling a Dominican flag which his father had bought at a Dominican parade in New York City. I did not object to his wearing it in the house. The problem was that he was sitting with two of his white friends in front of one of their homes in our suburban neighborhood. I felt that he did not need to call attention to his ethnicity, that it was my duty to protect him from unnecessary rejection or mistreatment. What might seem to him a proud marker of his identity could be misinterpreted as defiance, as a way of throwing his difference in the face of our mainly white community. Upon reflection, I realized that I was being unfair. The fact that I have not validated myself by highlighting my linguistic and cultural identity does not mean I should expect my children to make the same choice, especially since this denial has caused me some suffering.

A newspaper article made me reflect further on these internalized negative attitudes. I read that a new Harlem Renaissance is at work, with African-American graduates of Harvard moving back to the historically black neighborhood. This decision was "psychologically soothing" for one investor, who said, "I don't have to live next to a white

Jocelyn Santana.

family. I have effectively integrated. I have gone to predominantly white schools. I work in a white firm and I can live anywhere I want." By this logic, it should be psychologically soothing for me to live in Washington Heights, the Upper Manhattan neighborhood where many Dominicans reside and where I lived with Mami when I moved to New York. I balk at this—Washington Heights remains for me the place I had to leave and where I did not want to raise my children. I still hear Mami's voice: "One does not come to the United States to live at the bottom of society. We have come here to work hard and make a better life for ourselves."

It is mainstream America that has defined these neighborhoods as "bad places." I bought into the belief that making it in this country meant moving out and separating myself from others like me, staying at a comfortable distance to prevent being confused with "them." But no matter where I go or where I live in this country, I have learned that I am seen as one of "them." Now I know that native blacks and whites and immigrants alike have pre-conceived notions about the Dominican me, the woman me, the color brown in me.

The Next Generation

Will I ever go back to Washington Heights and buy a brownstone? Not I, but maybe my daughter will. My American-born daughter, Darilyn, loves to speak Spanish and calls herself a Dominican. Perhaps she, like some members of the current generation of affluent African Americans, will develop an idealism that views a move back into the ethnic neighborhood as additive rather than subtractive.

Educating my daughter has given me the opportunity to carefully reconsider my attitudes toward Dominican and American cultures as I see her facing some of the same dilemmas I did. As I was taught, I teach my daughter that academic success is a Dominican value. Using my story as a frame of reference to compare "there" and "here," I attempt to instill in her the belief that there will be a payoff later for succeeding in school now. I promise her that I will support and protect her as much as I can as we cross cultural

and linguistic boundaries together. I do not hide the fact that not every barrier will be overcome, but I teach her that she must rise above the systemic forces of social injustice.

Like the dissertation reader and the children in my life, my friends force me to continually reassess my identity and my life choices. A friend posed one of the deepest questions I have had to confront: "What did it cost you to make it?" I have paid the price of reinventing myself by denying and devaluing some of my native linguistic and cultural capital. The lure of becoming an American woman proved irresistible!

Ironically, my academic studies to master English and the pursuit of my version of Americanization led to temporary financial troubles—including a large student loan debt—and to personal encounters with institutionalized "isms" in the highly competitive settings of a state university and an urban public school system. Despite my achievements, I have endured the pain, embarrassment, and suffering of dealing with individuals and institutions that devalue my intelligence and humanity because I am a brown Dominican American with an accent.

Despite my identity dilemma and the societal pressures that have created it, I still believe in the dream that has led to my American reality. The negative experiences of my journey do not obliterate my love for this country and the conviction that here I've had the opportunity to achieve all my professional and personal dreams. I am here to stay. The United States is my home. Since I received my college education in English, my intellectual identity is now most comfortable in the language I so desperately struggled to master. I use my English to understand what happened to my Spanish.

Achieving linguistic wholeness will mean recovering, accepting, and learning to love the devalued parts of me. I want to be complete in the circumference of a life composed of Spanish and English, the Dominican and American me. I am undergoing the decolonization of my soul: English and American are not superior to Spanish and Dominican. After more than two decades of Americanization, I have recognized that my Spanish and my Dominicanness are the sources of my linguistic gift and personal worth. I was able to learn and love English because of my solid command of Spanish, and because my Dominican family taught me the power of words and human dignity. It is so liberating to realize that my Spanish is not all gone, that I still have enough left in me to recuperate what has been lost. My Spanish is still inside me, blending with my English and embellishing my voice. ❀

brownstone: type of row house common in New York City

Harlem Renaissance: period of intellectual, literary, and artistic creativity in Harlem in the 1920s

linguistic and cultural capital: language and cultural knowledge and skills that serve as a valuable resource to an individual or group

los americanos son inteligentes: Americans are intelligent

mainstream: reflecting the majority or dominant culture

THE OBSTACLE OF RACE

Silvio Torres-Saillant and Ramona Hernández

Concepts of race differ in the Dominican Republic and the United States, and Dominicans who migrate must find their place in a new and unfamiliar racial-ethnic spectrum. Silvio Torres-Saillant, a literary scholar and cultural critic, and Ramona Hernández, a sociologist, show how Afro-Dominicans encounter both opportunities and challenges as "people of color" in U.S. society.

Blacks and mulattoes make up nearly 90 percent of the Dominican Republic's close to 8 million inhabitants. However, Dominicans have had to endure the aberrant negrophobia of the ruling class from colonial times to the present. Anti-black feeling has been promoted in the media, in school textbooks, and in speeches by some prominent political leaders.

Historically, Dominican society can be seen as the cradle of blackness in the Americas. The island of Hispaniola "served as port of entry to the first African slaves who arrived in Spain's newly conquered territories following the transatlantic voyage of Christopher Columbus in 1492."[1] Nonetheless, the dictator Trujillo spent vast public resources to promote an image of national identity that stressed the Hispanic European roots of the country's population, and omitted any mention of an African heritage. Joaquín Balaguer, a Trujillo associate who ruled the country during seven presidential terms from 1960 through 1996, wrote a book in the 1980s that overtly proclaimed the inferiority of blacks and urged Dominicans to strengthen their Spanish identity.[2] The obnoxious racial lessons perpetrated by the Dominican ruling class have proven so enduring that as late as 1996 it was possible for conservative politicians and their liberal allies to use negrophobic discourse in the presidential campaign to defeat the popular black contender José Francisco Peña Gómez.

The members of the Dominican lower classes, the overwhelming majority of whom are of African descent, can do little to combat the media, the conservative intellectuals, and the school system in the Dominican Republic. When Dominicans come to the United States, however, they escape the ideological artillery that sustains negrophobic thought in the homeland, and have a greater possibility of coming to terms with their real ethnicity. In North America—a racially segregated society where the color of one's skin has often mattered more than the content of one's character in obtaining jobs and opportunities—Dominicans may find it appropriate to assert their blackness. Generally darker than Cubans, Puerto Ricans, and most other Latinos, Dominicans are aware that the larger white society does not differentiate racially between them and Haitians or other dark-skinned Caribbeans.

Becoming Black

Dominicans in the United States have become accustomed to speaking of themselves as "people of color" and ally themselves with other peoples of color in the struggle for survival. For instance, Rafael Guarnizo, a self-employed accountant who lives in Manhattan, refers to himself in a personal narrative as being "a black American, a Dominican American."[3] The assistant district attorney in Kings County, New York, is a young Dominican woman named Patria Frías who affirms her African heritage with conviction. Interviewed by *Raíces*, a magazine that seeks to bridge the gap between blacks and Latinos, Frías spoke about her refusal to remove her dreadlocks even though her hairstyle made some peers in the legal profession uncomfortable.[4]

While some members of the Dominican diaspora community may go so far as to uphold radically Afrocentric views of Dominican culture and ethnic identity, the common pattern for Dominicans is to recognize that they have an alternative identity in relation to the racial labels that predominate in the United States. "I was black to white America; I was some strange Spanish-speaking person to black America," says Rosa Bachleda, the Dominican founder of an interracial group of women artists called Not Just Black and White.[5]

Whatever specific words individual Dominicans choose to articulate their racial or ethnic identity, once in the United States they invariably overcome the legacy of denial regarding the African part of their heritage. That change most likely stems from their coming to environments where many people of color come together to share social space and fight for equality. Dominican children in New York generally attend the public school system, which is overwhelmingly populated by nonwhite students. In college, too, they usually go to institutions of higher education that are public. In New York, for example, they have to interact on a daily basis with the majority of black, Latino, and Asian students who fill the classrooms of the City University of New York.

Class Differences

With this in mind, can we say that all Dominicans face racism? Ironically, it is neither the unskilled nor blue-collar workers who most dramatically suffer the oppressive weight of racial discrimination. Their own social segregation, their confinement to jobs populated mostly by people like them, keeps them for the most part from stepping outside their immediate surroundings.

As they hardly ever interact with people from the dominant sectors of society, they stay largely away from the settings where the drama of racism can be felt directly. It is really the professionals and those most qualified to compete for employment, education, and business opportunities in the mainstream who feel it in their flesh. It is they who get the chance to experience personally the extent to which their phenotype can limit their aspirations.

The case of young Dominican professional Heriberto Cabrera provides a pertinent example. After law school, Cabrera chose to work in the office of the Manhattan district attorney. However, he is hardly doing well in his chosen profession. Money continues to pose problems, and the big, lucrative cases elude him. He and his wife have two children, and the worry of insecurity sets in, to the point where he often wakes up in the middle of the night covered with sweat. The inability of Dominican and other young Latino lawyers to become partners in large law firms points to a dismal scenario for someone like Cabrera. "The notion that bright, well-educated Latinos can write their own ticket in the business world is a myth, especially in the legal profession, where the rules of racism are applied with the kind of precision characteristic of the best legal minds," he says.[6] ⊛

NOTES

1. Silvio Torres-Saillant, "The Dominican Republic," in *No Longer Invisible: Afro-Latin Americans Today* (London: Minority Rights Group, 1995), 110.

2. Joaquín Balaguer, *La Isla al revés: Haiti y el destino dominicano* (Santo Domingo: Librería Dominicana, 1984).

3. Alexandra Bandon, *Dominican Americans* (Parsippany, NJ: New Discovery Books, 1995), 74.

4. G. A. Watkins, "Childhood Vision Comes True for Young Dominican Assistant District Attorney," *Raíces* 2, no. 2 (1997): 19.

5. Bandon, *Dominican Americans*, 59.

6. Earl Shorris, *Latinos: A Biography of the People* (New York: Avon Books, 1992), 329.

Afrocentric: emphasizing African culture or identity

mulatto: person of mixed African and European origins

negrophobia: fear of black people, identity, or culture

raíces: roots

"THE PROFESSIONALS FEEL IT IN THEIR FLESH"

USE WITH: Units 44, 51, 52

DURATION: 1–2 classes

STANDARDS:

English Language Arts: 1, 2, 3, 10

Social Studies: 1a, 1b, 1e, 1f, 1g, 1h, 2e, 4b, 4c, 4f, 4g, 4h, 5a, 5b, 9b, 10c, 10d, 10i

Foreign Language: 1, 3.2, 4.2

GOAL: To expose students to the connections between immigration, class, and racism for Dominicans living in the United States.

OBJECTIVES:

- To compare the effects of racism on blue- and white-collar workers.
- To analyze the connection between upward mobility and racism.
- To develop a plan to counteract racism in the life of Heriberto Cabrera.

ACTIVITIES:

1. Open the class by showing students two pictures of black men. Tell students that one man is a lawyer and the other is a maintenance worker. Ask the class to write answers to the following questions:

   - Which man has the most difficulty with racism at work?
   - Which man has the most money? Which has a better life? How do you know?

2. Students discuss their answers and share their rationales.

3. Students read "Image and Identity" (unit 50) and "The Obstacle of Race" (unit 52).

4. Break the class into small groups. Each group works together to decide whether they agree or disagree with the assertion of Torres-Saillant and Hernández that professionals are more likely than nonprofessionals to experience and suffer from racism. Each group must state reasons for agreement or disagreement.

5. A group is assigned to read *"'Black Behind the Ears'—and Up Front Too? Dominicans in the Black Mosaic:" Dominicans in Washington, DC* (unit 44) and analyze the case of Maricela Medina. What benefits did she acquire by going "the African-American route" when she moved to Washington? What disadvantages might she also have experienced? The group presents their findings to the rest of the class.

Lesson plan prepared by Jocelyn Santana.

ASSESSMENT:

Students develop a plan to help themselves counteract racism or prejudice in their own lives. Encourage students to research the lives of Dominicans who have succeeded in the United States despite the "obstacle of race" (for example, an athlete such as baseball player Sammy Sosa).

MATERIALS:

- Newspaper or magazine pictures of two black men
- Newsprint and markers for small group work

I AM AN EXTENSION OF MY DOMINICAN MAMÁS

Jocelyn Santana

In this essay, adapted from her forthcoming memoir Dominican Dream, American Reality, *educator and writer Jocelyn Santana explores Dominican feminism across three generations in her family—a feminism based on sisterhood and strength.*

My grandmother was strong, not the way American women are, with their loud voices and blow-dried hair. Mamá was all about patience, silence, and lowered eyes. She was the polite gesture that had nothing to do with the demands of her ten children, and her *marido borracho en la calle.* Drunken husbands in the streets were the topic of conversation for the other women around, but not for her. For Mamá, such a disposition to speak ill of the one who touched her most private parts was inconceivable and for women *de baja clase.* Low-class women, who cursed and called their men *borrachones* in public, Mamá believed, were not real women, in the natural sense. She thought that bad spirits, those that were said to inhabit the bodies of *prostitutas,* possessed them. Whores, women who cursed, yelled, cried, and said they would rather die alone… Well, they were just not women.

Mamá had her reasons to feel this way. As a Catholic woman of God, she went to church every Sunday, and often during the week, to attend to the burdens of her spirit. She knew it was a sin to criticize others, so she never shared her thoughts with anyone, not even with God. She figured it was best to keep those things as far away from the church pews as possible and say ten Holy Marys each time she felt like judging the woman uptown, the one she thought about on her way to church on Friday nights. She was determined to forget *la querida,* the mistress, with *her* ten children, in the circumference of the black rosary.

Mamá was like the *robles* planted in the middle of the dusty roads in the distant town of Padre Las Casas. The oak trees stood still and bright, testaments to collisions and crashes that only left minor scratches on their trunks.

Mamá was understanding, you see. With twenty children to feed, my *abuelito* needed a real, good wife. Mamá was real and good, so much that she shared her meager weekly allowance with *la querida.* Mamá had her own ten kids to feed, but

MEL SHAW

Co-editor Jocelyn Santana and daughter Darilyn visit El Conuco Restaurant (2002), a major tourist attraction in Santo Domingo.

the whole town knew about the early morning exchanges between the two women by the church. Witnesses claim that they never made eye contact as Mamá gave her money, *plátanos*, rice and beans. Mamá would deposit the items gently near her feet, close enough to smell the body odor that her husband took home every Friday night. I know about the scent because Mamá told Mami—my mother—and Mami told me.

For a long time, I thought Mamá must have been crazy. Mami told me that long ago she vowed never to become like Mamá. When I heard about *la querida*, I vowed to become like Mami. Mami would not feed another woman's children or stay with an adulterous man. Mami would leave.

My father feels that, in all honesty, he did not treat Mami so badly. He took her to his house in a barrio of Santo Domingo near his relatives. Mami remembers that on Fridays he disappeared down the unpaved street where they lived and returned as a drunken ghost on Sunday nights. One morning, Mami took one piece of luggage, took me and the discolored pan in which she heated my milk, and headed back to Mamá's in Padre Las Casas. She left my father with his house, his weekend whores, and his drinking. In Mami's words, "Since I saw no progress or advancement for my life, I took my daughter and returned to my parents. I took nothing, except my daughter. I left him everything else."

I am an extension of Mamá's sisterly mother-

Mami and Mamá.

hood bonding and Mami's act of transgression. Mamá was taught to stay and never leave, but she resisted through a feminism based on the practical principle of sisterhood: the children have to be fed no matter what. I learn from that kind of strength. Deeds of courage are the legacy Mamá and Mami have left for me.

One of my greatest challenges has been dealing with accusations of being a "bad" mother and wife on account of my doctoral studies. Many saw my pursuit of a Ph.D. as a selfish act, and even some of my own relatives have classified me as a neglectful mother and wife. One of those relatives was "kind" enough to tell me that in the event my husband committed adultery or left me, which he eventually did, I had to forgive him. "After all," she said, "you have been in school too long. What do you expect him to do? Although he was raised here, you know, he is Dominican." I responded, "I guess that's the chance I have to take." Like Mamá and Mami I am willing to take a chance of abandonment and retaliation even from those who claim to love me. From these two women, I inherited the strength to perform my roles as a mother and a wife in the first person without regret or shame. I proclaim, "I am Mamá. I am Mami. I am me. *Yo soy yo.*" ❀

abuelito: grandpa
barrio: neighborhood
borrachones: drunkards
de baja clase: low-class
la querida: mistress
marido borracho en la calle: husband drunk in the street
mi español: my Spanish
Padre Las Casas: town in west-central Dominican Republic
plátanos: plantains
prostitutas: prostitutes
robles: oak trees

EXTENSIONS OF IDENTITY

USE WITH: Unit 54

DURATION: 1 class

STANDARDS:

English Language Arts: 1, 9, 10, 12

Social Studies: 1c, 4c, 4e, 4f, 4h

Foreign Language: 1.1, 1.2, 3.2, 4

GOAL: To explore identity formation through role models.

OBJECTIVES:

- To analyze personal identity.
- To gain understanding of the importance of family role models.
- To analyze a literary text.
- To practice writing skills.

ACTIVITIES:

1. Ask students: What makes you unique?

2. Students read "I Am an Extension of My Dominican Mamás" (unit 54) and analyze the situations of Mamá, Mami, and the author. Discuss how the three women are alike and different.

3. Students interview each other in pairs, asking the following questions:

   - Who are you?
   - Where did your name come from? Or, how was your name chosen?
   - Who do you look like in your family?
   - Who do you act like?
   - Who do you want to be like? Why?

ASSESSMENT:

Using the answers from their interview, students write their own "Extensions" essays (3–4 paragraphs minimum). Teacher grades essays.

Lesson plan prepared by Claudia Bedoya-Rose.

THE GENDER POLITICS OF SETTLEMENT VERSUS RETURN

Sherri Grasmuck and Patricia R. Pessar

Dominican families in the United States must weigh many factors in deciding whether and when to return to the Dominican Republic. When faced with this dilemma, Dominican women may see their interests as different from the interests of men. In this article, sociologist Sherri Grasmuck and anthropologist Patricia R. Pessar suggest that certain women choose to stay in the United States because of their newfound social and financial autonomy.

Reprinted from Sherri Grasmuck and Patricia R. Pessar, *Between Two Islands: Dominican International Migration* (Berkeley and Los Angeles: University of California Press). © 1991 by the Regents of the University of California. Used by permission of the publisher.

The return to the Dominican Republic can become highly contentious for many women. They struggle to maintain the gains that migration and employment have brought to them so they tend to postpone return. They realize that the sexual division of labor in the Dominican economy militates against wage employment for women of their training and class background. In this contest over return, migration may lose its character as a collective and unifying family project for social mobility. For certain middle-class and upper-working-class men, the conflict over return revolves around traditional male privileges. Migration can challenge these privileges, and many men seek to regain them back home.

Migration has brought societal and household-level changes to many Dominican immigrant men. Their first jobs tend to be on the lowest rungs of the prestige hierarchy. The status associated with those jobs may contradict the immigrant's self-identity and sense of worth. This is particularly likely for Dominican men, whose pre-migration employment often placed them in the ranks of the middle class or the upper working class.

Although such men experienced a decline in status by migrating, they are urged by others to subsume their individual identities and goals within the larger sphere of the household. Notwithstanding the social mobility realized at the household level, Dominican men in the United States sometimes become frustrated by their inability to translate household gains into public prestige.

Some men choose to pursue a financial strategy in which frugal living and savings are emphasized to ensure that the household will eventually return to the Dominican Republic. Not infrequently, this places the man at odds with his spouse, who has embarked on an opposing financial course. In several of the cases of divorce studied, what ultimately hastened the breakup was the man's return to the Dominican Republic with sufficient savings to reestablish himself, while the woman elected to remain in the United States.

To fully understand the profound changes in household authority within Dominican immigrant households and women's strategies to prolong their households' stay in the United States, we must recognize two elements. First, wage income is commonly assigned greater value than homemaking. Second, under some circumstances, such as when they gain regular access to wages, women are able to use this income as leverage to modify the terms of decision making about household budgeting and other domestic activities. In other words, once women are permitted control over a broader range of household decision making, they are reluctant to give up this newfound power.

These concerns lead to a reconsideration of Dominican settlement in the United States. Women's strategies for rooting the household in the United States include bringing dependents from the Dominican Republic. This strategy carries implications for the types of jobs immigrant household members will maintain or will accept. For example, savings are needed to meet the cost of sponsoring the children's migration. Since tax records are part of the portfolio of successful visa petitioners, the decision to recruit additional family members from the Dominican Republic greatly reduces immigrants' incentives or willingness to work for employers who pay "off the books."

Some Dominican women have been able to negotiate greater autonomy and decision-making rights within their households as a result of wage employment in New York. This has increased their marital satisfaction and encouraged them to think of New York as a permanent home. Yet, the success of the migration venture for them is dependent on the preservation of household bonds of solidarity, albeit renegotiated ones. When the household bonds are severed, the migration project of collective socioeconomic advancement often falters, because the individual resources of single members, especially women, are insufficient to sustain it. There is a painful irony associated with the fact that the newfound autonomy of many immigrant women may come at the expense of the collective social mobility of the household and, in many cases, lead to poverty. ✿

EDUCATION OF DOMINICANS THERE AND HERE

Jocelyn Santana

Dominican-born Jocelyn Santana, an educator in the New York City public schools, describes some of the challenges that Dominican students encounter when they enter U.S. classrooms. She calls for innovative programs to help these students learn core subjects while they improve their English and preserve their native Spanish.

With its proud educational tradition, Santo Domingo was once known as "the Athens of the New World." Less than ten years after Columbus landed, Roman Catholic missionaries established the first schools. The Autonomous University of Santo Domingo, created in 1538 as Saint Thomas Aquinas University, is the oldest university in the Western Hemisphere.[1]

Unfortunately, education in the Dominican Republic today does not live up to this heritage. While church-run schools serve the urban middle and upper classes, the majority of students struggle within a vastly under-funded and troubled public school system.

In 1990 a group of business leaders, teachers, and others drafted a ten-year plan to improve the schools. More than a decade after the government launched the plan, Dominican

A student at the Primaria de Camú.

A fourth-grade student recites in a Washington Heights classroom.

teachers, parents, and students agree that public education has improved markedly. New schools have been built, classrooms have more books and supplies, and rigorous standards have been set for teacher preparation.

But there remain deep inequities in the Dominican education system that the ten-year plan did not address. Underlying social and economic factors still keep many Dominican children from receiving high-quality schooling and staying in school. Most children and their parents, especially in the rural areas, live in a desperate state of impoverishment, and often children need to work to help support their families. In addition, school fees pose a barrier to attendance for many. Although public school tuition is free, there are many out-of-pocket expenses for students' families, especially the costs of uniforms and books. In

part because of these economic obstacles, fewer than 60 percent of students complete the fifth grade. Only about 40 percent of eligible children are enrolled in secondary school.[2]

Teachers' salaries are still barely above the poverty line. A recent conversation with a teacher in Santo Domingo revealed that the average salary of a public school educator teaching the morning and afternoon sessions is between 12,000 and 14,000 pesos per month—approximately $240 to $280.[3]

Dominican Students in U.S. Classrooms: Varied Backgrounds

Dominicans represent the fastest-growing minority group in New York City and several other U.S. cities such as Providence, Rhode Island, and Lawrence, Massachusetts. As

more Dominican students enroll in U.S. schools, educators and policy makers can benefit from an understanding of the Dominican educational system and the background these newcomers bring.

Dominican students enrolling in American schools encounter a new language, a new culture, and new educational methods, as well as teachers and other students from an array of different backgrounds. A range of factors influence their chances of academic success, including their socioeconomic background, prior schooling, knowledge of English, and attitudes toward American culture. The types of programs they encounter in schools here are also key to determining how fast they progress.

Students who attended school regularly in the Dominican Republic and who have developed both content and language skills in Spanish seem to make an easier transition into American schools. Their solid knowledge of Spanish makes it easier for them to learn English. For example, Raysa is the child of two Dominican doctors who moved to New Jersey three years ago. She emphasizes that her skills in Spanish have helped, not hindered, her adaptation to U.S. schools:

> I have been enrolled in school continuously... I had a very [good] command of Spanish when I arrived in this country. The school I attended in the Dominican Republic provided me a good foundation in math, science and even some English. My parents always help me with my homework. We live in a high-level income neighborhood where everybody speaks

High school students in Santo Domingo.

LINDA-ANNE REBHUN

MEL SHAW

An elementary school in Padre las Casas, Azúa.

English. There are always magazines, newspapers, books, dictionaries and comic books in my house. On weekends, I go to the museums, to visit friends, the local library or bookstores to learn new things. I still speak, write and read Spanish. I did not replace Spanish with English. I just added English to my skills.[4]

Conversely, students with fragmented schooling in the Dominican Republic typically have more difficulties adjusting to U.S. schools. In most cases, their poor literacy skills in Spanish make their second language learning even more difficult. Special mention should be made of children who are left in the care of grandmothers and aunts while their parents migrate to the United States. These "left-behind children" often fall behind in school in the Dominican Republic. By the time they finally rejoin their parents in this country, they may have repeated grades or dropped out of school entirely.

Wilfredo is an eighth grader in New York City. His school attendance has been intermittent, partly as a result of the realities of migration:

My family is like other immigrants. They have been many places before finding Massachusetts after living in the Dominican Republic. My parents are aware of my school problems and they care but they do not have a choice. I attended school in a small town in the Dominican Republic as a child. After that, we moved to *la capital* [Santo Domingo]. There I went to about three schools. From there, we ended up in Puerto Rico waiting for the visa. I did not really go to school much there. In New York City, I went to a couple of schools but I had to leave because my father and brother had found jobs in a factory near Boston. They put me in an eighth-grade class with ESL help. I cannot really read Spanish or English. I could not do most of the homework. I think I will get a job with my relatives in the factory.

Other students have to deal with family responsibilities, overprotective parents, and even social segregation during their time in school. Carmen, a high school student who was born in the Bronx, says:

My parents are working-class, I guess, because they both work in a shoe factory in New Jersey. I have always attended public schools in the Bronx, except for one year that my parents moved back to the Dominican Republic. I am still considered an ESL student because when I take the LAB test my counselor tells me I scored below the fortieth percentile. I do not really know what that means. It is such a dumb test. I am in bilingual education and take some ESL classes. I take most of my classes in Spanish and then I have some English classes.

All of us are mainly Dominican and Mexican. We all take the classes in the basement and I hardly see or talk to regular kids, you know, Americans. I have teachers too who have only been in the country for a couple of years. They can hardly speak any English. I live around mostly Dominicans and do not have any American friends. I feel better around Dominicans. My parents do not let me go out too much because of the drugs and the dangers in the street. I cannot stay for after-school programs because they run until it gets dark. They cannot help me with my homework but I do the best I can. On weekends, my parents work so I have to take care of my two younger brothers. We watch a lot of television. One day I would like to go to college, but I do not know if I will be ready.

Programs Needed for Immigrant Students

Entering U.S. schools, Dominican students, like those of other immigrant groups, may feel a sense of shock and dislocation, low self-esteem, and fear. The education of these children is often a challenge.

A significant factor in meeting their needs is the availability of English as a second language (ESL) and bilingual education programs. Many Dominican parents choose transitional bilingual education programs, which give students instruction in the main subjects (math, science, language arts, and social studies) in Spanish, along with ESL classes to help them learn English, until they are ready for classes taught entirely in English. The parents who make this choice often want to make sure their children preserve their Spanish language and Dominican culture. Some schools offer other program options, such as "dual language" and "sheltered English."[5] Unfortunately, most schools still do not offer all the programs necessary to address immigrant students' specific needs.

The challenge of meeting these needs is especially visible in New York City, where more than 10 percent of public school students are Dominican. In the city's Region Ten, which includes Washington Heights, 85 percent of newly enrolled immigrant children are of Dominican descent. For a generation of Dominican children in New York, many educational reforms have come too late. Large numbers have dropped out of high school and become part of the grim statistics documented in the 2000 census. Analysts of the census figures found that among Dominican adults twenty-five years of age or older, 53 percent in New York had not completed high school, compared to 49 percent nationwide. A positive finding is that U.S.-born Dominicans seem to be doing somewhat better: in 2000, only 19 percent of Dominicans born in the United States had not completed high school by the age of twenty-five.[6]

To respond to these problems, New York school districts are working to increase the number of Dominican teachers and principals in the schools. In addition, new schools are addressing the needs of immigrant high school students, a group at particularly high risk. Gregorio Luperón Preparatory School in Washington Heights was a transitional high school for newly arrived immigrants, and has become a diploma-granting school. With a Dominican principal and a cadre of mostly Dominican teachers, the school is a success story. It has implemented practices that address the challenges of poor prior schooling and other impediments to the achievement of a high school diploma in English. The High School of World Cultures in the Bronx is a similar institution; 56 percent of its student population is of Dominican descent.

But there is an urgent need to provide effective programs for Dominican and other immigrant students throughout the U.S. educational system. These children and their families often come to the United States believing that hard work and an American education will enable them to achieve a better life. U.S. educators face the challenge of creating educational programs that can help Dominican and other immigrant students realize their dreams. Meanwhile, Dominican students like Diana hold on to the legacy of their parents. "My parents have taught me not to give up," she says. "They have taught me that education is the one thing I will have all of my life." ❀

---

bilingual education: instruction that is partly or entirely conducted in two languages

ESL: English as a second language

NOTES

1. Citizenship and Immigration Canada, "Learning in the Dominican Republic," Cultural Profiles Project, http://www.settlement.org/cp/english/dominican/index.html.

2. Ibid. In 1999 the Ministry of Education began providing free textbooks to children in public elementary school.

3. At the 2004 exchange rate of approximately 50 pesos to US$1.

4. For this article, I interviewed various students in 2001 (names have been changed). Their accounts reflect the varied educational backgrounds and schooling experiences of Dominican students.

5. In dual language programs there is a 50/50 balance in the use of the two languages each day. Primary instruction is given in the students' native language, while second-language fluency is developed through activities that focus on meaning and comprehension. Students learn two languages and are educated in both.

   Sheltered English seeks to make academic instruction in English understandable to students learning it as a second language. Students in these classes are "sheltered" in that they do not compete academically with native English speakers. In the sheltered English classroom, teachers use physical activities, visual aids, and the environment to teach important new words for concept development in mathematics, science, history, home economics, and other subjects.

6. Ramona Hernández and Francisco Rivera-Batiz, "Demographic Explosion: Dominicans Will Become Third Largest Hispanic Population in the United States by 2010, New Report Says," *CCNY News*, City College of New York, October 9, 2003.

"I'M PART OF THREE REALMS..."

Interview with Silvio Torres-Saillant

Silvio Torres-Saillant, literary scholar and cultural critic, was the first director of the CUNY Dominican Studies Institute at the City College of New York. Born in the Dominican Republic, he migrated with his family to Brooklyn in 1973. In this interview he recalls the humble circumstances of his childhood, his education in the Dominican Republic and New York, and his evolution as scholar who is at once Dominican, Caribbean, and Latino.

Silvio Torres-Saillant was interviewed by Ruth Glasser in New York City on May 8, 2003.

I was born August 11, 1954, in the city of Santiago. We lived in a *barrio marginado*, a low-income neighborhood, called Pueblo Nuevo. This barrio is a world away from the city center, from the places where the better-to-do people lived. I recall my father thinking that I needed to spend more time *en el pueblo arriba*. He felt that I had a greater chance of striking an acquaintance with a better class of people.

I went to local public schools. We studied geography and history, learning the capitals of all the countries. There was a great deal of emphasis on memorizing content. There was math, and *lenguaje*—it was not called

Silvio Torres-Saillant

[COURTESY OF SILVIO TORRES-SAILLANT]

español—where you learned how to write, you learned your grammar. In my childhood, knowing things was something you could brag about. You would go to the corner and ask each other, "Do you know what the capital of Greece is? Do you know who Socrates is?" "Oh, you know nothing! Do you know who Pindar is?"

The underclass thought that you became *gente,* by knowing things. I recall one time, it could have been one of my duties as a Boy Scout, that I had to go door-to-door selling magazines. People would make comments about how well spoken I was. I always thought that knowledge was something I wanted to pursue, but it wasn't clear to me exactly how. I thought I wanted to be a lawyer. I imagined myself in a courtroom, deploying language in ways that would change the world.

My father was very haughty about the things that he knew. He would say things like, "I am the person with the best knowledge of the Spanish language in the entire Cibao region." He would spend time quoting Scriptures, so we all learned about Solomon and David. We in the family learned all the philosophers, historians, major players in world history. We were familiar with many names through discourses we used to hear from our father.

But a part of our poverty had to do with the fact that my father, even with his knowledge, was not able to work because of his trouble with the Trujillo regime. At one point his name was listed in something called the Foro Público as a person to be watched, an enemy of the regime. He was a journalist and a poet, and in looking through his newspaper columns, the examiners had found that the name of Trujillo was never mentioned. That omission was suspect in a country where you got places by showing that you were more *trujillista* than anybody else.

My mother's family was from an area called La Guajaca, a rural section of the northwest. She had several menial jobs. At one point she was working in a cigar-making shop, and another time she worked in an assembly-line shirt factory. She was a skilled seamstress, so she made my sister's dresses, the boys' shirts, and quite often our pants as well. She was a very talented woman, with aspirations to become a singer. I could get a glimmer of those yearnings when she would sing to us.

She had to devise ingenious ways to keep us fed. She learned how to cook delicious meals with almost no money, bartering with merchants in the area. I remember a time when we ate *arroz* and *aguacate.* She only had rice but she had a lot of rice so she would bring a couple of pounds of rice to the shop to

exchange for an avocado or two.

I worked from very early on. My mother was of the generation that believed children should have an education but they should also learn a trade. When I was in the third grade I was already working in a shoe factory and going to school. I was apprenticed to a *cortador,* a leather cutter. That's what I trained in. I would go to school until three, and to work after that. But I was needed on the job for longer hours, so I switched to night school in the third grade and became a worker during the day.

I was in *la zapatería* when the U.S. arrived in 1965. A detachment landed at the Santiago airport. That airport was only used for military purposes, so we knew, and we followed the war on the radio. I remember the old people speaking about how unfair it was that the revolutionaries were on the ground while the government and the Yankees were in the air shooting down on them. There was an unevenness of military power involved. I also recall people going to *la capital,* to Santo Domingo, to join the fight against the Marines. The government forces didn't need to recruit, they had the army and the Yankees. When you "joined the effort" it usually meant you joined the revolutionaries—the *constitucionalistas,* as they were called, because they were fighting to restore the constitution.

My memories get clearer when you get closer to 1966, when Balaguer is brought by the U.S. government to the occupied country and Juan Bosch is also allowed to return. The funny

thing is that years later when Aristide is overthrown in Haiti the U.S. brings him back as president, but the U.S. didn't bring Bosch back as president; they brought him back to give him a chance to compete against Balaguer, their favorite. I recall very clearly my sentiments of being on Bosch's side and being disappointed when he "lost." Well, we know he didn't lose, I mean it *entre comillas.*

It was very clear that my mother was economically asphyxiated. My father was not efficient enough at providing for the family, so it fell on her to make sure we got ahead. When the exodus began, she saw migration as an option. My eldest sister was the first person who came to this country. She married a person who had been brought by his mother to the United States and then eventually she followed him. While my sister was living in New York, she got a temporary visa for my mother.

Arriving in New York

My mother brought me to New York in 1973. We lived in the Brownsville section of Brooklyn. I recall people looking different from people I had known. There were people who were black, and people who were white, and the materiality of those categories became so clear. People who were black were living in black neighborhoods. It was a vague experience of racial spaces. I suppose in Brooklyn College I learned to think about race in American terms. Before that, I was eyeing everything with curiosity.

I enrolled in Brooklyn College, began taking English as a second language. Then when I began to feel confident about my English I took my first history class. I decided I was not going to major in Spanish because of fear of English. My major was broadcasting, but my primary interest was always literature. I did broadcasting because I wanted to feel that I had majored in something that could turn into a job. Then I could go on and do the literature.

After my daughter was born I moved to Washington Heights, and became very involved in the Dominican community. I was a member of the organization that founded the Dominican parade in 1982. So I was identified by many people as this bright young man who is studying at the university. I began doing research on Dominican history, preparing to deliver community-sponsored lectures on February 27 (Día de la Independencia), and August 16 (Día de la Restauración). I began to get a feel for the Dominican past. So that was the turning point, my being identified as a person who had assets that the community needed.

I entered New York University, the only graduate school where I applied. I felt lucky that people would want me; I didn't have a sense of empowerment and entitlement. I did my master's and completed the courses for the doctorate. Then I got to that gray area when

people finish their coursework, but they still have the dissertation to write. They are no longer in school and do not qualify for financial aid or student loans. So I worked as a caseworker for the Human Resources Administration in the Office of Special Services for Children, which deals with cases of abuse and neglect.

My master's thesis was on the European romance as a genre. I looked at the romance tradition in various European literatures: German, Spanish, Italian, English, French, what in Spanish would be *novelas de caballería.* I still remained loyal to the idea of world culture, which meant you were knowledgeable about the Western tradition. Meanwhile, I worked as a shipping clerk in a casting supply store in midtown Manhattan's jewelry district.

I took a course with Haydee Vitali, a Puerto Rican member of the Spanish department at NYU. We read some of the classics of Puerto Rican, Cuban, and Dominican literature. I remember her making references to writers outside of the Hispanic Caribbean, in the other linguistic blocs. Then I thought, let me do an independent study with her. I would do the Spanish Caribbean for the course and the French and the English Caribbean as an independent study course, then put all of that together into one comparative paper. That became the basis for my dissertation proposal, which I

wrote with Vitali and Earl Minor among the members of my committee. Eventually that became the doctoral thesis. After extensive revision, it also became my first book, *Caribbean Poetics,* published by Cambridge University Press in 1997.

Becoming a Caribbeanist

I began to discover that Dominican culture is not so much Latin American as it is Caribbean. Sometimes, it's possible to see more similarities between Dominicans and other Caribbeans, even if they speak different languages, than between Dominicans and other Latin Americans. There are more discernible similarities between a Dominican and a Haitian than between a Dominican and a Chilean.

So that identified me as a Caribbeanist. With the advent of the Dominican Studies Institute, my need to speak on things Dominican caused me to enter into dialogue with other Latinos. I have often had to behave as the official Dominican voice in the academy, speaking about the exclusion of Dominicans from everything. Later I began speaking about things Latino, also. I am now one of the associate editors for the journal *Latino Studies,* one of the senior editors for the *Encyclopedia of Latinos and Latinas in the United States,* published by Oxford University Press, and the director of the Latino–Latin American Studies program at Syracuse University.

I now feel that I'm part of three realms: the Dominican experience, the Caribbean as a cultural area, and the Latino space within the United States. There's that Mexican history of the Southwest that dates back hundreds of years, not disconnected from the experience of Puerto Ricans and Cubans who came beginning in the nineteenth century, or Dominicans whose massive exodus starts in the 1960s. I'm now wrestling to put together a history that encompasses those different chronologies and different forms of insertion into the American experience. ✿

academy: higher education
aguacate: avocado
arroz: rice
Caribbeanist: scholar who studies the Caribbean
Cibao: central region of the Dominican Republic
Día de la Independencia: Independence Day
Día de la Restauración: Restoration Day
en el pueblo arriba: in the upper part of town, where better-off people live
entre comillas: within quotation marks
español: Spanish
gente: respectable people
lenguaje: language
novelas de caballería: romances of chivalry, a type of Spanish novel
trujillista: loyal to Trujillo
zapatería: shoe factory

Caribbean Connections

THE DOMINICAN REPUBLIC

PART FOUR

HAITIAN-DOMINICAN RELATIONS

Haitian art for sale on the malecón *(seaside boulevard) in Santo Domingo.*

HAITI

Sherezada Vicioso (Chiqui)

MIGUEL GÓMEZ

Born in Santo Domingo, Sherezada Vicioso, known as Chiqui, lived in New York for eighteen years before returning to the Dominican Republic in 1981. Her poetry collections, essay collections, and plays have won many awards. In this poem, Vicioso imagines Haiti in various ways and alludes to the contradictory emotions many Dominicans feel about this neighboring country.

Haití
te imagino vírgen
antes de que piratas precursores
te quitaran tus vestidos de caoba
y te dejaran así
con tus senos redondos al aire
y tu falda de yerba desgarrada
apenas verde,
marrón tímida.

Haití
te imagino adolescente
olorosa a vetiver, tierna de rocío
sin esta multitud de cicatrices
con que te integraron al mercado de mapas
y con que te ofrecen multicolor
en las aceras de Puerto Príncipe
en Jacmel, en San Marcos, en el Artibonito
en un gran baratillo de ojalata.

Haití
caminante que afanosa me sonríes
interrumpiendo siestas de veredas
ablandando piedras, asfaltando polvo
con tus pies sudorosos y descalzos.
Haití que tejes el arte de mil formas
y que pintas las estrellas con tus manos
descubrí que el amor y el odio
como tú se llaman.

Spanish poem reprinted from *Viaje desde el agua* (Santo Domingo: Ediciones Visuarte). © 1981 by Sherezada Vicioso (Chiqui). Used by permission of the author. English translation by Daisy Cocco De Filippis.

HAITI

Sherezada Vicioso (Chiqui)

Haiti,
I imagine you a virgin
before forerunning pirates
had removed your mahogany dress
to leave you thus
with your bare, round breasts
and your torn grass skirt
barely green,
timidly brown.

Haiti,
I imagine you an adolescent
fragrant of vetiver, tender with dew
without the numerous scars
you are displayed and sold in the
maps market wrapped in multicolor banners
on the sidewalks of Puerto Principe,
In Jacmel, in San Marcos, in the Artibonite
in a dramatic tin plate bargain.

Haiti,
traveler who eagerly smiles at me
interrupting the quiet of paths,
softening stones, paving dust
with your sweaty, bare feet
Haiti who can give art a thousand shapes
and who paints stars with your hands
I found out that love and hate
share your name.

vetiver: a grass from tropical
   India cultivated for its
   aromatic roots that yield an oil
   used in perfume

JACK SCHIFFER

HAITIAN–DOMINICAN RELATIONS

Samuel Martínez

The history of Haitian-Dominican relations is one of mutual grievances and mistrust. People of both nationalities, but especially many Dominicans, believe themselves to be utterly different from and incompatible with their neighbors on the other side of the island. These perceived differences are expressed in linguistic, religious, and racial terms, and provide leaders on both sides with a rationale for not trying harder to improve relations between the two countries. Among Dominicans, openly racist expressions of hostility toward Haitians abound.

According to the organization Human Rights Watch, people of Haitian descent in the Dominican Republic have been denied basic rights. The Dominican government makes it difficult for Haitian immigrants to obtain legal residency documents, so the vast majority are undocumented. Thousands of Haitians have been deported from the Dominican Republic without due process. Even the Dominican-born children of Haitian immigrants are frequently denied Dominican citizenship, and are vulnerable to deportation.

In this article, cultural anthropologist Samuel Martínez argues that cultural and linguistic differences are not the true source of the tensions between the two peoples. Rather, he suggests that Dominican politicians have used anti-Haitian feeling, especially resentment of immigrants, for political gain.

Adapted from Samuel Martínez, "Not a Cockfight: Rethinking Haitian-Dominican Relations," *Latin American Perspectives* 30, no. 3: 80–101. © 2003 by Sage Publications, Inc. Reprinted by permission of Sage Publications, Inc.

Many people believe that "the problem" between the Dominican Republic and Haiti began with Haiti's political domination over the entire island in the nineteenth century. According to the popular Dominican depiction of the country's history, Haiti "invaded" the eastern portion of Hispaniola in 1822 and ruled the entire island until 1844. But accounts by noted Dominican historians do not support this view. They contend that Haiti did not invade the eastern part of the island, but was instead invited by its neighbors to enter.[1] The Haitian government did not act out of greed or distrust of its Spanish-speaking neighbors, but rather to bolster the eastern side of the island against the threat of attack by France or another European power.[2]

Once in power over the entire island, the Haitian government was of course not universally popular in the Spanish-speaking east. A small minority, made up of Catholic clergy and white *criollo* landowners, opposed Haitian control from the beginning.[3] But the rest of the population seemed initially to regard Haitian rule as the lesser of two evils. After all, the Haitian army had liberated Afro-Dominicans from slavery in 1801 and again in 1822. For nearly twenty years of their twenty-two-year reign, the Haitian "occupiers" held power not with their own troops but with regiments recruit-

ed from the Spanish-speaking black, mulatto, and white men of the eastern part of the island.[4] Furthermore, the Haitian government brought about greater prosperity through land reform and the opening of ports in the east to legal trade with other nations.[5] Blacks and mulattos in the east regarded Haitian rule as an improvement over the Spanish colonial government and preferred it to an independent but white-dominated state.

Thus, the period of unification with Haiti (1822–44), so often identified as the founding moment of the Haitian-Dominican conflict, was neither an "invasion" nor an "occupation," and the history of this period does not point to a fatal hatred

between the two countries. Unfortunately, the myth that the two states and their people have always been at odds with each other is still being etched into the minds of many Dominicans by the country's schools and official information media.

The political destruction of popular presidential candidate José Francisco Peña Gómez shows how powerful this anti-Haitian bias remains. During his campaigns for the Dominican presidency in 1994 and 1996, Peña's Haitian ancestry made him the target of openly racist slurs and innuendoes that he was secretly disloyal to the Dominican Republic. Nevertheless, nearly 50 percent of Dominicans voted for him.[6]

JON ANDERSON

Picking up garbage from a batey next to La Duquesa dump. These men are called "buzos" (divers) and are a mix of both Haitians and Dominicans. Many of them are former cane cutters, reduced—due to the present economic decline of the industry—to foraging for resellable bottles, clothing, even rotting food.

Jean-François, a Haitian sugar cane cutter who has lived in the Dominican Republic for more than ten years, at a cane brake outside of San Pedro de Macorís.

Considering that a near-majority of Dominican voters chose *el haitiano*—the nickname by which Peña was widely known on the streets of Santo Domingo—to be their president, could anti-Haitianism really have so powerful a hold on the Dominican imagination as most observers seem to think?[7] There is considerable evidence that large segments of the Dominican population, especially those who have frequent daily contact with Haitians, do not reject all things Haitian.[8]

The Immigration Issue

There is a Haitian-Dominican struggle taking place on the island of Hispaniola, but it focuses on the specific issue of immigration. The struggle is not over the island but over control of the large Haitian immigrant population in the Dominican Republic—as many as half a million people, by some estimates. It is a contest between politicians who seek to score points against their opponents by raising a scare about uncontrolled immigration.

In other words, history, language, and culture are not the main sources of tension between Haiti and the Dominican Republic. Rather, Dominicans' anti-Haitian feelings stem from anti-Haitian propaganda, reinforced by popular Dominican resentment of immigrant laborers from Haiti who are willing to work for low wages.[9]

Does this mean that relations between the two nations will improve? Not if one considers recent examples of other social groups—Hutus and Tutsis in Burundi and Rwanda, or Croats, Serbs, and Bosnian Muslims in the former Yugoslavia—who share significantly more culturally than Haitians and Dominicans, but even so have killed each other en masse. Yet I think it is still important to be as accurate as we can in specifying what really divides the island of Hispaniola into two social entities. Focusing on the cultural distance between the two nations distracts from the root causes of their conflict. ✵

criollo: Dominican-born
el haitiano: "the Haitian"
mulatto: of mixed African and European descent

Dominican children of Haitian descent sing the national anthem during an annual citizenship awareness campaign by MUDHA (El Movimiento de Mujeres Dominico-Haitiana).

COURTESY OF JOCELYN SANTANA

NOTES

1. Franklin J. Franco, *Historia del pueblo dominicano*, ed. Raymundo González, Michiel Baud, Pedro L. San Miguel, and Roberto Cassá (Santo Domingo: Sociedad Editorial Dominicana, 1993), 176–77; Frank Moya Pons, *La dominación haitiana*, 1822–1844 (Santiago, Dominican Republic: Universidad Católica Madre y Maestra, 1972), 34.

2. Moya Pons, *La dominación haitiana*, 22–23.

3. Franco, *Historia del pueblo Dominicano*, 182–84.

4. Ibid, 181.

5. Ibid, 186–88.

6. Peña Gómez died of cancer in May 1998.

7. Silvio Torres-Saillant, "The Tribulations of Blackness: Stages in Dominican Racial Identity," *Latin American Perspectives* 25, no. 3 (1998): 133.

8. Carlos Dore Cabral, "Los dominicanos de origen haitiano y la segregación social en la República Dominicana," *Estudios Sociales* 20, no. 68 (1987): 57–80.

9. Bernardo Vega, "Etnicidad y el futuro de las relaciones domínico-haitianas," *Estudios Sociales* 26, no. 94 (1993): 31.

THE MASSACRE RIVER

Michele Wucker

The Massacre River, which follows part of the border between the Dominican Republic and Haiti, is named for a slaughter of French pirates that took place under Spanish colonial rule. But it is better known for a more recent tragedy, one that has played a symbolic role in Haitian-Dominican relations for more than sixty years. In this piece, author Michele Wucker describes the massacre of approximately 15,000 Haitians on the Dominican side of the river by dictator Rafael Trujillo's forces in October 1937.

Medias montañas,
Medios rios,
y hasta la muerte compartida.

Between them mountains,
Between them rivers,
And even a shared death.

—Manuel Rueda, "Cantos de la frontera" (Songs of the border)

The Artibonite River begins high in the Dominican Republic's Cordillera Central mountain range. It runs west, then curves south, parallel to the Carretera Internacional, the highway along the north-south border dividing the island of Hispaniola into east and west. The road is an international highway in the sense that it is the only direct route through the very center of the island, right along the Dominican-Haitian border. Rather than the grand thoroughfare its name suggests, the International Highway is a maze of rocks, crevasses, and quicksand strung together through the mountains that helped give Haiti its name, from an indigenous Taíno word meaning "high place" or "mountain." It can take a whole day to travel, though it is less than two hundred kilometers long, beginning in the south at San Juan de la Maguana and ending in the north at Dajabón, by another river, the Massacre.

The Artibonite River links the two countries. The Massacre River, and the terrible events that occurred in 1937 along the border formed by its waters, separates them…

…

Smooth, sweet Dominican rum was poured liberally at the festivities in the border town of Dajabón on the night of October 2, 1937. Doña Isabel Mayer, a wealthy Dominican who owned much of the surrounding land, was giving a banquet at her home in honor of the President himself, Generalissimo Rafael Leónidas Trujillo Molina, Great Benefactor of the Nation and Father of the New Dominion. For Trujillo, the trip was a break from the headaches of the capital. He had just received reports that opponents of his regime were plotting against him. In his own

Reprinted from *Why the Cocks Fight: Dominicans, Haitians, and the Struggle for Hispaniola* (New York: Hill and Wang). ©1999 by Michele Wucker. Reprinted by arrangement with Writers House, LLC as agent for Michele Wucker.

sinister way, Trujillo had sent out his spies and gunmen to satisfy himself that he was not materially threatened. Still, the incidents troubled him. This trip was his second to the remote northwest border. It took place just two months after he had gone there in August to inspect the beginnings of the new International Highway, the center point of his grand plan to link the north and south and to fortify the Dominican presence on the border. So little work had been accomplished on the highway that he and his entourage had had to ride in on mule back to get to the project that drew a line between two points through nowhere.

The border itself was officially only eight years old. When Dominican President Horacio Vásquez and Haiti's President, Louis Borno, drew a permanent border in 1929, the strokes of their pens had created a large foreign population on Dominican land. After so many years of ambiguity, the people who lived in the central regions and who were now arbitrarily assigned a new country were not about to move just so they could live on Haitian-Dominican territory. Haitians did not stop speaking Kreyol, even though the land they lived on now happened to be Dominican. With time, the people might have begun to match the nationalities the new boundaries assigned them. But for Trujillo, later was not soon enough.

A decade earlier, waves of Haitians had crossed into the Dominican Republic to find work cutting cane on the vast sugar plantations, which were pushing to export more and more to a market that paid more than twenty cents a pound for the sweet white stuff. But in 1929, when Black Monday hit, catapulting world markets into the Great Depression, sugar fell immediately to just four cents a pound, then later to two. With the market all but destroyed for Dominicans' biggest export, Haitian workers were no longer needed. Throughout the 1930s, therefore, Dominicans had been seeking ways to send the Haitians packing. In July 1937, a new law forced foreigners to register with migration officials. Later that summer, Dominican authorities deported eight thousand Haitians who did not have proper papers. But these deportations barely assuaged the Dominicans, who were angry about the country's economic straits. For six years, Trujillo had ordered local military posts to submit to him thrice-monthly reports of the results of their patrols of the Dominican-Haitian border.

On his first trip to the border in August 1937, Trujillo was surprised to see so many Haitians around, even though a thousand or more had been coerced into working on the new highway. It also struck him as strange that there were no cattle on the grassy expanses in the valley around Pedro Santana. Peasants and town officials at each little town along the new highway responded that Haitians had stolen their livestock. Trujillo called Lieutenant Colonel Manuel Emilio "Niñí" Castillo, chief military official of the north of the Dominican Republic, to meet him in Dajabón to discuss the alleged Haitian incursions across the border.

By October, rumors were flying about "incidents" concerning Haitians. A few days before Trujillo's visit, the Montecristi provincial governor had complained that three hundred deported Haitians had returned to the hills around Montecristi. In response, the Interior Ministry had been alerted and the army mobilized. Whispers passed that just south of Dajabón, Dominican soldiers had killed a group of Haitians. In Sabaneta, it was said, Haitians had died. Other reports circulated of deaths in confrontations between Dominican soldiers and Haitians awaiting deportation from barbed-wire detention camps.

The tension did not dampen the festivities surrounding Trujillo's visit; indeed, they seemed to heighten the revelry. Amid the jovial atmosphere at Doña Isabel's banquet for him, Trujillo assured the guests: "I have learned here that the Haitians have been robbing food and cattle from the ranchers. To you, Dominicans, who have complained of this pillaging committed by the Haitians who live among you, I answer: I will solve the problem. Indeed, we have already begun. Around three hundred Haitians were killed in Bánica. The solution must continue." For emphasis, the drunken dictator banged his fist on the table.

In the wee hours of October 3, the formal killing of Haitians began. No longer a series of isolated incidents, the confrontation on the border became a massacre. "That day, such horrors took place under the torrential rain that your mouth tasted of ashes, that the air was bitter to breathe, that shame weighed down on your heart,

Every market day at Dajabón on the Río Massacre, Haitians from the town of Juana Méndez (Ouanementhe in Kreyol) come to sell various homemade goods as well as items they receive from U.S. aid programs (new clothing for example). Rather than wait on line to cross the border, many try to cross the river to get a head start. Border guards patrol the shore with a mix of jokes, threats, stones thrown, and occasional physical force, as they attempt to stem the tide, but it is an impossible task.

and the flavor of all life indeed was repugnant. You would never have imagined that such things could come to pass on Dominican soil," the Haitian author Jacques Stephen Alexis wrote later in his novel about the massacre, *Compère Général Soleil.* (Alexis himself became a martyr in 1961, stoned to death in Haiti for his efforts to unseat Dictator François Duvalier.)

Trujillo's soldiers used their guns to intimidate but not to kill. For that, they used machetes, knives, picks, and shovels so as not to leave bullets in the corpses. Bullet-riddled bodies would have made it obvious that the murderers were government soldiers, who unlike most Dominicans had guns. But death by machete can be blamed on peasants, on

simple men of the countryside rising up to defend their cattle and lands. Even a bayonet leaves wounds enough like those of a simple knife that the true authors of the crime can be masked. This elaborate façade left out one crucial detail: if the massacre was, indeed, the result of a Dominican peasant uprising against the Haitians, why were there no casualties on the Dominican side? And why did a number of Dominicans, at a great risk to their own lives and livelihoods, hide Haitians in efforts to protect them from Trujillo's murderers?

In the early fall of 1937, the border patrols were heightened; yet reports that came in every ten days failed to mention their sinister achievements at Manzanillo Bay, Tierra Sucia, Capotillo,

El Aguacate, La Peñita, El Cajuil, Santiago de la Cruz. But the tales of survivors brought out the truth. Trujillo's men searched the houses and estates of the region one by one, rounded up Haitians, and initiated deportation proceedings against them; once the paperwork was done, the Dominican government had "proof" that the Haitians had been sent back to Haiti. The Haitians then were transported like cattle to isolated killing grounds, where the soldiers slaughtered them at night, carried the corpses to the Atlantic port at Montecristi, and threw the bodies to the sharks. For days, the waves carried uneaten body parts back onto Hispaniola's beaches.

Often, the soldiers did not even bother with the charade of

covering up their crimes. Entire families were mutilated in their homes. For Haitians not actually in their homes—in the streets or in the fields—the soldiers applied a simple test. They would accost any person with dark skin. Holding up sprigs of parsley, Trujillo's men would ask their prospective victims: *"¿Cómo se llama ésto?"* What is this thing called? The terrified victim's fate lay in the pronunciation of the answer. Haitians whose *Bateyes* uses a wide, flat *r*, find it difficult to pronounce the trilled *r* in the Spanish word for parsley, *perejil*. If the word came out as the Haitian *pe'sil*, or a bastardized Spanish *pewehi*, the victim was condemned to die. The Dominicans would later nickname the massacre *El Corte*, the Harvest: so many human beings cut down like mere stalks of sugarcane at harvest time.

Yet the Haitians who lived from cane cutting escaped the blades of the bayonets and machetes. Trujillo, having gauged just how far he could take his maniacal plan, stayed clear of the plantations owned by the Americans, as Robert Crassweller has recounted; these owners refused to hand over their workers. Even so, strange things happened on the sugar cane fields, which had drawn Haitians to the eastern end of the island in the first place. In late September, Ingenio Porvenir, a sugar mill near the southeastern coastal town of San Pedro de Macorís, had requested and received permission to import Haitian workers for the 1937–38 harvest. But in the first week of October, while Trujillo's henchmen were carrying out the massacre, the sugar mill mysteriously had its permit revoked.

For Haitians who had worked their way to professions more lucrative than cane cutting, *El Corte* showed no mercy. The few who managed to escape to safety in Haiti arrived across the border in the town of Ouanaminthe (pronounced Wahna-ment) with grisly reports of their ordeals. A man named Cime Jean fled to Ouanaminthe from El Fundo during the massacre, barely escaping the hands of the Dominican soldiers. After an early morning of work, he reported, he had returned home to see Dominican soldiers entering his back yard. Thinking their presence had to do with an arrest, he fled before they saw him. When he returned hours later, he found slain on the ground outside his house nearly all his family: his forty-year-old wife, his parents-in-law, his three children, his nephew and the nephew's six children, two cousins, his daughter-in-law and her two children. Cime Jean's son escaped with his life but not his mind, tormented by the horrors he had seen. When Cime Jean passed by his neighbors' homes, he saw the same brutality repeated. Telling Haitian authorities at Ouanaminthe about what he had seen, he estimated the dead at sixty. His story was just one of tens of thousands.

Loyal servants of Dominicans were not spared, nor were Haitian husbands and wives of Dominicans. Sometimes, if they were lucky, the victims convinced their murderers to let their children flee to Haiti. "The children cry in Spanish now. Who will understand them in Haiti?" the Dominican Freddy Prestol Castillo wrote in his novel about the massacre, *El masacre se pasa a pie (You can cross the Massacre on foot).*

As the killing progressed, reports of the carnage leaked out of the Dominican Republic. Not wanting to bother with criticism from the world, Trujillo finally, after the massacre had gone on for more than a week, ordered an end on October 8. The worst excesses ceased, though some of Trujillo's men took an additional week or so to finish off the remaining details, giving up the fiction of machetes and kitchen knives and resorting to rifles to complete their vicious assignment more efficiently.

By the time *El Corte* was finished, Trujillo's men had the blood of at least 15,000 Haitians on their hands. Haitian President Elie Lescot put the death toll at 12,168; in 1953, the Haitian historian Jean Price-Mars cited 12,136 deaths and 2,419 injuries. In 1975, Joaquín Balaguer, the Dominican Republic's interim Foreign Minister at the time of the massacre, put the number of dead at 17,000. Other estimates compiled by the Dominican historian Bernardo Vega were as high as 35,000. ❁

Doña: title of respect for an older woman

indigenous: native to a particular place

Taíno: indigenous people living on Hispaniola when Columbus arrived

Kreyol: language of Haiti (Haitian Creole)

PEREJIL

Edwidge Danticat

Born in Port-au-Prince in 1969, Edwidge Danticat was raised by an aunt in Haiti after her parents emigrated to New York. When Danticat joined her parents in Brooklyn at the age of twelve, she spoke only French and Haitian Creole. Two years later she published her first writing in English. In 1995 her collection of stories, Krik? Krak!, *was enthusiastically received and nominated for a National Book Award. She has published three novels to wide acclaim:* Breath, Eyes, Memory *(1994),* The Farming of Bones *(1998), and* The Dew Breakers *(2004).*

The Farming of Bones *is historical fiction set in 1937, when the Dominican dictator, Generalissimo Rafael Trujillo Molina, ordered the slaughter of Haitians on the Dominican side of the border. The story is told from the perspective of Amabelle, a young Haitian woman who is a servant in the house of a Dominican army officer. In this excerpt, Amabelle and her traveling companions, Yves, Wilner, and Odette, try to flee back to Haiti during the massacre by crossing the Artibonite River. In the chaos, she has become separated from her lover Sebastien, a cane cutter. If Amabelle and her companions are caught by Dominican soldiers, they will be challenged to pronounce the Spanish word* perejil. *Saying instead the Kreyòl word* pèsi, *and thus betraying their Haitian origins, will mean certain death.*

As we walked out of the palm grove, we found a tree-arched path leading down to the river. From a distance, the water looked deep and black, the bank much steeper than I remembered. Chin-high grass surrounded the spot Wilner chose for our crossing. The bridge lay far ahead, the curve of its iron girders dotted with night lights. The lamps moved from one end of the bridge to the next, making the distant sentinels seem like giant fireflies.

We waited for some time to see if some guards would be coming that way. There were none in sight except for the sentinels at the bridge.

"We can perhaps cross now," Wilner said.

There was a splash from upstream; something had dropped from the bridge.

"They are throwing corpses into the water," Odette whispered.

"Don't listen," responded Wilner. "We need only look for the guards on patrol. I will go in last."

The marshlands led abruptly to the water's edge. The river

From *The Farming of Bones* by Edwidge Danticat. (New York: Soho Press) © 1998 by Edwidge Danticat. Used by permission of the publisher.

reached up to our chests when Odette and I slipped in together. Odette turned her face back to the bank where Yves was still feeling his way in and to Wilner who was still watching the bridge.

A strong scent of wet grass and manure wafted through the current as we forded farther in. I tried to find footholds in the sand, wedges to anchor my feet. The water was so deep that it was like trying to walk on air.

When we were nearly submerged in the current, I yanked my hand from Odette's. I heard her sniffle, perhaps fearful and shocked. But I was only thinking of one thing: If I drowned, I wanted to drown alone, with nobody else's life to be responsible for.

An empty black dress buoyed past us, inflated by air, floating upon the water. It was followed by a clump of tree branches and three empty sisal knapsacks. A man floated past us, face down. I swam towards him and moved his head to the side.

Sebastien?

No.

I turned the head down again, wishing I knew a ceremonial prayer to recite over the body.

The water guided Odette downstream. She was not paddling or swimming but simply letting herself be cradled by the current; her head dipped under now and then, and when it came up again, she opened her mouth wide to gulp in the air.

I swam after her, grabbed her waist with one hand, and fended my way across with the other. When she raised her face above the current, she looked frightened, but stifled her coughs as the water spilled out of her mouth.

EDUARDO HOEPELMAN. COURTESY OF THE CUNY-DOMINICAN STUDIES INSTITUTE LIBRARY, CITY COLLEGE.

Edwidge Danticat.

Behind us on the shore, someone was calling to Wilner, "¡He! ¡He!"

We stopped our struggles immediately, letting the current carry us downstream.

I reached for Odette's mouth and sealed it with both my hands when the shot rang out. Wilner did not even have time to reply.

During the dull silence after the shot, the soldier called out to his friends not to fret, that it was him, Segundo, and he, Segundo, was fine. Odette bit deep into my palm, scraping the inside flesh with her top and bottom teeth.

It is the way you try to stun a half-dead bird still waving its wings, a headless chicken courageously racing down a dirt road. I kept one hand on her mouth and moved the other one to her nose and pressed down hard for her own good, for our own good. She did not struggle but abandoned her body to the water and the lack of air.

The soldier who had shot Wilner continued marching upstream. Perhaps if he had wanted to, he could have seen us, but maybe the river itself,

though good for discarding the corpses, was considered not favorable for shootings.

I covered Odette's body with mine and framed her in my arms as Yves and I continued swimming towards the shore.

Yves was the first to land on a sandbar on the other side of the river. He crawled back on his belly and pulled Odette away from my chest. Taking hold of a boulder, I eased myself out of the current.

We lay Odette facedown. Even though she was still breathing, she would not gain consciousness. It was as though she had already made her choice. She was not going on the rest of the journey with us.

All I had wanted was for her to be still, to do her part in helping us live.

Yves was staring down at Odette as though our futures were written in those eyes that she refused to open. She had saved us at the square, so we wanted to save her too.

He picked her up and carried her onto the dusky plains in the dark. Following the track inland, we approached a cluster of parrot trees whose furry leaves looked like soft hands reaching down from some higher place, encouraging us to pause once again and rest.

As we sat there with Odette under a canopy of trees in the middle of a grassy field, she spat up the chest full of water she had collected in the river. With her parting breath, she mouthed in Kreyòl "pèsi," not calmly and slowly as if she were asking for it at a roadside garden or open market, not questioning as if demanding of the face of Heaven the greater meaning of senseless acts, no effort to say "perejil" as if pleading for her life. Que diga amor? Love? Hate? Speak to me of things the world has yet to truly understand, of the instant meaning of each bird's call, of a child's secret thoughts in her mother's womb, of the measured rhythmical time of every man and woman's breath, of the true colors of the inside of the moon, of the larger miracles in small things, the deeper mysteries. But parsley? Was it because it was so used, so commonplace, so abundantly at hand that everyone who desired a sprig could find one? We used parsley for our food, our teas, our baths, to cleanse our insides as well as our outsides. Perhaps the Generalissimo in some larger order was trying to do the same for his country.

The Generalissimo's mind was surely as dark as death, but if he had heard Odette's "pèsi," it might have startled him, not the tears and supplications he would have expected, no shriek from unbound fear, but a provocation, a challenge, a dare. To the devil with your world, your grass, your wind, your water, your air, your words. You ask for perejil, I give you more. ❀

Generalissimo: Trujillo
Kreyòl: language of Haiti (Haitian Creole)
perejil: "parsley" in Spanish
pèsi: "parsley" in Kreyòl
Que diga amor?: Should I say "love"?

CROSSING THE MASSACRE RIVER

USE WITH: Units 61, 62

DURATION: 1 class

STANDARDS:

English Language Arts: 1, 2, 6, 8, 10

Social Studies: 2d, 3a, 3b, 3d, 4d, 4c, 4f, 4h, 6f

Foreign Language: 1.1, 1.3

GOAL: To explore the role of geographic factors during the Haitian massacre of 1937.

OBJECTIVES:

- To trace the geographic route between the Artibonite and Massacre rivers.

- To describe the connections between a historical essay and work of historical fiction.

ACTIVITIES:

1. Students read "The Massacre River" from *Why the Cocks Fight: Dominicans, Haitians and the Struggle for Hispaniola* (unit 61), paying special attention to geographic descriptions and localities. On a map of the Dominican Republic, students work in small groups to locate the various places mentioned in the reading. Using markers and other available indicators, students chart the distance from the Artibonite River to the Massacre River.

2. Students read "Perejil," from *The Farming of Bones* (unit 62). Each student writes a brief response and shares it with the class. The class discusses the historical event described in the chapter.

3. Break the class in two groups and ask each one to list the ways that history and fiction blend. Use the following questions to guide the discussion:

    - List the historical event discussed in "The Massacre River" that is also found in "Perejil."

    - In what ways, if any, does Danticat choose to adapt the event or maintain its historical accuracy? Why?

ASSESSMENT:

- Find an interview with Edwidge Danticat on the Internet where she discusses *The Farming of Bones* and her use of history. Students summarize her position in an essay. Teacher assesses essay.

- Websites and their content change frequently. Two that have

Lesson plan prepared by Jocelyn Santana.

featured interviews with Danticat are Haiti Global Village (http://www.haitiglobalvillage.com/sd-marassa1-cd/d-conversations.htm) and Penguin Putnam (http://www.penguinputnam.com/static/rguides/us/farming_of_bones.html).

MATERIALS:

- Markers or highlighters

- Blank paper and detailed maps of the Dominican Republic

TRUJILLO ON TRIAL

USE WITH: Units 61, 62

DURATION: 3 classes

STANDARDS:

English Language Arts: 1, 2, 3, 4, 7, 8, 9, 10

Social Studies: 1a, 1c, 1d, 1e, 2b, 2d, 4h, 10d

Foreign Language: 1, 2, 3, 4

GOAL: To examine a tragic event in Haitian and Dominican history.

OBJECTIVES:

* To demonstrate the ability to conduct research.

* To present information to the class about the 1937 massacre of Haitians by the Trujillo regime.

ACTIVITIES:

1. Students read "The Massacre River," from *Why the Cocks Fight: Dominicans, Haitians and the Struggle for Hispaniola* (unit 61), and "Perejil," from *The Farming of Bones* (unit 62).

2. Introduce the following prompt to students: The world is shocked by the 1937 massacre of Haitians by the regime of General Rafael Trujillo. Several countries decide to form an international group to investigate Trujillo. A committee consisting of a reporter, a historian, a linguist, a psychiatrist, and a Haitian woman convene to reconstruct the event and try to understand Trujillo's motivations in order to determine his fate.

3. Divide into groups to research various aspects of the 1937 massacre. Each group member assumes one of the following roles and conducts the corresponding research:

   * HISTORIAN: Provides historical background on Haiti and the Dominican Republic, and on the relations between the two countries.

   * REPORTER: Reports the facts of the massacre.

   * LINGUIST: Examines the significance of the word *perejil* (parsley) and the broader importance of language in the events surrounding the massacre.

   * PSYCHIATRIST: Researches Trujillo's likely personality disorders, including obsessions and examples of narcissism. Possible sources include vignettes from *Memory of Fire: Century of the Wind,* by Eduardo Galeano, and from *Something to Declare,* by Julia Alvarez (see list under "Materials").

Lesson plan prepared by Elise Weisenbach.

- ❖ AMABELLE, A HAITIAN WOMAN: Provides an eyewitness account of the 1937 massacre as described by Edwidge Danticat in "Perejil" from *The Farming of Bones* (unit 62).

4. Role-play and report findings about the history of Haiti and the Dominican Republic, the massacre of Haitians in 1937, and Rafael Trujillo's personality. The class will decide Trujillo's fate.

ASSESSMENT:

Group work, oral presentation, journal entry.

MATERIALS:

- Julia Alvarez, *Something to Declare* (New York: Penguin, 1998). See especially "A Genetics of Justice."

- Eduardo Galeano, *Memory of Fire: Century of the Wind* (New York: Pantheon Books, 1988). See especially the following vignettes:

    "1930 Santo Domingo: The Hurricane"

    "1936 Ciudad Trujillo: In Year Six of the Trujillo Era"

    "Procedure Against the Rain"

    "Procedure Against Disobedience"

    "1937 Dajabón: Procedure Against the Black Menace"

    "1937 Washington: Newsreel"

    "1939 Washington: Roosevelt"

    "1939 Washington: In Year Nine of the Trujillo Era"

    "1956 Santo Domingo: In Year Twenty-six of the Trujillo Era"

    "1961 Santo Domingo: In Year Thirty-one of the Trujillo Era"

    "1961 Santo Domingo: Defunctísimo"

LITTLE HAITI

Michele Wucker

In this article author Michele Wucker describes daily life in Little Haiti, a neighborhood in Santo Domingo where many Haitian immigrants live and work. Ironically, the suspicions and stereotypes faced by Haitian immigrants in Santo Domingo are similar to those encountered by Dominican immigrants in San Juan, Puerto Rico (see unit 23).

Tucked behind the tourist-filled Colonial Zone and spreading up to the Duarte shopping district, Little Haiti in Santo Domingo lies at the new crossroads between the Dominican Republic and Haiti. It clusters around the Modelo market, whose massive arched roof spreads over a labyrinth of stalls where Dominicans sell jewelry, handicrafts, Haitian artwork, vanilla, cheese, carved wood, leather goods, and candy. Strung along the front entrance, at the top of a staircase leading down to the street, are bottles of rum filled with herbs and spices, a Dominican medicinal concoction called *Mama Juana*. At the back of the covered market are the fish vendors. Down the back steps and outside is a great shed where fruit and vegetable sellers hawk their goods and where poultry merchants pile squawking chicken cages into pyramids next to their butcher blocks in the open air filled with flies.

You hear more Kreyòl than Spanish on the streets here. Many of the Haitians are passing only a few days, long enough to sell the truckloads of canned goods they bring from Port-au-Prince and buy enough food to load up again and make the trip back—one day of driving and two more days to clear customs at the border. A life-size statue of St. Lazarus peers out of a little *botánica*. The store sells religious articles honoring the spirits of Vodou disguised as Roman Catholic saints who can answer the prayers of the faithful. When colonial plantation owners forbade their African slaves from worshipping

Reprinted from *Why the Cocks Fight: Dominicans, Haitians, and the Struggle for Hispaniola* (New York: Hill and Wang). © 1999 by Michele Wucker. Reprinted by arrangement with Writers House, LLC as agent for Michele Wucker.

A brightly painted Haitian "tap-tap" bus in Santo Domingo's Little Haiti neighborhood.

the spirits of their motherland, the slaves used the names of Christian saints to conceal the identities of their African spirits. St. Lazarus is really Papa Legba, the Afro-Caribbean god of cross-roads who protects travelers who wander in and out of Little Haiti. Next to him, merchants sell bright little bottles of magic bath-water that trucks have brought from Haiti. The bottles carry their own magical promises: they will make you young, restore your health, enhance your beauty, bring you money, etc. The potion called *Vini vini* will convince a lover to come to you. *Ven acá* (come here) will do the same. You can believe in the powers of the magic water if you want. In a world where reality is something less than what you'd like it to be, seizing on a myth is often the only way to survive.

At the edges of the market, the loading docks and parking lots are filled with tap-taps—giant Haitian trucks painted like circus wagons—waiting to be loaded with goods. *Esperance, Travail, Christ Capable*—Hope, Work, Christ Can Do It—read the slogans painted in bright red, yellow, and blue on the front. Past the loading docks, the streets spoking out from the market are filled with shops where mer-chants peddle cloth, pots and pans, grains and sugar in massive bags threatening to burst, spare auto parts piled on greasy tables. In luxury Rocky and Montero jeeps, the Dominican owners of the shops drive past the tap-taps to survey the scene.

By day, the glaring sun beats down on the cooks frying food in the street, on the vendors selling oranges and coconuts from their wooden carts, on the men who simply stand around. In the cool of the night, or in the dark corners of certain tenement hotels in the afternoon, drug dealers peddle their goods, aware that in any place where people come to buy there is a market for the products of night as well as of day. Drug authorities raid this neighborhood often, hauling off either suspects or bribes. The Haitians are easy prey. Caught between worlds, their home is no longer Haiti. Nor is it the Domin-ican Republic, which does not welcome them. If they do not go along with the police, they can be deported or simply thrown in jail and forgotten.

Down the street and around the corner from the Modelo market, the walls are covered with graffiti: *Abajo Haiti! Fuera los Haitianos!* Down with Haiti! Haitians Get Out! These slogans are scribbled all around town, on the Haitian embassy, not far from the American embassy and the Dominican President's house, and on the walls around the Feria market in southwestern Santo Domingo. Under the scrawls are letters spelling ORDEN (ORDER), the name of an anti-Haitian group. The Haitians make easy scapegoats.

The merchants who do the best business work out of a huge street front room filled with tables. Store owners stream in and out of the wide doors as they look for wholesale clothes. From a table in a corner of the room, Ferdinand Alexy sells shirts and shoes. He walks with God: the wooden pendant he wears around his neck guarantees it; on the round disc is painted a Christ in agony, with blood dripping from the crown of thorns. Ferdinand, now twenty-eight years old, came to Santo Domingo's market in 1981, when his mother decided that life was better here than in Haiti. She traded clothes, and her son followed her path. Business is good enough to support Ferdinand's three children, ages one, two, and nine. He can even send some money back to his uncle, sister, and brother who still live in Haiti's Artibonite Valley. The family itself earns enough for food, but the fifty dollars a month Ferdinand can send back helps them get extras. He doesn't want to live in Haiti. "There's no security there," he says.

After four years in Little Haiti, Ferdinand's wife, Antoine, won't return even though she misses her family in Port-de-Paix. She waits anxiously for news of them in letters or through friends who arrive every day on the tap-taps that come from Haiti. "I'm not happy here," she says. "The Dominicans don't want us here." She learned a little Spanish, but it is hard because she has little contact with Dominicans: "I stay at home, I keep to myself." The Haitians here have learned to become invisible in order to survive. ✸

---

botánica: store selling religious and medicinal items
Colonial Zone: the oldest part of Santo Domingo, built by the early Spanish colonists
Kreyòl: language of Haiti (Haitian Creole)
Port-de-Paix: city on Haiti's north coast
Vodou: indigenous religion of Haiti

PART FIVE

THE NATIONAL GOES GLOBAL: DOMINICAN MUSIC AND BASEBALL

Young boys sit atop the outfield wall at Tetelo Vargas Stadium in San Pedro de Macorís holding nets affixed to poles to snag balls during batting practice before a Dominican winter league game.

MERENGUE: SYMBOL OF NATIONAL IDENTITY

Paul Austerlitz

In this article, ethnomusicologist Paul Austerlitz briefly traces the history of merengue and its development into a symbol of national identity for Dominicans living on the island and in the diaspora.

Merengue started in the mid-nineteenth century as ballroom dance music and a cousin to the European-descended *danza* then popular throughout the Caribbean. Merengue was distinguished by two features: it was danced by independent couples rather than in groups, and it contained Afro-Caribbean rather than European rhythms. Merengue was briefly popular in Dominican ballrooms, but was rejected by the elites because of a dance style that they considered lewd, and because of the music's African elements. The rural Dominican majority, however, adopted merengue and infused it with even more African influences.

Different types of merengue developed in several areas of the Dominican Republic, but only the Cibao region's version gained prominence. By the early twentieth century, *merengue típico cibaeño*, performed on the tambora, the güira, the button accordion, and the alto saxophone, was the top social music and dance in Cibao's countryside and barrios.

When the United States Marines occupied the Dominican Republic from 1916 to 1924,

Adapted from Paul Austerlitz, "Merengue: Music, Race and Nation in the Dominican Republic," in *Africana: The Encyclopedia of the African and African American Experience*, eds. Kwame Anthony Appiah and Henry Louis Gates, Jr. (New York: Basic Civitas Books). Copyright © 2000 by Afropaedia LLC. Reprinted by permission of Basic Civitas Books, a member of Perseus Books, L.L.C.

Dancing to orquesta merengue in New York City, 1990.

PAUL AUSTERLITZ

they met widespread resistance. Rural populations waged guerrilla warfare, while the urban upper classes mounted an international protest on the diplomatic front. The diplomatic campaign went hand in hand with a passionate cultural nationalism in which islanders embraced all things Dominican. The song "La Protesta," written during the eight-year occupation, shows how this patriotism spread to merengue.

Prior to the U.S. occupation, upper-class Dominicans had rejected both local Afro-Caribbean and modern North American music. They favored European music such as the waltz, polka, and *danza*. With the U.S. occupation, however, composers in the Cibao city of Santiago began to write music based on merengue and other local forms. Influenced by this trend, the leader of the Cibao's top dance band, Juan Espínola, became popular by performing refined merengues for ballroom dancing. By the 1920s and 1930s these ballroom dance bands also became influenced by jazz-tinged popular music that the Marines had introduced into the Dominican Republic. Of course, many of those who were against the Yankee occupation did not totally embrace the music brought by the invaders, but in 1933 another Santiago bandleader, Luis Alberti, had the idea of fusing merengue with big-band jazz. This new merengue style soon found a permanent place in the dance band repertoires.

Meanwhile, poorer residents of rural and urban barrios in the Cibao region continued to dance to accordion-based merengue. Two types of *merengue típico*

cibaeño were popular, and both are still played today. One was a three-part sectional form simply called merengue; the other was a one-part form called the *pambiche*. While it is probable that both already existed before the U.S. occupation, the *pambiche* is often said to have originated during this period. As the story goes, U.S. Marines sometimes went to local fiestas but were unable to dance merengue correctly, combining fox-trot with merengue steps. Imitating the North Americans, Dominicans in the town of Puerto Plata created a dance called "Yankee-style merengue." The new dance became associated with a song about Palm

Beach, the Florida city. The new style of music therefore was called *pambiche*, a Dominicanization of the words Palm Beach. The anecdote about this music's origin shows how a politically dominated people could still make a strong cultural statement. Dominicans couldn't contend with U.S. military might, but their superiority on the dance floor was unquestioned, and they even created a new genre out of the Marines' choreographic clumsiness!

The Dominican dictator Rafael Trujillo rose to power in 1930. In spite of his own African blood, Trujillo supported a racist idea of Dominicanness that excluded African contribu-

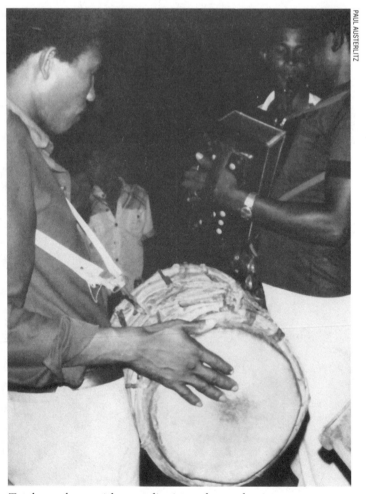

Tambora player with accordionist and saxophonist.

Merengue musicians playing accordion, marimba, tambora, and güira for tourists in Santo Domingo, Dominican Republic, 1985.

tions to the nation's culture. He elevated merengue to a national symbol, but favored a "cleaned-up" version of the music in which the African content was not apparent. In 1936 Trujillo brought Luis Alberti's band, renamed Orquesta Presidente Trujillo, from Santiago to the capital city of Santo Domingo to play big-band arrangements of merengue at high-society balls. From then on, the country's dance bands were required to perform newly composed merengues praising the dictator. This national music became a staple of radio broadcasts.

New Influences

After Trujillo was assassinated in 1961, the Dominican Republic opened to outside influences as never before. Bandleader Johnny Ventura and arranger Luis Pérez incorporated salsa elements and rock 'n' roll performance style into an exuberant, faster merengue. This new form of merengue abandoned jazz band instrumentation in favor of a smaller *conjunto* format consisting of tambora, güira, piano, bass, singers, and two to six wind instruments.

The women's movement in the mid-1970s facilitated the development of female merengue bands. Millie y los Vecinos in particular became very popular through their lyrics that empowered women. A member of the group, Jocelyn Quezada, described how many women identified with the lyrics of their songs:

We were making a statement, because Dominican men are very male chauvinist; I mean, women stay home and cook. So, when we stood up in front of a band…women in the audience would identify with us. And the songs that we used to sing, we were attacking men: if you don't take care of your woman, you're going to lose her. So we had a lot of women fans, we still do.[1]

Throughout the late twentieth century, typically rural, accordion-based merengue remained important. While rural groups and those playing for tourists stuck to the traditional style, groups in the Cibao city of Santiago developed a new form of *merengue típico* that added conga drums and electric bass to the traditional line-up of accordion, saxophone, tambora, and güira. These groups became popular during the merengue boom, and today, they perform alongside top merengue bands in nightclubs throughout the Dominican Republic and in the diaspora. Because it combines both tradition and modernity,

Merengue icon Johnny Ventura and his band.

Dominicans sometimes call this music *merengue típico moderno*.

At the same time, urban musicians have adopted aspects of rural merengue. In the late 1990s, for example, the New York City–based Dominican group Fulanito gained fame with their dramatic use of merengue accordion patterns, combined with rural sounds, urban hip-hop, and house music.

Merengue has gone beyond national borders. Massive out-migration followed Trujillo's assassination, and by 1990, hundreds of thousands of Dominicans were estimated to be living in New York City alone. Access to the international Latin music markets gained new audiences for merengue among non-Dominicans; it even usurped salsa's position as the most-requested Latin Caribbean dance by the late 1970s. Bandleaders Wilfredo Vargas and Juan Luis Guerra led the way in the "internationalization of merengue." Merengue became an important marker of identity for Dominicans in the diaspora, serving as a form of resistance to the North American culture that surrounded them.

Still popular today, Guerra's songs often offer social commentaries on Dominican society, focusing on topics such as social injustice, poverty, and immigration. "Visa para un Sueño"[2] is one of his most famous songs, almost an anthem to the hardships of immigration that so many Dominicans have faced. ❀

conga: tall, tapered single-headed drum played with the hands
conjunto: combo
güira: metal scraper
merengue estilo yanqui: Yankee-style merengue
merengue típico: folk merengue
merengue típico cibaeño: Cibao-style folk merengue
merengue típico moderno: modern folk merengue
tambora: double-headed drum played with sticks
visa para un sueño: visa for a dream

NOTES

1. Paul Austerlitz, *Merengue: Dominican Music and Dominican Identity* (Philadelphia: Temple University Press, 1997), 117.
2. From *Grandes Exitos de Juan Luis Guerra y 440* (compact disc, Karen Publishing Co., 2000).

VISA PARA UN SUEÑO

USE WITH: Units 19, 66

DURATION: 1 class

STANDARDS:

English Language Arts: 1, 2, 4, 6, 10

Social Studies: 1g, 4b, 4c, 5b, 10c

Foreign Language: 1, 2, 3, 4.2

GOAL: To examine the visa process through merengue music.

OBJECTIVE: To interpret merengue lyrics.

ACTIVITIES:

1. Listen to "Visa para un Sueño" (Visa for a Dream), by Juan Luis Guerra, and follow the song lyrics (available in Spanish inside CD cover).

2. Discuss the lyrics and their meaning through the following questions:
   - What kind of visa is the song referring to?
   - What is the dream?
   - People are often refused visas. What are their options in that case? How do you know this?
   - In the second stanza, in "everyone has his price," who is "everyone?" Explain.
   - How do you think some people feel as they apply for a visa? What might be their worries and hopes? Support your answer with references to the lyrics. "At the Consulate," the excerpt from *Muddy Cup: A Dominican Family Comes of Age in a New America* (unit 19), also addresses the visa process and can be used in conjunction with this lesson plan.

ASSESSMENT:

Assess students' ability to accurately interpret the song and describe the visa process and its effects. For example, the teacher can group students into pairs and ask them to role play an American consul at the U.S. embassy in Santo Domingo and a Dominican citizen applying for a visa. Each pair writes a script of questions and answers that might form part of the visa interview.

MATERIALS:

- "Visa para un Sueño" by Juan Luis Guerra (track 4 on *Grandes Exitos de Juan Luis Guerra y 440*, compact disc, Karen Publishing Co., 2000)
- CD player
- Song lyrics (available in Spanish inside CD cover)

Lesson plan prepared by Mike Croft.

MERENGUE: SYMBOL OF NATIONAL IDENTITY

USE WITH: Unit 66

DURATION: 1 class

STANDARDS:

English Language Arts: 1, 3, 4, 9, 10

Social Studies: 1c, 1d, 4b, 4c, 4f, 5a

Foreign Language: 1, 2, 3, 4.2

GOAL: To explore the meaning of national identity.

OBJECTIVE:

- To compare symbols of national identity in the Dominican Republic and the United States.

ACTIVITIES:

1. Read "Merengue: Symbol of National Identity" (unit 66).

2. Ask students:

   - What is national identity?

   - What kinds of symbols do people use to represent national identity?

   - Why do many Dominicans consider merengue to be a symbol of national identity?

   - How did merengue become such a symbol?

   - Over the years, have you identified (or associated your life experiences) with the lyrics of a song?

3. As a class, brainstorm symbols of national identity in the United States. Would most people agree that these symbols are representative of the United States? Why or why not?

ASSESSMENT:

Each student chooses a symbol of national identity (can be associated with any country). The student brings in a photograph or other example of this symbol and explains to the class how it expresses national identity. Teacher assesses for comprehension of the term national identity and correct use of symbols.

Lesson plan prepared by Anne Gallin.

"IT'S NOT JUST ABOUT DANCING..."

Interview with Pedro Tavarez

Pedro Tavarez was born in 1966 in Villa Juana, a neighborhood of Santo Domingo. When he was eighteen he moved to Washington Heights in northern Manhattan to finish high school at Louis D. Brandeis High School on 84th Street. Pedro received his B.A. in public administration and is currently working toward a Master's degree at John Jay College of Criminal Justice.

In addition to his job at the New York City Department of Education, Pedro spent ten years playing the tambora and conga drums in numerous bands. He reflects on his experiences as a percussionist and on his life, spent half in the Dominican Republic and half in the United States.

Pedro Tavarez was interviewed by Anne Gallin on November 1, 2003, in New York City.

I didn't have any formal training as a musician. It was a family thing, something in my genes, I guess. My grandfather used to live in Puerto Rico, and every time he came to the Dominican Republic he used to bring some kind of instrument. I remember him giving me a güiro, a maraca. I was probably six or seven years old. Eventually I started playing for all the little groups.

My family used to get together for birthday parties, baptisms, christenings, and each time we would bring some kind of instrument. We used to gather almost every Sunday and play music and dance all day long—music from Johnny Pacheco,

Dancing to accordionist Adolfo Díaz's merengue típico moderno group in New York City, 1990.

Pedro Tavarez teaches Connecticut teacher Karianna Rosenberg to play the tambora, a double sided drum.

Eddie Palmieri, the Fania All Stars, Willie Colon. The other musicians used to bring their own congas, bongos, and güiras.[1] They would play a record and we would play along with it. So it became a huge party for the whole neighborhood.

I started to play professionally when I came here, in my mid-twenties. A group needed a tambora player. They asked me, "Would you like to play for us?" and I said, "But I never played." They said, "Neither one of us has played professionally." Then another group called me to join them and I started jumping from one group to another until I was able to put my own band together with my friends. It was called The Latin Band. My friend was

the musical leader, and I was the manager. I used to get in touch with the club owners and set the price and then pay the rest of the musicians.

We would practice once a week and perform at least twice a week. On Fridays and Saturdays, sometimes we would play in two different places in the same night. Well, I was young then, and we had the energy to jump from one place to another. We were doing it not just for the money, but for fun. Most of us were single guys, and we liked the adventure.

New and Old Bachata

When I was growing up I was exposed to salsa and merengue, so that's why I like salsa so much. The younger

generation likes bachata, because that's what they hear every day. Personally, I really don't like the new types of bachata. Of course I can dance it, I can play it. But it's not the same bachata that I listened to years ago. I like the old bachata, because it used more instruments. Now it's just the guitar.

Bachata lyrics are all about the same. This person is suffering because that person left him. We call that *amargue*. "You left me and what am I going to do? I'm going to kill myself." But some groups like Aventura are singing other kinds of lyrics. And I've always liked Juan Luis Guerra because he doesn't write just *amargue* or melancholic lyrics. He writes about the things that affect people's lives—politics, economics, religion—and people struggling to live better.

Bacharengue is a combination of merengue and bachata. It's merengue because it's fast, but it's bachata because it has the guitars.

Favorite Musicians

For merengue, I love Johnny Ventura because I've been listening to him ever since I was born. Wilfrido Vargas, yeah. Fernando Villalona, he's part of my upbringing. And I like Oro Sólido very much because it's one of the most dynamic groups.

I think Juan Luis Guerra is one of the best composers who can really say who we are as Dominicans. I don't know if you remember his song about the discovery of America, "El Costo de la Vida" (The Cost of Living).[2] It talks about the fact

that we still live as they did when Christopher Columbus came to America. It talks about the building of the lighthouse in the Dominican Republic: we know that they took a lot of money from the people just to build something that wasn't really necessary.[3] He tells exactly what's going on. And this is a big deal because we have somebody who could actually travel internationally and bring merengue music to other people. He's a smart guy, he knows how to deal with the public, so people don't see merengue just as music to dance or move the hips to, but also as music to listen to. I would say that most people really pay attention to the lyrics. It's not just about dancing but also about what he's trying to say.

Johnny Ventura was a big star in the 1970s. He used to

live in Villa Juana, so he represented us. And he became, for many years, the most famous merengue player internationally. He's very educated, a very nice guy, very humble. And of course, poor, black... He had all that negative stuff that could prevent somebody from succeeding, but then he did it. He made it, so he's a big role model to all of us. If he made it, we can also.

As for female performers, Millie Quezada, to me she's the best. Fefita la Grande plays what's called typical merengue, *merengue típico,* and I like her too. But for modern merengue it's definitely Millie.

I like the music from La Banda Gorda also. The song "Aquí, Pero Allá" is definitely not just about the Dominican Republic. It's about Dominicans living elsewhere and that's a

COURTESY OF PEDRO TAVAREZ

Pedro Tavarez plays the tambora (two-sided drum) behind the singers of his group, the Latin Band.

reality. That's the way you feel about the Dominican Republic, always dreaming about going back. That brings up issues for people who want to stay here, and people who want to go back. That is definitely a great song that we identify with.[4]

His Future Back Home

I always thought that I would go back to the Dominican Republic and stay there. I never thought about the United States as a land for me to stay in. My mother retired not too long ago and she bought a house there. It's always on my mind that whenever I retire or get tired of being here, I will definitely go back and live in the Dominican Republic. There's more to do there. You have more time to enjoy yourself, your family, outdoor activities and friends, and, well, the music itself. Something there calls me back to live and stay there til I die.

I like the idea of raising kids there, then eventually bringing them over here so they could complete high school and get a nice job, and then moving back there. That's the way I did it, so I would like to have my kids do the same thing. That way they have both countries' influence. Because it has been a good experience for me to have been part of both cultures. ✵

bongos: two small single-headed drums joined side by side, played with the hands

conga: tall, tapered single-headed drum played with the hands

güira: metal scraper

güiro: wooden scraper

maraca: shaker filled with small wooden balls

merengue típico: folk merengue

tambora: double-headed drum played with sticks

NOTES

1. The güiro is made of wood and is mostly used to play salsa and charanga. It is related to the maraca. The güira is a metal instrument and is mostly used by merengue and bachata players.

2. From *Grandes Exitos de Juan Luis Guerra y 440* (compact disc, Karen Publishing, 2000).

3. President Joaquín Balaguer spent millions of dollars to build a lighthouse commemorating the arrival of Christopher Columbus in the Americas. The project was widely criticized in the Dominican Republic.

4. From Peña Suazo y su Banda Gorda, *Aquí, Pero Allá* (compact disc, MT & VI Distributors, 1999).

INTERVIEW WITH PEDRO TAVAREZ

USE WITH: Unit 69

DURATION: 2 classes

STANDARDS:

English Language Arts: 1, 4, 5, 7, 9, 10

Social Studies: 1a, 1c, 1d, 1e, 4b, 4c, 4f, 4h, 5b

Foreign Language: 1, 2, 3, 4.2

GOAL: To analyze an interview with a Dominican musician.

OBJECTIVES:

- To develop Spanish language skills by writing and conducting a mock interview.
- To familiarize students with the experiences of Dominican musicians in New York City.
- To practice the use of Spanish grammar features (*ser* and *estar*, interrogative, the indicative and subjunctive moods).

ACTIVITIES:

1. Students read "'It's not just about dancing . . .': Interview with Pedro Tavarez" (unit 69).

2. Divide the class into two sections. Section 1 discusses Pedro Tavarez's life while section 2 discusses Dominican music and musicians.

3. Divide each section into groups of three and distribute instructions and criteria for simulating an interview with Pedro Tavarez.

4. Student groups write their interview questions and answers and then conduct the interview in front of the class. Teachers may wish to specify that the interviews be conducted in either Spanish or English.

ASSESSMENT:

Teacher assesses the essay and oral presentation for grammar and cultural content.

MATERIALS:

- Criteria for simulated interview

Lesson plan prepared by Elise Weisenbach.

CRITERIA FOR SIMULATED INTERVIEW

Section 1: Biography of Pedro Tavarez

Names of students in group: _____

_____

_____

• Pretend that you are interviewing Pedro Tavarez. You want the students at your school to learn about his life and about life in the Dominican Republic.

• Based on the interview with Pedro that you have read, create interview questions and responses using the information in column 1.

• Select one person to play the role of Pedro Tavarez. Other students will be the interview panel for an oral presentation to the class. If the interview is conducted in Spanish, be sure to incorporate the grammar in column 2.

1 Content	2 Grammar
Date of birth Place of birth Education Occupation	Ser/estar Present, imperfect, preterite tenses
What Tavarez used to do with his family when he was young His experiences as a professional musician	Imperfect and preterite tenses
His hopes for returning to the Dominican Republic Lifestyle on the island The value of being part of two cultures	Future tense, perfect tense

CRITERIA FOR SIMULATED INTERVIEW

Section 2: Dominican Music and Musicians

Names of students in group: _____

_____

_____

- Pretend that you are interviewing Pedro Tavarez. You want the students at your school to learn about the music and musicians of the Dominican Republic.

- Based on the interview with Pedro that you have read, create interview questions and responses using the information in column 1.

- Select one person to play the role of Pedro Tavarez. Other students will be the interview panel for an oral presentation to the class. If the interview is conducted in Spanish, be sure to incorporate the grammar in column 2.

1 Content	*2 Grammar*
Types of music: bachata, merengue, bacharengue, salsa Names of instruments commonly used	Interrogative words—at least three of the following: *cómo, cuál, por qué, qué, quién*
Musicians and composers: traditional favorites, contemporary favorites	Expressions of like/dislike or preference: *gustarle, encantarle, fascinarle, preferir* Expressions of personal opinion: *para mí, en mi opinión* Comparisons (at least two): *más que, menos que, tan como, tanto*
What the world will learn about Dominican culture and social issues from song lyrics	Future tense Subjunctive mood: expression of volition, expression of emotion, impersonal expression
If you had the opportunity to play with a famous Dominican musician, whom would you choose?	Imperfect subjunctive "If" clause with conditional tense

Colmados like this one have long provided residents of poor neighborhoods with a place to socialize and listen to music.

BACHATA: A MUSIC OF THE PEOPLE

Deborah Pacini Hernandez

In the early 1960s, at the end of Trujillo's reign, thousands of rural Dominicans began an exodus from the impoverished rural areas of the country to the cities, looking for work. Crowded into shantytowns ringing Santo Domingo and Santiago, many were unable to find secure employment and were forced to eke out a living as street vendors or day laborers. Out of this situation of struggle and desperation, a new music, bachata, was born.

In this article anthropologist Deborah Pacini Hernandez describes the evolution of bachata, from its roots in the Dominican countryside to its birth in the barrios of Santo Domingo and its subsequent emergence on the world stage.

Adapted from *Bachata: A Social History of a Dominican Popular Music,* by Deborah Pacini Hernandez. Reprinted by permission of Temple University Press. © 1995 by Deborah Pacini Hernandez. All rights reserved.

Before the development of a Dominican recording industry and the spread of the mass media, guitar-based trios and quartets were almost indispensable in the Dominican Republic for a variety of informal recreational events such as Sunday afternoon parties. These spontaneous gatherings that took place in back yards, living rooms, or in the street were known as *bachatas.* Dictionaries of Latin American Spanish define the term bachata as *juerga, jolgorio,* or *parranda,* all of which denote fun, merriment, or a good time. In the Dominican Republic, in addition to the emotional quality of fun and enjoyment suggested by the dictionary definition, the term bachata referred specifically to get-togethers that included music, drink, and food. The musicians who played at bachatas were usually local, friends and neighbors of the host, although sometimes reputed musicians from farther away might be brought in for a special occasion. Musicians were normally recompensed only with food and drink, but a little money might be given as well. Parties were usually held on Saturday night and would go until dawn, at which time a traditional soup, *sancocho,* was served to the remaining guests. Outside of these Saturday night gatherings, another place where people could listen to bachata was in the neighborhood *colmado,* a small grocery store found throughout shantytowns and poor working-class barrios. *Colmados* served as a space for exchanging news, information, ideas and culture. Women often visited *colmados* several times a day to buy household necessities, while men typically visited them in the evening and on weekends to buy beer and cigarettes, and to play dominoes on tables set up in front. In order to enhance the *colmado's* social functions, owners typically had some sort of sound system—most commonly a record player and a small record collection, which they kept up-to-date by purchasing a few carefully chosen bachata records on a regular basis. *Colmados,* then, served as key loci for the dissemination of bachata in urban areas—especially to women and children, who could not frequent the *barras,* where it was also played. Middle-class people, however, had little if any contact with bachata and continued to listen to other types of music that they did not associate with the urban poor.

A Negative Image

Among Dominicans there is considerable disagreement as to exactly when the term bachata came to refer to a particular kind of music. According to bachata musicians themselves, it was in the 1970s that the guitar-based music they recorded came to be identified by the term bachata. By then it had lost its more neutral connotation of an informal (if sometimes rowdy) backyard party and acquired an unmistakably negative cultural value implying rural backwardness and vulgarity. For example, on hearing one of these recordings, a middle- or upper-class person might say something like *"¡Quítate esa bachata!"* ("Take that bachata off!"). Thus this style of guitar music made by poor rural musicians came to be synonymous with low quality. The condemnation fell not only upon the music and its performers, but upon its listeners as well; the term *bachatero,* used for anyone who liked the music as well as for the musicians, was equally derogatory.

In the late 1970s and 1980s, the worsening social and economic conditions of bachata's urban and rural poor constituency were clearly reflected in bachata. The tempo became noticeably faster, and the formerly ultra-romantic lyrics inspired by the Cuban *bolero* (ballad style music) became more and more concerned with drinking, womanizing, and male bragging. Increasingly, they began to express *desprecio* toward women. As bachata's popularity with the country's poorest citizens grew, the term bachata, which earlier

DEBORAH PACINI-HERNANDEZ

Many women survive by working in the informal sector selling fruit on the street.

had suggested rural backwardness and low social status, became loaded with a more complicated set of socially unacceptable features that included illicit sex, violence, heavy alcohol use, and disreputable social contexts such as seedy bars and brothels.

In bachata, one guitar plays lead, embellishing by picking rather than strumming, and another plays rhythm. The bongo and maraca (or güira) players mark the typical four-four time rather discretely, although sometimes in musical breaks the bongo player might add a few displays. Traditionally, the lead guitar player also composed and sang lead, while the other musicians provided choruses, although as bachata groups have professionalized, some are now fronted by a vocalist who does not play, thereby relegating the lead guitar player to a secondary role.

Bachata is essentially a vocal genre, meant to tell stories—there is no such thing as an instrumental bachata. Besides its characteristic guitar-led instrumentation, one of bachata's defining features is its highly emotional singing style. Bachata's vocals, like those of other rural musics (such as U.S. country and western and Colombian *carrilera*), are often sung in close harmony, usually in thirds. The backup vocal parts in bachata are often in call-and-response form; sometimes the backup singers simply repeat a phrase such as "no, no, no" between solo lines; at other times the chorus might repeat the last line of a verse, or the singer and vocalists might engage in a dialogue.

Although bachata has its roots in rural musical forms, bachata musicians today are known for their ability to interpret the urban experience. Popular language is one of the most important markers of *barrio* identity, and the ability to use language creatively is a highly valued skill. Indeed, the most successful *bachateros* are those who best command a Dominican urban street language that offers a rich variety of words, phrases, and proverbs for expressing their thoughts and feelings. In bachata, as in U.S. rap, language, spoken or sung, empowers a speaker. Through the control of words, a singer can construct alternative realities. This is taken to the extreme in the widely used *doble sentido*, or double meaning, in which words and their meanings are manipulated for humorous effect. These songs, like Dominican popular speech in general, are full of hidden or ambiguous meanings that subvert official meanings. Ethnomusicologist Aristides Incháustegui attributes Dominicans' ability to simultaneously conceal and reveal information to the repression of the Trujillo regime:

> During the Trujillo era words didn't work properly. So the Dominican became a specialist in speaking in masked messages. It was something so ingrained in our consciousness that you couldn't say things, that it entered our genes, and when children are born, they already know how to play with words.

Rising Popularity

In 1991, a talented young musician, Juan Luis Guerra, and his vocal group 440, released a recording titled *Bachata rosa*. It became one of the most successful recordings in the recent history of Latin music and, according to some, brought bachata out of obscurity. Guerra was far removed from the social and material realities of the desperately poor *bachateros*, whose musical style he interpreted. His background is solidly middle-class: his mother was a lawyer, his father a civil servant, and his friends and relatives were all from the more comfortable layers of Dominican society. He studied music at the National Conservatory and later received advanced musical training at Boston's Berklee College of Music. His 1985 album *Mudanza y acarreo*, which contained complex and sophisticated interpretations of a variety of Dominican regional musics, had established him as one of the country's most accomplished musicians. However, when he released *Bachata rosa* in 1991, some Dominicans were scandalized that such a talented and promising musician was dabbling in the disreputable bachata. Nevertheless, with the release of *Bachata rosa*, suddenly bachata music was embraced by all sectors of Dominican society. Musicians of all stripes rushed to record songs, and bachata records were included in the programming of major Santo Domingo FM stations and could be purchased in the city's best music stores.

It was precisely because of bachata's low social status that Guerra's experiments with the bachata genre in *Bachata rosa* made such an impact on the Dominican musical landscape. While the country's cultural establishment may not have been paying attention to bachata prior to *Bachata rosa*, stylistic changes that had been developing at the grassroots level were being well received by a younger generation of Dominicans attracted by bachata's earthy vitality.

Today, more than ten years after *Bachata rosa* was released, musicians are using sophisticated mixers and songs have increased considerably in tempo and are far more lively and danceable than a decade ago. Younger audiences have encouraged bachata musicians to include more merengues in their repertoires and as a result, bachata-merengues now comprise as much as half of many bachata ensembles' repertoires. There are many other well-known performers besides Juan Luis Guerra. Raulín Rodríguez, Blas Durán, Antony Santos, Joe Veras, Zacarias Ferriera, and Aventura are just a few. Raulín Rodríguez, in particular, makes a deliberate point of writing lyrics about romantic love. His music is lively and danceable and, like Guerra, he has reestablished bachata's credentials as a romantic music among the middle class and

---

"Soledad" is a famous bachata about a man whose lover has been taken away from him by her father, preventing them from getting married. Soledad *means loneliness.*

Soledad

Raulín Rodríguez

Soledad, no se lo que a mí me pasa
Cada vez que yo recuerdo, no se lo que a mí
  me pasa
Cada vez que yo recuerdo, mi primer amor
  la que yo quería ya de mí se olvidó
Que mi primer amor la que yo quería ya
  de mí se olvidó

Decía que era imposible, que no podíamos
  casarnos
Decía que era imposible, que no podíamos
  casarnos
Su padre se la llevó me ha dejado solito,
  ¿Ahora qué hago yo?
Su padre se la llevó me ha dejado solito,
  ¿Ahora qué hago yo?

Y si ella a mí me quería, ¿Por qué me negaron
  su amor?
Y si ella a mí me quería, ¿Por qué me negaron
  su amor?
Ay yo la quería tanto, no la he podido olvidar
  no no
Ay yo la quería tanto, no la he podido olvidar

Soledad, es lo que siento en mi alma
Es lo que siento en mi pecho, esta soledad que
  me está matando
Es lo que siento en mi alma, es lo que siento
  en mi pecho
Esta soledad que me está matando

(chorus)
Ay ay ay, que me está matando
Ay ay ay, que me está matando
Ay ay ay, que me está matando ✺

Loneliness

Raulín Rodríguez

Loneliness, I don't know what's happening to me
Every time I remember, I don't know what's
  happening to me
Every time I remember my first love, the one I
  loved, she forgot me
That my first love, the one I loved, she forgot me

She said it would be impossible, that we couldn't
  get married
She said it would be impossible, that we couldn't
  get married
Her father took her away, left me all alone;
  what am I to do now?
Her father took her away, left me all alone;
  what am I to do now?

And if I was the one she loved, why did he deny
  me her love?
And if I was the one she loved, why did he deny
  me her love?
Ay, I loved her so much, I haven't been able to
  forget her, no no
Ay, I loved her so much, I haven't been able to
  forget her

Loneliness, I feel it in my soul
It's what I feel in my heart, this loneliness that's
  killing me
It's what I feel in my soul, it's what I feel in my
  heart,
This loneliness that's killing me

(chorus)
Ay, ay, ay, it's killing me
Ay, ay, ay, it's killing me
Ay, ay, ay, it's killing me ✺

mass media. One example is "Soledad" (see sidebar).

Female performers have remained peripheral in bachata music. Some observers believe that while Dominican men were able to articulate their emotional pain, their vulnerability, their frustrations, and their anger through bachata songs, women did not have comparable opportunities. Women were frequently portrayed as the aggressors and men as victims. Given that both men and women experienced the difficulty and anguish of shantytown life, it seems peculiar that *bachateros* did not unite with women in order to cope with their shared troubles.

Two female bachata singers, however, were able to break this marginalization. Mélida Rodríguez emerged in the 1960s, during bachata's formative period. She had an extraordinarily expressive voice and composed her own songs. Unfortunately, Rodríguez recorded only one LP and a few singles before she died at a very young age. The songs she left, however, are truly haunting and compelling statements of her experiences of social and economic dislocation. Aridia Ventura offered a unique female perspective that differs from that of the male bachateros. Her song "La Fiesta," like many bachatas, expresses contempt for a former lover—but from a female point of view.

Today, bachata has practically become a household word throughout Latin America, and in many areas of the United States and Europe. Many Dominicans, once appalled at the rudeness and vulgarity of the music, are now surprised—and some are even proud—to see that bachata has acquired an international profile, bringing the music of the Dominican Republic to the attention of worldwide audiences. ❀

barras: bars
bongos: two small single-headed drums joined side by side, played with the hands
desprecio: disrespect
güira: metal scraper
Mudanza y acarrero: Moving and carrying along
maraca: shaker filled with small wooden balls
sancocho: stew of meat and root vegetables

BACHATA: A MUSIC OF THE PEOPLE

USE WITH: Unit 71

DURATION: 1–3 classes

STANDARDS:

English Language Arts: 5, 10

Social Studies: 1c

Foreign Language: 1, 3.2, 4.1

GOALS:

- To expose students to the history and development of bachata.
- To analyze the social conditions involved in the process of mainstreaming bachata.

OBJECTIVES:

- To discuss the historical development of bachata.
- To compose a bachata song.

ACTIVITIES:

1. Listen to *"Soledad"* (Loneliness), by Raulín Rodríguez, and follow the song lyrics (unit 71).

2. Students read "Bachata: A Music of the People" (unit 71) and discuss the historical development of the music, using comprehension questions created by the teacher.

3. In pairs, students write a bachata song about a lost love, following Raulín Rodríguez's dramatic style.

ASSESSMENT:

Teacher assesses student creativity and understanding of the bachata genre as reflected in the student-composed song.

MATERIALS:

- "Soledad" by Raulín Rodríguez (track 4 on *Soledad,* compact disc, Ringo Records, 1997)
- CD player
- Song lyrics (unit 71)

Lesson plan prepared by Jocelyn Santana.

SAN PEDRO DE MACORÍS: BASEBALL MECCA

Rob Ruck

American GIs, part of the armed forces that occupied the Dominican Republic in 1965, playing baseball with Dominicans in Santo Domingo.

MAY 5, 1965, JACK LARTZ (USIA)

Reprinted from *The Tropic of Baseball: Baseball in the Dominican Republic* by Rob Ruck, by permission of the University of Nebraska Press. Copyright © 1991 Meckler Publishing.

After the World Series marks the season's end in the United States, writes baseball historian Rob Ruck, baseball springs back to life in and around the Caribbean. There, against a backdrop of orange and purple skies and to the rhythms of salsa and merengue, some of the best baseball in the world is played each winter. From Venezuela through Cuba, Puerto Rico, and the Dominican Republic, and into parts of Mexico and Central America, baseball is played with an intensity that goes beyond mere passion. "It's more than a game," former Dominican manager Winston Llenas said. "It's a national fever. Here, in the Dominican Republic, it's almost a way of life."

Latin America, and the Dominican Republic in particular, have been sending talent to the United States major leagues since the early 1960s. And if the Dominican Republic has become the epicenter of Caribbean baseball, says Ruck, the small city of San Pedro de Macorís is its mecca. Of the hundred-plus Dominicans to have played in the majors by 1988, over a third came via San Pedro de Macorís. In this article, Ruck explores the reasons for this connection.

San Pedro de Macorís, with a population of only 100,000, lies on the southeastern end of the island. Its success at producing so many baseball players who have made it to the major leagues is attributed to the influence of three groups who lived and worked in the region in the early 1900s. They are the Cubans and North Americans who built and ran the sugar mills at the turn of the last century, and the English-speaking West Indian islanders who worked in the sugarcane fields and mills.

In the 1870s, four or five thousand Cubans fleeing the Ten Years' War for independence from Spain arrived in the Dominican Republic, settling in the southeastern plains around San Pedro de Macorís. Many of the Cuban exiles played baseball, a game which took hold in Cuba in the 1860s. By the 1890s, San Pedro claimed center stage in the Dominican sugar industry. At the same time owners of sugar mills began hiring seasonal workers from St. Kitts, Tortola, Antigua, Montserrat, and other English-speaking islands, who were paid lower wages than Dominicans.

Harvesting sugar cane, Central Romana. La Romana has recently become the site of luxury resorts and baseball training camps. Some of the would-be baseball stars trained in La Romana are descendants of "los ingleses," immigrants from the English-speaking Caribbean who came to the area to work in the sugar cane fields.

The West Indian workers became known as Cocolos because many of them were from Tortola, which was a difficult word for Spanish-speaking Dominicans to pronounce.

Although the early migrants stayed only for the cutting and grinding season, usually beginning in December or January, more and more began to remain year-round at the sugar mills. The *bateyes*, clusters of shacks in the fields, were crowded with seasonal male employees and offered few amenities. The estates, where more women and children could be found, were no better. Medical, educational, and recreational facilities did not exist. To complicate matters, the Cocolos were not accepted by Dominicans. To survive, they maintained an English-speaking community in the *bateyes* that favored West Indian culture, especially the game of cricket, which they played in free time and during the summer months of the *tiempo muerto* when the sugarcane grew. These cricket teams reflected the Cocolos' tendency to organize institutions that helped make their life better, including mutual aid societies and trade unions. Many Cocolos were followers of Marcus Garvey, the charismatic Jamaican black nationalist who created the Universal Negro Improvement Association. They stuck together and tried to find collective solutions to their problems.

In 1916, the U.S. Marines invaded the Dominican Republic and governed until 1924. During this time they built a baseball field by the ocean in San Pedro de Macorís. Although Cubans had introduced the sport to Dominicans years before, it quickly grew in popularity and the Marines stationed near San Pedro played against Dominican teams on many occasions.

In 1932, dictator Rafael Trujillo enacted a law that called

for at least 70 percent employment of native-born Dominicans in the sugar industry. Although many of the Cocolos returned to their homelands, those who remained watched their children grow up as Dominicans, speaking Spanish and playing baseball. Cricket had helped the Cocolos build their community and come to terms with life in the Dominican Republic. Baseball would help their sons and grandsons "Dominican-ize," just as the game helped to

ABOVE: Boys sitting in the dugout of a ballfield in Consuelo, a sugar mill town outside San Pedro de Macorís that has sent more than a dozen players to the major leagues. BELOW: A fire-eater entertains the crowd at Estadio del Cibao during a game between the home team, Las Aguilas from Santiago, and the Leones of Escogido from Santo Domingo.

"Americanize" generations of immigrants in the United States a century ago. By the 1940s, baseball replaced cricket at the sugar mills, and with the game gaining more and more adherents in other regions, it soon became the favorite sport throughout the country. By 1987, all four of the Dominicans who played in the major league All-Star game were from San Pedro, and two of them were the grandsons of Cocolos. Rico Carty, Pedro Guerrero, George Bell, Alfredo Griffin, and Sammy Sosa are among the *peloteros* with Cocolos roots.

Is there a connection between cricket, baseball, and the high number of professional players from San Pedro de Macorís? It is true that historically the major concentration of baseball talent in San Pedro was on the sugar estates with the most English speakers and the best cricket players. Whether the fact that San Pedro de Macorís produces some of the best baseball players in the world can be attributed to cricket and an English heritage remains unknown. What we do know is that baseball is still the favored sport in the Dominican Republic, and Dominican boys of all ages dream of becoming professional baseball players someday. ❀

bateye: cane cutters' camp
Cocolos: people from the English-speaking Caribbean islands working as sugarcane cutters in the Dominican Republic
pelotero: ballplayer
tiempo muerto: idle season
Universal Negro Improvement Association: grassroots organization based in the United States and the Caribbean in the early twentieth century, which sought to promote black unity and economic self-reliance
West Indian: from the English-speaking Caribbean islands

ROB RUCK

A young man looks on as Dominican summer league players practice at Estadio La Romana in La Romana. The players belong to one of the many U.S. major league teams operating academies in the country.

DOMINICAN BASEBALL

USE WITH: Unit 73

DURATION: 1–2 days

STANDARDS:

English Language Arts: 1, 4, 10

Social Studies: 1b, 1c, 1d, 3g, 4b, 4c, 4e, 4h, 9b

Foreign Language: 1, 3.2, 4.2

GOAL: To draw connections between the lives of Dominican baseball players in the Dominican Republic and the United States.

OBJECTIVE:

To outline facts of baseball's development in the Dominican Republic.

ACTIVITIES:

1. Ask students:

   • Do you like baseball?

   • What is your favorite team?

   • What countries do its players come from?

   • Who are some famous Dominican baseball players?

   • What do you know about their lives before the majors?

   • How do Dominican players get to the U.S. major leagues?

2. Students read "San Pedro de Macorís: Baseball Mecca " (unit 73).

3. Students divide information from the text into segments and transfer that information onto large index cards with notes on one side and a picture, symbol, or word clue on the other. Or, the teacher can assign a segment to each student. For example, one card might say, "In 1916, the U.S. Marines invaded the Dominican Republic and governed until 1924. During this time they built a baseball field by the ocean in San Pedro de Macorís." Symbols on the other side of that card might be a U.S. flag and the years 1916–24 superimposed on a map of the Dominican Republic, with a few baseballs drawn around the map.

4. Students divide into two baseball teams. One team lines up as batters on one side of the room while the other team assumes positions on the "field." A pitcher standing in the middle of the room pitches each batter a squoosh ball or other soft ball. The student catches the ball and shows the symbol side of the card to her/his teammates, to help jog memories and give a reference for the information. The teammates have to guess the time period

Lesson plan prepared by Lola Lopes.

and segment of text from the article. Depending on how well they answer, the batter goes to first, second, or third base or gets a home run. Scoring: A completely correct answer is equal to a home run (one point); partial answers can be equal to first, second, or third base. The teacher is of course the umpire and keeps points! The team with the most points wins the game.

ASSESSMENT:

Students discuss the successes of Dominican players in the United States. How do you think their baseball fame might affect them personally, in the United States and back in the Dominican Republic when they make visits home?

MATERIALS:

- Large index cards

EPILOGUE | A JOURNEY OF CONNECTIONS

Jocelyn Santana

As co-editor of this book and the Dominican member of the trio, it falls to me to write a closing piece. The more I read and reread the book, the more the theme of connection emerges as a central force in shaping a Dominican identity. Those of us in the diaspora share a relentless need to hold on to *nuestra dominicanidad,* our Dominicanness. It has taken us this far and will carry us forward into the future.

After twenty-five years in the United States, I call myself a Dominican American and realize that I carry the individualities of the Dominican collective in me. I am each Dominican in *Caribbean Connections* and each Dominican is me. Like fingerprints, each of us is unique, and like fingerprints, we remain connected to the hand of our Dominicanness. The power of our story is in this connection—in our ties to the Dominicanness we refuse to let go of or exchange for the illusion of a permanent American citizenship. We remain Dominicans and become Americans all at the same time.

Our immigrant experience is an all-inclusive model that allows connections to the new and the old. We want to stay connected to each other and to our land, to the smells and sounds and the picturesque coasts. We even find ways to transport our favorite seasonings and foods in the same planes that take us from NY to the DR and back again.

Caribbean Connections: The Dominican Republic is a collection of the history of our lives in the Dominican Republic and the United States, and about what happens in between the trips we take back and forth. In telling these stories, we hope to pave a path for other Dominicans and Dominican Americans to continue the narrative of our experiences.

Home

United States, you have no choice
but to let the dream,
never intended to materialize,
run free in my life.
Some of it is my Dominican me;
Some of it I acquired from you.
Here we are, together, me in you
and you in me.
I've had stories to tell
and stories to learn.
It's up to you to keep fighting me
and calling me names.
I am really one of you;
And . . . I'm also one of them.
I hope you get used to me
real soon.
You see, this too is my home.
I moved in a long time ago.

¡Hola, América!
What are you going to do with me?

I am you,
the fruit of your seed;
I am part of you;
you are part of me.

What are you going to do with me?

I am here to stay.
I pledged an accented allegiance
to what you stand for.
I have become me in you:
Alien . . .
Minority . . .
Dominican . . .
Indivisible . . .
Your creation . . .
Your reflection . . .
Partaker of "liberty and justice"
for me?
for all?

What are you going to do with me?